Understanding modernisation in criminal justice

CRIME AND JUSTICE

Series editor: Mike Maguire

University College of Wales, College of Cardiff

Crime and Justice is a series of short introductory texts on central topics in criminology. The books in this series are written for students by internationally renowned authors. Each book tackles a key area within criminology, providing a concise and up-to-date overview of the principal concepts, theories, methods and findings relating to the area. Taken as whole, the *Crime and Justice* series will cover all the core components of an undergraduate criminology course.

Published titles

Understanding modernisation in criminal justice
Paul Senior, Chris Crowther-Dowey and Matt Long

Understanding youth and crime
Sheila Brown

Understanding crime data
Clive Coleman and Jenny Moynihan

Understanding white collar crime
Hazel Croall

Understanding justice 2nd edition
Barbara A. Hudson

Understanding crime prevention
Gordon Hughes

Understanding violent crime
Stephen Jones

Understanding risk in criminal justice
Hazel Kemshall

Understanding psychology and crime
James McGuire

Understanding community penalties
Peter Raynor and Maurice Vanstone

Understanding criminology 2nd edition
Sandra Walklate

Understanding modernisation in criminal justice

by Paul Senior, Chris Crowther-Dowey and Matt Long

McGraw Hill
Open University Press

Open University Press
McGraw-Hill Education
McGraw-Hill House
Shoppenhangers Road
Maidenhead
Berkshire
England
SL6 2QL

email: enquiries@openup.co.uk
world wide web: www.openup.co.uk

and Two Penn Plaza, New York, NY 10121-2289, USA

First published 2007

A catalogue record of this book is available from the British Library

ISBN 13: 978 0 335 22065 6 (pb) 978 0 335 22066 3 (hb)
ISBN 10: 0 335 22065 7 (pb) 0 335 22066 5 (hb)

Library of Congress Cataloging-in-Publication Data
CIP data has been applied for

Typeset by RefineCatch Limited, Bungay, Suffolk
Printed in the UK by Bell and Bain Ltd, Glasgow

The McGraw-H

Contents

Series editor's foreword

This book is the latest in Open University Press' well established *Crime and Justice* series, which has been running since 1996. Paul Senior, Chris Crowther-Dowey and Matt Long provide a comprehensive discussion of a topic of major importance to anyone who works in, studies or writes about public and voluntary sector agencies, especially those in the criminal justice field. The central focus is on New Labour's concept of 'modernisation' and its application through a range of significant reforms to the police, courts, prisons, probation service, youth justice services and community safety partnerships, as well as attempts to mould and incorporate private and voluntary sector agencies into new 'managerialist' frameworks of service delivery. As the authors make clear, much of the thinking behind the concept has a long history, and many elements of so-called modernisation – notably the emphasis on business principles of efficiency and effectiveness, the reconceptualization of 'service users' as 'customers' and 'consumers', and the promotion of competition, contracting out and quasi-markets – were essentially continuations of the Thatcher and Major governments' efforts to reform the public services through the neo-liberal 'New Public Management' agenda. However, they argue that the New Labour agenda has been different in important respects, being influenced, at least in its early days, by the philosophy of the 'Third Way' (with its focus on rights and responsibilities), and placing a much stronger emphasis on 'partnership' and on the setting and monitoring of targets for service delivery. The authors ask to what extent the resulting 'performance' and 'audit' culture, together with the increasing involvement of new players in what was previously essentially a field monopolized by state agencies, has impacted in practice upon issues, such as diversity, individual rights and professional autonomy and discretion, all of which are of central importance in the criminal justice arena. They also explore the changing nature of central, regional and local structures of governance, and the increasing complexities of the relationships between them.

This book provides a nice balance between, on the one hand, broad theoretical chapters which situate the above changes within the framework of major sociological themes, such as late modernity, globalization and the growth of neo-liberalism and, on the other, chapters with a strong empirical focus which explore their impact in specific areas of criminal justice. Overall, it maintains faith with the core aim of the series, which has been to produce short but intellectually challenging introductory texts in key areas of criminological debate, in order to give undergraduates and graduates both a solid grounding in the relevant area and a taste to explore it further. Although aimed primarily at students new to the field, and written as far as possible in plain language, the books are not oversimplified. All the authors set out to 'stretch' readers and to encourage them to approach criminological knowledge and theory in a critical and questioning frame of mind. Moreover, as with previous authors in the series, Senior, Crowther-Dowey and Long have not only provided balanced summaries of previous literature, but have taken the debates further and put forward their own distinctive views and interpretations.

Other books previously published in the *Crime and Justice* series – all of whose titles begin with the word 'Understanding' – have covered criminological theory (Sandra Walklate), justice and penal theory (Barbara Hudson), crime data and statistics (Clive Coleman and Jenny Moynihan), youth and crime (Sheila Brown), crime prevention (Gordon Hughes), violent crime (Stephen Jones), community penalties (Peter Raynor and Maurice Vanstone), white collar crime (Hazel Croall), risk in criminal justice (Hazel Kemshall), social control (Martin Innes), psychology and crime (James McGuire), victims and restorative justice (James Dignan), drugs, alcohol and crime (Trevor Bennett and Katy Holloway), public attitudes to criminal justice (Julian Roberts and Mike Hough), desistance from crime (Stephen Farrell and Adam Calverley), prisons (Andrew Coyle), political violence (Vincenzo Ruggiero) and race and crime (Colin Webster). One (Walklate) is already in its third edition, four are in second editions, and other second editions are in preparation. All are topics which are either already widely taught or are growing in prominence in university degree courses on crime and criminal justice, and each book should make an ideal foundation text for a relevant module. As an aid to understanding, clear summaries are provided at regular intervals, and a glossary of key terms and concepts is a feature of every book. In addition, to help students expand their knowledge, recommendations for further reading are given at the end of each chapter.

Mike Maguire

List of acronyms

ACPO	Association of Chief Police Officers
APA	Association of Police Authorities
ASB	anti-social behaviour
BCU	Basic Command Unit
BMA	British Medical Association
BME	black and minority ethnic groups
BSIA	British Security Industry Authority
BV	Best Value
CAD	computer aided dispatch
CCTV	closed circuit television
CDA	Crime and Disorder Act (1998)
CDRPs	Crime and Disorder Reduction Partnerships
CID	Criminal Investigation Department
CIRCLE	Community Involvement Revitalizes Community Long-Term Engagement
C-NOMIS	Custody-National Offender Management Information System
CRAMS	Case Recording and Monitoring Systems
CRP	Crime Reduction Programme
DAT	Drug Action Team
DETR	Department of the Environment, Transport and the Regions
Dip	Drug Intervention Programme
ESF	European Social Fund
ETE	Education, Training and Employment
EU	European Union
Europol	European Union Law Enforcement Organization
FBI	Federal Bureau of Intelligence
HMIC	Her Majesty's Inspectorate of Constabulary
IMF	International Monetary Fund
Interpol	International Criminal Police Organization

KWNS	Keynesian Welfare National State
LSC	Learning and Skills Council
MAPPAs	Multi-Agency Public Protection Arrangements
MDT	mobile data terminal
NAFIS	National Automated Fingerprint Identification System
NCIS	National Criminal Intelligence Service
NCS	National Crime Service
NHS	National Health Service
NHTCU	National Hi-Tech Crime Unit
NIM	National Intelligence Model
NOMS	National Offender Management Service
NPIA	National Policing Improvement Agency
NPM	new public management
OECD	Organization for Economic Co-Operation and Development
Ofsted	Office for Standards in Education
OLASS	Offender Learning and Skills Service
OPEC	Organization of the Petroleum Exporting Countries
PCSO	police community support officers
PCTs	primary care trusts
PFI	Private Finance Initiative
PITO	Police Information Technology Organization
PPAF	Police Performance Assessment Framework
PPU	Public Protection Unit
PSOs	probation service officers
RDAs	regional development agencies
ROMs	regional offender managers
SEU	Social Exclusion Unit
SOCA	Serious and Organized Crime Agency
SRB	Single Regeneration Budget
SWPR	Schumpeterian Workfare Post-National Regime
TDPF	Transform Drug Policy Foundation
VCS	voluntary and community sector
YJB	Youth Justice Board
YOTs	Youth Offending Teams
ZTP	zero tolerance policing

Introduction

The modernisation of criminal justice is an ongoing set of reforms and this book provides a detailed account of the impact of such processes in the context of crime and public policy in the twenty-first century. It is argued that an appreciation of the analytical and practical significance of the concept of modernisation enriches understanding of criminal justice and crime reduction policy. Our understanding of modernisation is based on recognition of the equal significance of two factors in criminal justice reform: on the one hand, the permanence of change and uncertainty; and, on the other hand, the enduring significance of structural influences that tend to channel change and reform in particular, sometimes predictable, directions. More than this, it is an explanation of the relationship between ideas about modernisation and the various ways in which these conceptions have a material effect on the decisions and actions taken by criminal justice professionals. The following chapters outline the policy frameworks devised by modernisers who are committed to making the criminal justice system work better as it achieves its main priorities and aspirations. In principle, modernisation is all about developing coherent strategies that ensure the system achieves politically constructed aims and objectives in the most effective way. In practice, the good intentions of the architects of modernisation are thwarted by unintended and paradoxical influences on their activities. Consequently, considerable time and space in this text is dedicated to dealing with the permanence of paradox, which is almost a defining feature of the modernisation of criminal justice policy and practice. Most of the following pages concentrate on a particular period in the modernisation of crime and public policy, namely the first decade of the new millennium. To be even more precise, it describes the emergence of different ideas about modernisation and how they were adopted and adapted by three successive New Labour governments in the UK, commencing in 1997 and taking us through the first decade of the twenty-first century. Significantly, modernisation is global in its origins and workings and is therefore not unique to New Labour, yet for the purposes of clarity we use the UK as a case study to explore this phenomenon in detail.

Under the leadership of two New Labour Prime Ministers, Tony Blair and Gordon Brown respectively, a major programme of modernisation was set in train which redefined the ideas, values, structures and processes found in criminal justice policy in particular and social policy more generally. Our aim is to address the complex ideas associated with this ambitious and unfinished governmental project and their impact on the workings of the police, courts, prison, youth justice and probation services. The focus of our analysis is not limited to the core players in criminal justice and takes on board the key part played by other statutory agencies, as well as the voluntary and private sectors. The latter point demonstrates that modernisation is an inclusive strategy where all agencies and citizens are encouraged to be involved in developing a safe and secure society in the most effective and efficient way possible. A premise of this book is that whenever we wish to understand criminal justice matters from a criminological or penological perspective the influence of modernisation is never far away. This observation applies to everyone who is interested in crime as an observer of or participant in the crime reduction industry. Before elaborating this it is necessary to place modernisation into a concrete historical context.

It would be disingenuous if we have created the impression that modernisation belongs exclusively to New Labour in the twenty-first century. This is far from the truth. For example, some of the key factors underlying the emergence of modernisation can be identified in the aftermath of the Second World War (1939–45), a date that is not arbitrary in its selection. After this event societies throughout the world embarked on major social programmes of reform, demonstrated in the UK by the creation of the welfare state responsible for the provision of health, education, housing, personal and social service, income maintenance and, last but not least, law and order. Similar structures have been erected throughout other European as well as Antipodean and American liberal democracies. In the UK these services were initially funded by the taxpayer and were addressed to meet a complex range of social needs. Some were free to all at the point of need (i.e., health) and others were made available in a more selective way (housing, income maintenance) through so-called means testing. Taking this as a starting point, governments from then on have been addressing the workings of this complex piece of machinery with an emphasis on changing and reforming its perceived inefficiencies and deficiencies.

Up until the 1970s there was widespread governmental and public support for a welfare state but the Conservative party, first elected in 1979, set out to reform and change this system through the introduction of a particular set of reforming tools which achieved the label New Public Management (NPM). (Clarke and Newman, 1997). The thinking behind NPM is considered throughout the book not least because it had a profound influence on the welfare state, including criminal justice, but primarily because it has been taken forward, albeit in a moderated guise, by New Labour as part of its modernisation strategy commencing in 1997. More crucially, New Labour's contribution will be adopted and adapted by future governments rather like they did with the Conservative legacy, whatever political hue future governments may be, and even though the word 'modernisation' may not be used explicitly. It is necessary to situate modernisation in the context of a range of social changes occurring in the late twentieth century, mainly driven by the growth of neo-liberalism throughout Europe, the United States and the Antipodes. A major trend underpinning the modernisation agenda is globalization, which has resulted in the hollowing out of nation states (Jessop 2003). While the impact of globalization varies significantly from country to country, and though there is some localization (Robertson 1992), a general outcome is that states are proving unwilling or unable to regulate the global economy and its impact at a local level. There is also an increased emphasis on 'responsibilization' (Garland 1996) where individual citizens and communities are required to take more responsibility for their personal welfare and security. These changes are examined in particular detail in relation to criminal justice in England and Wales. It is necessary to consider the manifestation of the changes (referred to above) under a series of governments, including Thatcher, Major and Blair. The focus is, however, mainly on Blair's New Labour regime.

Modernisation is quite clearly associated with government and politics and it is shown throughout this book that change and reform occurs as a consequence of political choices and decisions. Between the 1970s and mid-1990s most liberal democracies were embroiled in a dispute about the role of government. This debate has continued in more recent times and in short, on the one hand, are neo-liberals or the political right who argue that society should operate according to the principles of the marketplace. The ethos expressed by these people is that individuals should be free to choose and take personal responsibility for themselves and their families. Government should be kept to a minimum, they believe, and should merely guarantee the preservation of the conditions necessary for a free market. Accordingly, the welfare state should be removed or residualized. The perspective on crime held by the neo-liberals is that criminals are people who lack self-discipline and who are motivated to commit crime because of their innate greed and nastiness. On the other hand, there is the social democratic left who continue to recognize the need for a more interventionist government to regulate the economy and to take seriously the welfare of all citizens in a particular society. However, such support is provided with more caution and the belief is that where possible people should become more responsible. Offenders are regarded as a problem but also individuals who may be in need of not only punishment but also some support.

By the mid-1990s there was a move beyond 'left and right' (Giddens 1994) culminating in an emerging consensus on what should happen to reform and change the public sector – the so-called 'Third Way'. The basic assumption of this perspective is that governments are not able to significantly influence the global economy and that while they can address some of its worst effects this is limited by finite economic resources and political clout. While reform and change is possible it is only of a rather limited nature. As far as crime goes, there have been reductions of some offences but there is a perception that society is more violent and a less safe place. Criminal justice policy is full of contradictions and paradoxes, something we explore in depth throughout, where care and control are frequently hybridized with some notable paradoxes. Under New Labour, Tony Blair, the Prime Minister (1997–2007) emphasized his government's intent to be *'tough on crime, tough on the causes of crime'*. This created an ambivalent approach in crime and public policy, which attempted to address social exclusion but in practice its policies excluded people through mass imprisonment and the criminalization of young people with an assault on anti-social behaviour. This book shows how from the 1980s onwards all political parties tended to adopt and adapt each other's ideas and that this observation would appear to be accurate for any governments in the foreseeable future.

Increasingly the workings of domestic governments have been influenced by developments in other countries, most notably the European Union (EU) and OECD and many of the ideas covered in this book should have global resonance. Modernisation is not unique to the UK, although we argue in line with the authors of an OECD report assessing the modernisation of government across the world that modernisation is contextually specific (OECD 2005). Similar issues may increasingly affect governments throughout the world and they are all required to change and reform in response to developments elsewhere in an increasingly small world. Factors, such as global warming, the international terrorist threat, cybercrime and organized crime know no barriers and governments everywhere are being required to modernise under difficult and austere socioeconomic and political conditions. Although they share much in common, the examples given refer to a high degree of abstraction and each nation state confronts an uncertain world in its own particular way.

The aforementioned point is acutely clear if our focus is shifted towards criminal justice matters. Most jurisdictions have police, courts and correctional agencies orientated towards crime control and the maintenance of internal security. On the surface criminal justice in Perth, Australia operates in much the same way as it does in Nottingham, the United Kingdom. There are offenders who are arrested, charged, prosecuted, sentenced and punished. These statutory authorities will be situated alongside other statutory agencies as well as the private and voluntary sectors. Communities will play a part too, not only as actual and potential victims and witnesses of crime but in preventing their own victimization. The aforementioned two countries are governed by political parties that speak a similar political language and which are affected by very similar problems. Very similar crimes as well as similar social conflicts, arising from racialized social divisions affect them both. However, their respective government and administrative structures are very different, while their approach to reform and change is driven by different contextual factors and their lexicon of reform is somewhat different. This is in line with a lesson learnt from comparative criminology: there are profound differences existing between different countries; and it is very difficult to make generalisations about seemingly very similar phenomenon (Mawby 1999; Cavadino and Dignan 2006). Take as another example the different legal systems in England and France, which readily illustrates the difficulties arising from making comparisons of autonomous systems. For this reason, this book develops a conceptual framework, which it applies to understand a specific manifestation of modernisation, precisely the criminal justice system in England and Wales.

It is arguably difficult enough to cover developments in the main agencies in one jurisdiction, without addressing many of the complications and contradictions a comparative perspective would introduce. However, the conceptual framework is there to test out change and reform in the criminal justice sector in other parts of the world. It is hoped that the model can be refined and revised to make sense of the correctional agencies in South Africa and Sweden, for example, but to do that in a short book like this one would lead to oversimplification.

Having established the general aims of this book it is now necessary to rehearse its structure and contents.

Structure of the book

The purpose of Chapter 1 is to account for the emergence of the concept of modernisation in political debate, especially in the late 1990s. The sociological concept of modernisation pre-dates its usage in late twentieth and early twenty-first centuries and is clearly underpinned by the principles belonging to the Enlightenment project of modernity. This is called **modernisation (1)**. This chapter, however, is not concerned with examining the technical debates being conducted in sociological theory, rather the distinctive conceptual meaning of modernisation in the context of political philosophy and practical attempts to govern society, hence modernisation (2). The chapter shows how modernisation was at the heart of New Labour's (1997–) unfinished and ongoing governmental project. This example is limited to a single time and place, although the factors bringing about modernisation have been evidenced throughout other parts of the world. Modernisation was initially a component of the so-called 'Third Way', noted above, an idea developed through the influential writings of the social theorist Anthony Giddens (1999, 2007). The 'Third Way' refers to a raft of reforms and programmes intended to update or modernise government and public sector activities. This was partly achieved through a response to the Conservative-led (1979–97) neo-liberal reforms of the state and government. For example, modernisation was partly a continuation of managerialism or the New Public Management (NPM), including the '3Es' (economy, effectiveness and efficiency), which were associated with privatization, quasi-markets, organizational restructuring, downsizing and contracting. Modernisation did not abandon these changes altogether, introducing other value frameworks to compensate for the worst excesses of the free market ethos held by neo-liberals. For example, modernisation also includes an attempt to rethink the process of management itself, demonstrated by initiatives, such as 'best value', the emphasis on public consultation, democratization and joined-up partnership working.

The above paragraph refers to many complex changes and while one should resist imposing philosophical coherence where it does not really exist there is a pattern to modernisation. Students of modernisation have identified three trends: (1) the facilitation of effective planning; (2) reform of the policymaking process; and (3) collaborative inter-agency working. This chapter will look at each of the above in a little more detail. Taking the first development, effective planning can be seen in the type of fiscal control exercised by the government. For example, in England and Wales the so-called Comprehensive Spending Review and the use of Public Service Agreements introduced in New Labour's first term in office (1997–2001) ensured a strong fit between planning for long-term goals and the financial resources required to achieve such ends. Taking the second factor, the government in question used specific tools to produce policy outcomes, resulting in less concern with how policy goals should be attained and greater interest in creating innovative ways of working. An example is the '4Cs' belonging to the best value initiative. In contrast to managerialism, for modernisers of government there is more importance attached to outcomes instead of simply measuring outputs. Quality is, at least in principle, as important as quantity. And third, collaborative working through partnerships involving statutory, as well as private and voluntary agencies is a core component of modernisation. This is also related to David Garland's (2000) 'responsibilization strategy', which also makes individual citizens and communities more responsible for their own welfare.

Throughout the chapter the tensions existing between the NPM of the neo-liberals and strategies of modernisation are explored. It would appear that the NPM is still an integral part of modernisation showing how the past continues to inform and influence change and reform in public policy.

Chapter 2 revisits the contextual background leading to the modernisation debate – the pre-modernisation agenda – and also shows how the present and future is influenced by the past. For example, there is a clear thematic continuation connecting modernisation with the neo-liberal/conservative concept of NPM. It is argued that although the principles of the NPM were still there they were transformed. Thus, it is not feasible to reduce modernisation to the sum parts of the NPM because both have their distinctive features. Despite this it is necessary to broaden and deepen our understanding of the main principles associated with the NPM to offer an explanation of the reasons why public policy is characterized by authoritarian austerity. This chapter advances our debate by showing the preconditions necessary for what we call the disciplinary and censorious side to modernisation. This so-called 'pre-modernisation' agenda ran between 1945 and 1997 comprising therein two periods. First, there was the era alluded to earlier in this chapter running from 1945–79, sometimes called the welfare state settlement. (Clarke and Newman 1997). In this section we account for the growth of the welfare state as a complex bureaucratic structure. This was followed by a second period, the 'managerial society' era (1979–97). During this period the welfare state and the principles of welfarism attracted censure from the government and it was gradually dismantled to be replaced by the 'managerial state' (Clarke and Newman 1997).

In Chapter 3 the ideas, discussed in the two preceding chapters, are scrutinized in more detail in order that we can develop a framework to apply towards the analysis of the modernisation of criminal justice. The chapter highlights those features of modernisation that are distinctive from NPM, also showing how tenets of both impact on the criminal justice sector. Taking NPM first, there are at least eight tendencies, including a move towards disaggregating units, such as Next Steps agencies, and regulatory agencies as the first. Second, the deprofessionalization of practitioners, which has the effect of limiting the role of experts in particular policy fields, such as probation or police officers. Third, criminal justice professionals have a greater management role with additional responsibilities but this is not backed up with any authority. Fourth, working in the criminal justice sector involves performance measurement where there are clear standards and procedures. The courts, for instance, are required to process criminal cases much more speedily. Fifth, the outputs practitioners produce are emphasized and there is a preoccupation with managing by results. Police officers are expected to catch more criminals, for example. Sixth, competition is promoted throughout the sector in the hope that this will improve performance. For example, private prisons and private policing were expanded to compete with public prisons and police. Private sector styles of management is the seventh factor, introduced with the aim of making public sector agencies, like probation, run like corporate and commercial organizations. Finally, the courts, police and correctional agencies were exposed to greater discipline in an attempt to increase parsimony in resources using mechanisms such as the quest for value for money. Attempts at cost-cutting are also used, usually meaning services are required to do more work for the same or in some instances less money.

The chapter then examines Rhodes (2000a) characterization of the NPM, consisting of six dimensions – privatization, marketization, corporate management, regulation, decentralization and political control. These were introduced throughout the criminal justice system, albeit with an uneven application. Governments achieved this through the censure of agencies that failed to comply with these aims and objectives. At a later date these dimensions were revised as part of attempts to modernise government, being replaced with the following principles – mixed economy of provision, contestability, performance management, deconcentration and regionalization, audit and inspection, penal populism and risk management, pluralization, joined-up justice, and responsibilization. The last three forming distinctive contributions explicitly associated and developed under New Labour in the United Kingdom. Of course, these principles will be reconfigured in variable forms within and across societies and agencies.

The chapters following in Part two of this book concentrate on the application of these principles in the key sectors of the criminal justice system. In doing this it considers the reform orientation of each agency and the political tactics employed by the government. The extent to which the former agencies may be **reform vulnerable**, meaning that they are regularly subjected to external drivers requiring organizational change, is debated. The structure of such organizations is flexible and malleable. In criminal justice, the probation service has been shown to be the most vulnerable (see Chapter 5). Other agencies are characterized as being '**reform resistant**' in thwarting attempts to change a particular way of working. It will be seen how the police, courts and prison services are all to varying degrees quite adept at resisting wholesale reform and their functions remain essentially unchanged since their inception. All organizations may also be to some extent '**reform transformative**'. This concept refers to those times when an agency accepts change and uses it to its own advantage and to further its interests, notably some elements of the voluntary and community sector.

Modernisation is a political exercise and this work argues that there are three main political tactics, namely **censure, compliance** and **commitment**. The first, **censure**, occurred mainly as part of NPM and involves the use of penalties and sanctions against agencies that are reform resistant. The aim with censure is to create conformity primarily by the threat of sanctions, but if this fails then different forms of punishment are available. **Compliance** refers to those occasions when an agency goes along with a particular reform agenda. It may not fully subscribe to what is being imposed against it nevertheless it will go through the motions, observing the correct procedures and ensuring that the rules are adhered to. Finally, there is **commitment**, where an agency accepts the need to modernise and embraces it as an opportunity for further organizational development.

The diagram at the end of Chapter 3 summarizes all the debates covered in the opening chapters drawing attention to what we have referred to as the **permanence of paradox** in the modernisation of crime and public policy. Each of the criminal justice agencies are then examined with reference to this conceptual framework, drawing attention to the contradictions and ambivalence at the heart of the politics of modernisation.

In Chapter 4 we turn our attention towards the **modernisation of youth**

justice. Young people are frequently labelled as a problem in many societies and they are all too often demonized as a criminal 'other'. We review youth policy in England and Wales from an historical perspective. It is shown that from the mid-1980s onwards the government has extolled youth services arguing that 'delinquency management' is something to be emulated. The chapter charts the alleged success of delinquency management policies, beginning in the 1980s and leading on to the Criminal Justice Act (1991). This contextual background is important because it shows that political parties of all persuasions endorsed the need for a managed approach to youth justice. The delivery of youth policy by the Conservatives was beset with conflict, though, which cast this area of policy into an organizational, and identity, crisis. The bulk of the chapter concentrates on the rejuvenation of youth justice as a kitemarked service by New Labour and stands as the first major criminal justice project it undertook. Many of the ideas underpinning modernisation were first developed here. Its 'success' is subjected to critical scrutiny and the relevance of the different dimensions of modernisation are addressed and evaluated.

The **correctional services**, otherwise known as probation and prison, receive attention in Chapter 5. These agencies have also been affected by the modernisation agenda in recent years, albeit in different ways. Prison and probation have their unique histories with different occupational cultures that have a bearing on the nature of their particular organizational construction and response to change. It is shown that the implementation of changes in probation has been particularly problematic and that this service faces a serious crisis of mission. The main dimensions of modernisation are used to ascertain the paradoxical disjunctures that have materialized in the correctional services. In the early twenty-first century, a major debate took place about reforming the correctional agencies and there was talk about joining up prison and probation in a National Offender Management Service (NOMS) where, it is argued the principles of contestability and privatization were played out in what effectively became a mixed economy of provision.

Chapter 6 assesses modernisation and its impact on the organization and delivery of **crime reduction services** in local communities. It takes, as an example, developments in England and Wales from the 1990s onwards, considering the Crime and Disorder Act (1998) and the role of the Crime and Disorder Reduction Partnerships (CDRPs). This legislation, and the initiatives it spawned, rest on the premise that the solutions to local crime problems are more likely to be achieved locally. The chapter suggests that partnerships are a relatively new mode of governance (see Chapter 1) illustrated with reference to the role of local strategic partnerships that have driven forward a community safety agenda. There is a discussion of the relationship between the ideas of community safety, crime reduction and crime prevention. It then evaluates changing definitions of these interrelated ideas in the context of government policies, in particular those attempting to tackle crime in socially excluded communities. A joined-up framework of governance, consisting of CDRPs and the Social Exclusion Unit (SEU) was established to reduce crime and enhance community safety. It is concluded that partnership offers an opportunity for integrated policy-making, connecting a range of agencies but the organizational priorities of individual agencies lead to disincentives that weaken commitment to partnership working. Moreover, crime reduction goals often dominate partnerships at the expense of community safety and policies may exclude rather than include particular groups of offenders.

The **modernisation of the courts** is the topic addressed in Chapter 7. The court 'system' as it is now known consists of lay and judicial sentencers, legal professionals, clerks and the Crown Prosecution Service (CPS). This autonomous system is closely related to other players in criminal justice, including the police, prison, probation and youth justice services. The main focus of the chapter is on the magistrates' courts where 95 per cent of cases are processed. Towards the end of the twentieth century the reform and modernisation of the courts has been associated with cross-cutting and joined-up services, as well as innovations in IT. These developments have not occurred without problems, though. IT raises questions about data sharing, data protection and confidentiality, and the emphasis on joined-up practice threatens to compromise judicial independence and the separation of powers currently enjoyed by legal professionals. The chapter explores some of the tensions this creates.

Chapter 8 on **policing and modernisation** explores how public policing has responded to the post-1997 modernisation agenda. The continuities as well as the discontinuities between New Labour's modernisation agenda and the new managerial public sector reform initiated by the Conservative administrations post-1979 are explored. Developments over the last three decades are considered in order to properly contextualize trends in public policing. The impact of the key dimensions of modernisation specifically for policing are considered, while the political tactics used by successive Conservative administrations in the 1980s and 1990s, and New Labour more recently, help to explain the contemporary position in terms of reform orientation of public policing.

The **voluntary and community sector** (VCS) nowadays is a key actor in criminal justice policy and Chapter 9 explores attempts to modernise its functions. This book has concentrated overwhelmingly on statutory agencies but the voluntary and community sector has played a role in crime policy too. In England and Wales, for instance, this sector was made a key feature of the project of modernisation. The activities of this sector are most closely related to correctional services work, and volunteer and community involvement in the police and courts is rather limited. Drawing on the original research of one of the authors of this text (Senior *et al.* 2005) the chapter appraises the enhanced role of the voluntary and community sector under NOMS (referred to in Chapter 5). It is argued that market testing, competition and contestability all feature in discussions about the activities of the VCS. More than that, modernisation amounts to a challenge of the traditional ethos of the sector, but it nonetheless enjoys considerable government support and sometimes exercises its transformative reform orientation.

The final chapter returns to the conceptual and theoretical issues raised in the introductory chapters. Its purpose is to assess the contribution that modernisation has made and whether the theoretical framework, which underpins the approach, is sustainable upon examination of the impact in criminal justice practice and to ask questions about where this contribution will lead over the next decade and beyond. What are the continuities and discontinuities between the ideology, policy and social practice of modernisation across the criminal justice sector? What pitfalls and weaknesses have emerged which may inhibit the modernisation of particular agencies in the sector? What can we learn from the modernisation agenda about the future policy priorities of criminal justice?

Part One

chapter one

Understanding the concept of modernisation

The main purpose of this chapter is to account for the emergence of the concept of modernisation, introducing some of the concepts that are central to understanding crime and criminal justice policy. Many social scientists will be familiar with this concept although this is likely to be linked to their knowledge of the sociology of development, written by a group of sociologists writing in the 1960s and 1970s (Harvey 1989; Touraine 2001: 66–7; Savage *et al.* 2003). This book is not about that contribution to sociological discourse but modernisation as a political project set in motion by various governments, such as the New Labour governments in the United

Kingdom (1997–2008) (Driver and Martell 2006). For example, under the leadership of Prime Minister Tony Blair, the concept was mobilized at a particular moment in history when it was applied as a method of governance. Having said that, the idea of modernisation was a 'floating signifier' in various contexts prior to this period, many of them having no direct relevance to this text, but it had been crucial in the gradual reform of parliamentary party politics in post-Second World War societies, and its usage in the reconstruction of political thought and public policy. Modernisation in this sense was not the preserve of particular governments such as New Labour, and their Conservative forebears also referred to the concept, but its most distinctive features for the purpose of this book are an integral product of New Labour thinking and action. Future governments in the UK, and governments in other parts of the world, are all involved in modernising – or changing and reforming – government (OECD 2005).

Thus, although New Labour are the prime modernisers of government and public policymaking in the late twentieth and early twenty-first century Britain, it is neither altogether new-fashioned nor specific to that time and place. The sociological concept of modernisation pre-dates its use in public policy and is clearly underpinned by the principles advanced as part of the Enlightenment project of modernity (Lea 2002). However, this chapter is not primarily concerned with examining the technical debates being conducted in sociological theory, rather the distinctive conceptual meaning of modernisation in the context of political philosophy and its practical attempts to govern society and regulate crime, disorder and anti-social behaviour (Cabinet Office 1999). Crucially, modernisation is at the heart of ongoing governmental projects across the world and it is a component of the so-called 'Third Way', an idea developed through the influential writings of the social theorist Anthony Giddens (1999, 2007). The 'Third Way' refers to a raft of social democratic reforms and programmes intended to update or modernise government and public sector activities. Martin (2003: 165) provides a nice précis of the situation in the UK:

> A fundamental component of New Labour's Third Way is the emphasis on modernising government. This is sold as a package of reforms and programmes, which can be used to update government and public services, and which works as a means to move beyond the assault on public services that occurred under the Conservatives.

Naturally, similar processes are at work throughout society.

Modernisation and the 'Third Way' are both projects that have not been fully realized but they do have some distinctive features. They are closely related to the restructuring of state forms, in particular Jessop's (2000) account of the ongoing and incomplete transition from a Keynesian Welfare National State (or KWNS) to the Schumpeterian Workfare Post-National Regime (or SWPR) (Hay 1999; Jessop 2003). This partial transformation has been achieved through a response to the neo-liberal and New Right-led reforms of the state and government. For example, modernisation is partly a continuation of managerialism or the New Public Management (NPM), including the '3Es' (economy, effectiveness and efficiency), privatization, quasi-markets, organizational restructuring, downsizing and contracting-out (Newman 2000; Martin 2003; Clarke and Newman 2004). The NPM is scrutinized in more detail in the following chapters, which consider the police, courts, correctional agencies and voluntary and private sector agencies involved in crime policy. An important point here is that while the aforementioned elements remain they are combined differently by different governments. This is in line with the 'continuist' approach to understanding modernisation (6 and Peck 2004), suggesting that modernisation is not simply about discarding these earlier changes and reforms but rather the introduction of other value frameworks to compensate for the worst excesses of the free market ethos held by neo-liberal conservatives. Politicians belonging to the social democratic left subscribe to social values, such as equality of opportunity and social solidarity evidenced in the areas of childcare, schooling and education, social security and income maintenance. In terms of practice, modernisation also includes an attempt to rethink the process of management and governance itself, demonstrated by initiatives, such as 'best value' (BV) in the UK: this placed emphasis on public consultation, democratization and joined-up partnership working (Chapter 2 discusses BV at greater length and for the moment its conceptual significance is highlighted). This illustrates 6 and Peck's (2004) 'distinctivist' take on modernisation. As far as criminal justice is concerned the police, courts, correctional agencies (and any partnerships to which they may belong) work with the active or passive consent of communities to address crime and its effects.

The above paragraph refers to many complex changes and while one should resist imposing philosophical coherence where it does not really exist, there is a pattern to modernisation (6 and Peck 2004). Three trends of modernisation have been identified: (1) the facilitation of effective planning; (2) reform of the policymaking process; and (3) collaborative inter-agency working. This chapter will look at each of the above in a little more detail towards the end. It is argued that there are three main responses to these reforms: censure (Sumner 1990), compliance[1] and commitment. Censure refers to those instances when the state sanctions an agency for failing to deliver the quantity or quality of services it is supposed to. For example, police forces can be criticized if they fail to meet government targets, such as the reduction of street crimes (Fitzgerald *et al.* 2003). Later on in this book, it is shown that this tactic has a relatively short shelf life and compliance tends to replace it. Agencies are compliant when they give their consent to what is asked of them and initiate any changes and reforms requested of them. They do not necessarily have to like what they are doing but they will tick the boxes and go through the motions. Commitment is self-evident: it is when an organization believes in change and actively pursues it. Each of these political tactics is principally state-initiated but the responses by policymakers and practitioners at meso and micro levels vary considerably. For example, under neo-liberalism, or at least during the 1980s, censure was arguably the dominant political tactic but as part of the project of modernisation compliance and commitment are more evident than censure. Responsibilization also makes individual citizens and communities more responsible for their own wellbeing, bringing the state and citizenry closer together in a quasi-contractual partnership (Garland 2001). In some societies people are asked to look after themselves by taking precautions against crime victimization at home, work and in their leisure time.

Throughout the chapter, the tensions existing between the NPM of the neo-liberals and the modernisation project are explored. It would appear that the NPM is still an integral part of governing complex societies. The remainder of the chapter evaluates the conceptual significance of the uneven impact of these ideas on public policy in very general terms. The chapters in Part Two of this book, ground these ideas more firmly in the context of the concrete setting of criminal justice agencies.

This chapter consists of two main parts. The first renders explicit two distinctive, but interrelated, conceptions of modernisation: modernisation as social development and modernisation as a mode of governance. Both of these ideas are examined in their wider political economic context. In the second section there is a discussion on the concept of governance, drawing attention to the limitations of concentrating exclusively on the 'Westminster model' of government (Ryan *et al.* 2000). It is at this stage that the key conceptual themes relating to the modernisation of public policy are rehearsed.

Introducing modernisation (1) and modernisation (2)

Modernisation is an idea that has been around in one form or another for many years and its conceptual genealogy (history) is yet to be written, although 6 and Peck have made a significant start (6 and Peck 2004). The more modest aim of this chapter is to define and develop a conceptual framework for understanding modernisation in the context of criminal justice. The chapters following this one, each consider the consequences of this idea for the workings of each of the criminal justice agencies but before this can be done there is a requirement for the identification of some general and organizing principles. These initial sketches of what is essentially a slippery concept will no doubt be revised as modernisation is redefined by its architects, not just in the academy, but primarily among policymakers and political elites and also among practitioners and the wider citizenry. Modernisation is an unfinished undertaking or series of interrelated and incomplete projects. Nonetheless, we believe that there are some defining features of modernisation and the political economic context in which it is embedded that will determine, albeit softly, its future direction. Before this can be attempted it is necessary to clear up a few points about our approach to understanding modernisation.

It is argued that there are two broad approaches to modernisation: (1) modernisation as a stage in social development; and (2) modernisation as a governmental project or mode of governance. Hereafter and until further notice, these approaches are referred to as modernisation (1) and modernisation (2). There are arguably problems with this characterization because there is the danger of identifying conceptual conformity where it does not exist. There is also the plausible accusation that it does not attend to the diverse usage of the idea within different disciplines to describe different dimensions of the social world. In our defence the remit of this book is criminal justice matters and we will limit our focus to some of those disciplinary narratives on which it draws (and we may add, contributes back), in particular political science, social policy, sociology, and history. Psychology and law are seamlessly intertwined with the study of criminology and criminal justice in higher education though the contribution of these disciplines towards coming to terms with ideas of modernisation is, as yet, undistinguished. The conceptual frame of this book is therefore situated in a social scientific intellectual frame with a particular commitment to the sociologies of modernity, albeit a late modernity (Bauman 2000; Young 2007). This book is traditional, though critical, in its approach and does not take on board postmodern interpretations of the social world (Berger and Luckmann 1996). This latter point is important in relation to modernisation (1).

Modernisation (1): a stage in social development

Modernisation is often understood to refer to those gradual, albeit fundamental, social changes initially brought about by the Enlightenment project of modernity. It is primarily concerned with social cohesion. For example, the socioeconomic changes occurring in British society in the eighteenth and nineteenth centuries were partly brought about by the displacement of religious attitudes and beliefs by scientific ideas and the principle of rationality. Perhaps the leitmotif of this period was the belief that human beings could exert control or, at the very least, an influence over the social environment. The human subject is able to emancipate themselves from the state of nature (Bauman 2000). Added to this was a conviction that the outcomes of modernisation were social progress and a more civilized society (Elias 1978, 1982). The Enlightenment was very much the product of a European imagination but it was exported to other parts of the world through colonialism and imperial expansionism. Hence modernisation revealed some negative traits in the form of race science and the war crimes linked to the barbarism of the holocaust (Bauman 1989). Throughout the twentieth century scientific reason and rationalism impacted unevenly across the globe leading to uneven social development, degrees of civilization and modernisation (Bauman 1991; Lea 2002). Although this approach is only of indirect relevance it is necessary to consider it because it provides the necessary conditions for modernisation (2), especially a belief in progressive change based on scientific evidence, manifest in the form of 'evidence-based policy' and the 'what works' mantra which dominated criminal justice policymaking in the late twentieth and early twenty-first centuries (Wiles 1999; Davies *et al.* 2000; Hough 2004). This contradicts the 'nothing works' pessimism of the 1970s and 1980s where faith in the rehabilitative ideal and the notion that criminals could be reformed or treated waned (Martinson 1974).

Drawing on Durkheim's (1964) sociology and his account of the transition of societies based on organic solidarity to mechanical solidarity, modernisation (1) includes five broad developments: urbanization, differentiation, geographical and social mobility, economic and technological change, and individualization and loss of community (Leonardsen 2004). All nation states experiencing modernisation have varying experiences of each of these key ingredients for social cohesion and they are all related differently to modernisation (2).

Urban space has also attracted the attention of criminologists, not least the Chicago School and environmental criminology, and the growth of criminology as a discipline is related to urbanization because most crime and disorder is overwhelmingly concentrated in inner- and outer-city areas (Park *et al.* 1925; Fyfe 2001). This in turn has strong links with structural changes in the political economy. In the nineteenth century it was the process of industrialization and the growth of the manufacturing sector, specifically the factories and mills which led to the growth of cities. The cities of Victorian Britain are still with us but they are dramatically changed urban forms as capital is severed from labour in a knowledge and service economy where production by hand is more or less obsolete (Hay 1999). Cities are not expanding at the rate they once did because population rates are steadying as birth rates have declined, although the ageing population seems set to inflate (e.g. the pensions 'timebomb'). Urban areas in Britain are currently either in a state of disrepair and dereliction or undergoing regeneration and a renaissance. They are sites of opportunity for social advancement and prosperity or places 'on the edge' where crime and social exclusion is endemic (Hutton and Giddens 2000). Urbanization is essentially a key element of modernisation (1), but modernisation (2) needs to come to terms with complex political debates and realities as individuals and agencies seek political influence and compete for scarce resources to regenerate urban space and tackle social exclusion in the fields of crime, housing, education, health, social security and transport. There is the added problem that many initiatives, such as those applied in New Labour's first term in government (1997–2001), were area-based and targeted at particular zones (i.e., 'zero tolerance policing', Health Action Zones) and tensions materialized when apparently similarly deprived communities did not always benefit from the investment of resources. An example of this is the racialized disorders occurring throughout the north of England (Webster 2007).

The next feature of modernisation (1) is differentiation, which refers among many things to the increasingly complex range of tasks and functions performed in society. Again there are links to Durkheim's account of the move from organic solidarity to mechanical solidarity. This theme also touches on social differentiation including social divisions, such as class, ethnicity and race, gender, sexual orientation, and so on (Solomos and Schuster 2004; Walkerdine and Johnson 2004; Weeks 2004; Butler and Watt 2007). The aforementioned physical markers all differentiate people into distinctive social groupings. The inequalities associated with each of these social divisions are offset, at least rhetorically, by the universal values underpinning both citizenship and human rights (Silvestri and Crowther-Dowey 2007).

However, modernisation (1) has also tended to bring about greater individualization. In the nineteenth century, the movement of populations from small, close-knit rural communities to the densely populated and overcrowded 'company of strangers' in the cities weakened communal bonds. The huge, impersonal bureaucratic 'iron cage' of modern state institutions also created a further sense of existential estrangement and isolation (Weber 1964). The solidarity of belonging to a particular social class and the activities of some feminist and anti-racist groups did counter, to an extent, this growing sense of atomization. However, the arrival of neoliberalism, identity politics and postmodern discourses all challenged in different ways the universalizing qualities of the politics of class, gender and race/ethnicity. The new form of individualization can be seen in the cultivation of individuals less as citizens and more as consumers, sometimes 'flawed consumers', making individualized choices in a competitive marketplace (Bauman 1998). Social differentiation, then, is crucial for understanding a political project as ambitious as modernisation (2), especially the tension between discourses surrounding citizenship and consumerism (Bauman 2000). It is also clear that many crimes are committed by individuals who are excluded from full citizenship and for whom the means to the end of consumption is crime.

The other tendencies belonging to modernisation (1) also continuing to have resonance in contemporary society are geographical and social mobility. There are some contradictory developments with this issue. There is for instance nowadays more geographical mobility, inasmuch as global travel is relatively easy for the business classes and tourists. The other side of the coin is that it creates more opportunities for the movement of other groups of displaced and vulnerable people, such as asylum seekers, and the increased involvement of organized criminal gangs in people trafficking as well as terrorism (Kelly and Regan 2000; NCIS 2000;[2] Solomos and Schuster 2004; SOCA 2006). The arrival of significant numbers of these groups and people from other EU and non-EU countries has placed a struggling public sector under additional pressure and presents dilemmas for modernisation (2).

When it comes to social mobility most Western European societies, and the United States, are described as meritocratic, open and classless societies where all have the opportunity to become prosperous as a result of hard work (Devine *et al.* 2004). There is little evidence to support the realization of increased mobility, especially with regard to the redistribution of economic resources and social opportunities from the most wealthy to the needy and socially excluded. Inequalities continue to exist in relation to the distribution of crime (Dixon *et al.* 2006), as well as welfare benefits, especially pensions, social housing, long-term health care, disability insurance and higher education (Hills and Stewart 2005).

Despite this, there is a case to be made showing that fewer people are now chronically socially excluded compared to when, for example, New Labour first came into power in 1997 (Crowther 2004). This has been achieved less through redistribution and more as an effect of stealth measures (Jessop 2003; Lister 2004). Social policies with the aim of responding to the needs of the neediest continue to exist but they are not supposed to lead to any additional cost, or at least costs that are felt by crucial voters in so-called 'Middle England'. Elsewhere in the world social exclusion has worsened, attested to by the violence on the streets of American cities and the implosion of Aboriginal communities throughout Australia (Zimring 2007).

Finally, economic and technological change is as much an element of modernisation (1) as it is of modernisation (2), especially technological innovations. Along with new benefits, such as improved global communications, there are new risks attached to the Internet as well as the now permanent threat of terrorism in most societies (Matassa and Newburn 2003) and proactive responses to it such as the Prevention of Terrorism Act (2005) and calls for national identity cards in Britain. These are important issues for modernisation (2) but of greater salience is the reliance on information sharing within and across government departments and agencies (Laming 2003; Bichard 2004). These are also tied to the commitment of governments to building a knowledge-driven economy where there is an attempt to 'reconcile and realign the interests of financial capital and a knowledge-intensive productive capital' (Jessop 2003: 9).

Modernisation as a governmental project: modernisation (2)

The political economic context

The issues addressed in the previous section are extremely important in order that we can see how modernisation has unravelled itself. Out of the last two centuries or so of social development, (e.g., modernisation (1)) it is possible to identify a legacy and this goes some way towards explaining the emergence of the modernisation agenda. In particular it will be argued that modernisation is a consequence of three broad developments, with the globalizing hegemony of neo-liberalism coming first. Second, there is the restructuring of nation states and a reconfiguration of the politically determined economic and social priorities in public policy. Third, there is the so-called 'Third Way' in Anglo-American and Antipodean politics demonstrated by the move 'beyond left and right' (Giddens 1994, 1999).

Taking British society as an example, as noted earlier, Jessop (2000, 2003) has observed that the British capitalist state is experiencing an ongoing transformation by global economic forces, which are restructuring the KWNS into an SWPR (Jessop 1990; Hay 1999). This change refers to the overlapping of two strategies. First, throughout the 1980s there were the neo-liberal reforms inspired by a Conservative Prime Minister, Margaret Thatcher (1979–90), sustained by a belief in freedom of choice, natural rights and competition. The main ideas were rolling back the state and reduced taxation, resulting in the attempted residualization of publicly funded state welfare. There was deregulation and privatization, and the creation of the conditions necessary for a self-regulating free market. This project, characterized as a deliberate 'strategy of inequality' culminated in a fundamental contradiction in the British economic structure (Walker 1991; Butler and Watt 2007). As pointed out earlier, public sector reform did achieve a degree of residualization through rationalization, privatization and the application of the principles of 'new public management' (see Chapter 2). In the criminal justice sector the government encouraged the expansion of the private sector, such as the privatization of prisons and the expansion of private forms of policing (Crawford *et al.* 2005). However, the market alone could not ensure that the economy would remain internationally competitive. There is a discernible neo-liberal accumulation strategy, as well as the influence of New Right and neo-Conservative thinking calling for authority and discipline, an acknowledgement of a requirement for some government involvement in the form of a strong state. For example, governments at that time, rather like the Republican administrations in the US, had waged wars on crime and drugs (Garland 2000).

Second, following the fall of Margaret Thatcher, her replacement, John Major, attempted to drive forward these earlier reforms but the British economy started to show signs that it was entering into a conjunctural crisis. Consequently there was a need for state intervention on the supply side as part of an effort to train and reskill the labour force in order that Britain's, as well as other EU nation state's, economic competitiveness in the global economy could be maintained. In other words, the partial substitution of a KWNS to the SWPR (Crowther 2000a: 158).

The KWNS is supported by the principles of demand-side interventions whereas the emerging SWPR involves the government intervening on the supply-side. What this actually entails is the investment of resources in the productive capacity of the free market economy rather than an over-bureaucratic and socialized public sector. Hay (1996: 172) describes this in the following way, 'Instead of a minimal welfare state, welfare becomes restructured as Workfare, a mechanism for disciplining the labour market and promoting economic competitiveness'. A structural change of this kind is about more than simple retrenchment of social welfare. Instead welfare is 'restructured and subordinated to market forces' (Jessop 1994: 28). To further complicate the issue Hay (1999: 183) remarks that the 'fiscal fortitude' of the Treasury means that there are structural limitations to the project, especially because of an 'investment shortfall' (1999: 126). As such, the resources available for stimulating modernisation, economic and social renewal, and crime reduction are shared out inequitably. The developments described above are clear to see, at least at a discursive level, under the Major regime as well as under Blair's first regime (1997–2001). New Labour's thinking about modernisation is underpinned by the key elements of the ideal type of an SWPR inasmuch as the solutions to a range of social problems is to be found in the economic sphere, especially the inclusion of all able citizens of a working age in the labour market (i.e., 'Welfare to Work') (Lodemel and Trickey 2000). This latter aspiration is a precondition for the modernisation agenda and is one that is based more on American thinking about public policy than ideas associated with continental Europe (Wilson 1996).

The 'third way' and the continuation of the neo-liberalist agenda: the global political economy

In the context of the UK, New Labour's public policy reform continued the Majorite programme or, as Hay puts it, 'the Blair-Major hybrid [of] "Blaijorism" ' (1999: 163). This can be interpreted as an outcome of 'third way-*ism*', which holds the view that Keynesian-style macro-economic management cannot resolve contemporary economic crises currently existing in the globalizing economy. Individual nation states across the globe can only play a minor and often inconsequential role in attempting to regulate the working of their provincial economy in a global context (Giddens 1999; Hay 1999).

Among policymaking power elites, especially in Britain, the United States and the Antipodes, there is a general consensus that the solution to social problems involves not necessarily less government *per se* but smarter and more astute modes of governance. Modernisation may create the conditions for a more integrated and inclusive society yet this will only be realized if individuals and their families take personal responsibility for their own lives, especially through paid work (Mooney 2004). In short, the success of modernisation is largely dependent on the inclusion of the vast majority of the citizenry in the labour market. This assumption is not without its critics, though, because it fails to take into account the structural barriers getting in the way of permanent or secure employment for some sections of the population (Bauman 1998). The 'truly disadvantaged' in some isolated and segregated geographical areas are not likely to benefit from such social policies, especially as resources become more and more scarce (Wilson 1996). For example, it will be argued that modernisation involves the following:

- the devolution of responsibility downward from central to local government, although budgets continue to be set by the former;
- services have to be delivered more economically, effectively and efficiently;
- there is increased targeting of resources.

The resources made available to different agencies in different geographical areas varies substantially and the social problems modernisation is intended to deal with may be counterproductive, largely because economic interests override social interests. For example, in the late 1990s police services in England and Wales were required to address a range of crimes but some offences were prioritized at the expense of others. The reduction of volume crimes (i.e., burglary, car theft) received most attention and limited resources were dedicated to such offences. The police had to be cautious in how they used resources to achieve these targets. Due to an obsession with 'what gets measured, gets done' other crimes, such as paedophilia, were neglected.

Thus neo-liberalism has reworked the public sector, but in doing this it has ironically put the welfare state in crisis by eroding its capacity to modernise. Although the public sector and welfare state have not shrunk, and indeed have grown in some respects, they have been attenuated by a neo-liberal-led 'responsibilization strategy' (Garland 1996: 454–5) or conceivably 'emancipation' (Bauman 2000). The government insists that its capacity to intervene and regulate the inexorable logic of the globalizing economy is limited, but it simultaneously makes statutory, voluntary, not-for-profit and private agencies, and above all individual citizens at a micro level responsibility for their own general conduct and wellbeing.[3] As Bauman (2000: 30) puts it, '. . . the present day modernity is light at the top, having relieved itself of its 'emancipatory' duties except its duty to cede the business of emancipation to the middle and bottom layers to which most of the burden of continuous modernisation has been relegated'.

Also, as an upshot of neo-led reforms of the public sector, the welfare state no longer has available the resources and government support needed to deal with the needs of a diversifying and fragmented society. The subordination of social policy to the requirements of economic policy can result in the neglect of some social issues and possibly the stigmatization and demonization of some communities as crime prone. The basic role of the SWPR is to control economic and social policy under material circumstances which make this task more and more difficult.

Although the management of the political economy has changed under social democratic governments, such as New Labour, there are also continuities with their Conservative predecessors too. Before continuing it is necessary to consider the nature of the crime problem confronting New Labour during its time in office.

Modernisation and crime in context: drivers in global crime

In this section it is argued that there are eight key drivers in global crime, which are numbered and italicized below. The salience of each of these drivers is elaborated, particularly in Chapter 3, as well as in the remaining chapters. We will stay with the British example to ensure some continuity and clarity. Until a couple of years before New Labour were elected to govern in May 1997, crime rates had soared according to both police statistics and the British Crime Survey (Kershaw *et al.* 2001; Reiner 2007b). Since coming to power an overriding aim has been (1) *crime prevention and crime reduction*. From the mid-1990s onwards, there was a decline in the numbers of crimes recorded by the police and reported to Home Office researchers. Despite that the public perceived modern Britain to be a 'high crime society' and fear of crime was an intractable problem (Garland 1996, 2000). The reasons for declining crime rates and the high degree of fear of crime are complex but under the guardianship of four successive Conservative governments, there occurred the criminalization of a workless underclass (Young and Matthews 2003). Also due to (2) *penal punitiveness* (i.e., the 'Prison Works' agenda of the Major regime) and the (3) *decline of the rehabilitative ideal* there has been the expansion of the numbers incarcerated in an overcrowded prison estate making Britain one of the most punitive societies in Western Europe (Liebling and Maruna 2005; Padfield and Maruna 2006).

Under New Labour, crime went down by 30 per cent and the risk of becoming a victim became the lowest it has been for 20 years. Notwithstanding this the prison population continued to rise to its highest ever (Garside 2006; Jewkes and Johnston 2005), while the police were thrown into crisis by (4) *NPM* with some evidence of underpolicing and indeed the abandonment of some communities (Crowther 2004). To be fair, as acknowledged earlier, New Labour reversed some of the most exclusionary tendencies of their Conservative predecessors, for example, by tackling extreme poverty (Hills and Stewart 2005). Attention was also directed towards neighbourhood renewal, housing, education and making all able-bodied citizens employable. Despite addressing with some success the link between poverty and crime, the criminal justice system had actually been made responsible for a wider range of crimes (Solomon *et al.* 2007, quoted in Reiner 2007b). Among the list are paedophiles, Internet or cybercrime and the new global/international threat of terrorism and increasingly violent organized criminal cartels involved in drugs markets (NCIS 2000; Crowther-Dowey 2007).

While there were clear signs of a reduction of street crime and some crimes of violence, achieved in part by police reform, these were offset by the insecurities generated by the risks and hazards posed by the examples just mentioned (Home Office 2004). The (5) *assessment and management of risk* is now a central driver of crime policy, which was increasingly oriented towards (6) *public protection* (e.g., Multi-Agency Public Protection Arrangements and anti-terrorism legislation). The government also focused increasingly on fear of crime and quality of life issues, such as anti-social behaviour (Farrall and Gadd 2004; Burney 2005). For instance, the police and local authorities were given additional powers to deal with vandalism, graffiti art, fly tipping, the misuse of guns and fireworks, and incivilities or 'loutish' behaviour in general (Squires and Stephen 2005). Perhaps the most significant increased workload was brought about by the focus on victims and witnesses (Spalek 2006) and the development of (7) *victim-centred justice* (Goodey 2005). Since the early 1990s successive British governments have introduced so-called Victims' Charters in 1990 and 1996 (Home Office 2000b), followed by the Victims' Code of Practice, coming into effect in 2004 with the passing into law of the Domestic Violence, Crime and Victims Act (2004) (Spalek 2006). Although the Conservatives did launch the first Victim's Charter (Home Office 1990b), it was New Labour that invested much more resource into this area (Williams 2003).

Finally, there is (8) *the commercialization of crime control* where the private sector is a major provider of crime reduction and security services, ranging from the regulation of the night-time economy (Winlow 2001; Hadfield 2007) to private policing (Johnston 2000) and private prisons (Matthews and Francis 1996).

As far as modernisation goes, New Labour's broadbrush aims were to increase access to justice for the general population and to realize best value for taxpayers.

The modernisation of governance

The understanding of modernisation in this book is based on the assumption that although there is talk about modernisation being taken forward by various governments, our argument refers explicitly to the debate taking place in political science which focuses on the distinction between government and governance (Rhodes 2000b).

The government and modernisation

Approaches that examine government focus on the constitution and institutional approaches to policymaking concentrating on the relationship between legislative, executive and judicial elements of government. This is sometimes called the 'Westminster model' (Cope 2001) where the chief argument is that different players in government are involved in the implementation and interpretation of government policy. Governments also exist at different spatial levels, for example, the supranational, regional and local.

To illustrate the above point the modernisation of public policy first needs situating in the macro context of New Labour's aspiration to make government more modern. Constitutional and parliamentary reformers in New Labour had an ambitious agenda and aimed to achieve three broad objectives:

- The devolution of power and the transformation of government at local and national levels (i.e., Scottish Parliament and the Welsh and London Assemblies). The rationale for this was to ensure decision-making occurs in closer proximity to the communities actually influenced by decisions.
- To make government more accountable at a local level.
- To address any democratic deficit by developing the appropriate rights for citizens supported by the relevant institutions.

To flesh this out a little, New Labour tried to make Parliament more accountable by making the political process more transparent. For instance, there were more select committees, increased mechanisms for scrutinizing the House of Commons, and concerted efforts were made to educate the public about the nature of government, demonstrated by the Internet access enjoyed by all citizens. The constitution experienced reform (i.e., the Supreme Court, the independent judicial appointments commission). There were also major pieces of legislation to enshrine constitutional reform focusing on human rights (Human Rights Act 1998), in particular by making government more open (i.e., Freedom of Information Act 2000).

The aforementioned agenda was all about bringing people into the political process and to call politicians and policymakers to account. As well as increasing the government's accountability the aim is to make government more responsive to the citizenry. This can only be achieved by giving communities more opportunities to have a direct bearing on governmental decisions that affect their everyday lives. In local communities councillors come under more scrutiny and people are given a choice about the election of mayors. Because government is in the business of providing services to the public there is an overriding concern with accountability and the quality of the services delivered. The modernisation of government at a macro level impacts on all areas of public policy (i.e., crime and anti-social behaviour, education, health) as well as in the economic sphere (i.e., the independence of the Bank of England).

However, this institutional approach highlighting macro developments only tells part of the story and for that reason it is necessary to move on to consider the concept of governance and its utility for understanding the modernisation of crime and public policy.

The concept of governance

It is not our intention to jettison the concept of government altogether rather to realize its limits for understanding an agenda as complex as modernisation. Governance is the preferred concept because it refers to the co-ordination of different aspects of social life, which reflects better the ongoing developments in public sector reform. The governance literature emerging in the 1980s identifies three main modes: markets; hierarchies; and networks (Heywood 2000). While the concept may lack precision these three modes provide an insight into the context behind modernisation.

The market refers to a price mechanism, which is used to co-ordinate supply and demand. Hierarchies share much in common with bureaucracies, which describe traditional systems of power and authority co-ordinated in a top–down fashion. In addition to this vertical dimension networks are 'flat' and provide co-ordination through informal relationships between departments and agencies (Heywood 2000).

Governance is associated with new forms of public management of which there are four main tendencies. First, the 'steering' and 'rowing' metaphor, which states that the role of government is restricted to 'steering' or setting targets and defining objectives rather than 'rowing' or administration and service delivery. As noted earlier, the police may be set targets to reduce particular crimes. Second, the boundaries separating government from the market are becoming more and more blurred, demonstrated by public/private partnerships and the growth of the Private Finance Initiative (PFI). In criminal justice, there was a suggestion that correctional services could be provided by the voluntary and community, and private sectors, as well as by the traditional providers, the probation and prison services. The third development is the growth of policy networks involved in policy formulation (Rhodes 2000a). Rather than concentrating exclusively on the legislature and executive arms of government, a wider range of agencies from different sectors are implicated in policymaking. Nowadays, crime reduction involves multi-agency partnerships rather than relying exclusively on the operational responsibilities of single agencies. Fourth, governance occurs at multiple levels with the effect of supranationalism and federalism, as well as devolution (Heywood 2000). Cope (2001: 3) expresses this well in his observation that:

> There is thus a highly complex and dynamic set of interdependent and consequently interconnected actors, cutting across different levels of government and different sectors of society, involved in governing. Governance, according to Kooiman, 'takes place in interactions between actors on micro, meso and macro levels of social and political aggregation' (2003: 41). Governments do not govern on their own; they increasingly rely on other actors to govern society.

Governance and the modernisation agenda

The governance literature has been used to justify neo-liberal arguments, such as the minimization and lessening of government involvement in public policy. This book does not intend to become involved in an ideological dispute of this kind, though, but instead plans to use it to explain how the modernisation agenda operates in practice. The modernisation of governance has consequences for two main groups: (1) the agencies involved in the policymaking process or the internal environment; and (2) citizens and communities or the external environment. The space between the above is fluid and dynamic, with the former having more power and influence on the modernisation agenda.

In short modernisation is all about reforming and changing the public sector and governmental organizations and departments. The rationale of modernisation is to overcome overcompartmentalization of government departments by joining up government agencies to deliver services in partnership. This requires more interconnectedness between agencies through vertical and horizontal forms of integration of different levels of government, including the central, regional, local, as well as the supranational. In terms of governance, horizontal and vertical integration is a prerequisite in other social domains, including the public, private, voluntary and not-for-profit sectors. This is clearly a government-led type of governance as the former is able to discipline and regulate what goes on in the police, courts and correctional services, as well as hospitals, universities, schools, local government, privatized utilities and arguably the voluntary sector too.

It is already quite clear that all the main departments at Whitehall are being enlisted to participate in this process and that there are no exemptions. In other words, there is a disciplinary side to modernisation. Discipline may be exercised through the sovereign power of the state but it may also be internalized by agents who regulate their own conduct (Foucault 1991). This discipline is ensured through either one or a combination of three mechanisms or political tactics, namely censure, compliance and commitment. Taking the first political tactic, censure, this refers to those aspects of reform where modernisers can influence the behaviour of policymakers and practitioners through the use of reprimands, such as 'hit teams', whether real or symbolic. In very crude terms, if an agent or agency fails to deliver what it is supposed to deliver then there are sanctions in place. For example, underperformance will be met with a range of injunctions including a reduction or withdrawal of resources or verbal castigation. For instance, as part of the ongoing modernisation of the NHS there have been various *Commission for Health Improvement* inspectorate-led crackdowns on deficits, and Primary Care Trusts (PCTs) are cutting spending in areas where too much has been spent or if there is insufficient resource. In the field of education the activities of Ofsted is a further example.

Compliance is an altogether different mechanism and refers to those individuals and organizations who comply with the terms of an agenda. They may not agree to them fully but they give their consent. This may be seen as an example of hegemony (Gramsci 1971) where individuals give their consent, both actively and passively, to the socioeconomic status quo. The last political tactic, commitment, is where agents and agencies accept modernisation and co-operate with the architects of economic and moral change. As later chapters show this is widespread throughout the criminal justice sector.

The chapters in the remainder of the book are dedicated to different criminal justice agencies; before then the theoretical significance of this response is teased out. The basic point is that any attempt at strategic and structural reform is not simply about changing existing or making brand new legislation, rules, structures, procedures and processes. There is also the issue of communicating a reform agenda to those charged with driving forward modernisation and there is also the issue of their consent, however active or passive it may be.

Modernisation is also not just a product of social structural arrangements. It is also related to human and political agency. For example, modernisation is a set of political rationalities deployed throughout the policymaking process. Most crucially it is a method of governance realized through social structures and human agency. It is also a discourse and an emergent ideology. Ideology is a rather unfashionable concept these days, especially since the collapse of scientific socialism in the late 1980s but we would like to retain it. For the purposes of this text, ideology refers to a 'coherent logic' used to frame a range of different values and resources to justify particular decisions, actions and interventions (Hewitt 1992) as well as non-decisions and inaction (Lukes 1974). In this sense, though, we are not talking about the big picture ideologies or metanarratives of neo-liberalism or Marxism, but ways of seeing the world where there is a degree of coherence and semantic stability.

Modernisation as a set of political rationalities

Modernisation is a normative concept in political debate inasmuch as it is set against the traditional, hackneyed and out of date. Modernisation strategies have been central to the internal dynamics of governments and modes of governance. For instance, in the UK, New Labour has developed ideas about modernisation that are unique to them and are being translated into practice under their governance (Cabinet Office 1999). However, modernisation does draw on neo-liberal, New Right and conservative political rationalities, and the structural constraints they have created. Any future neo-liberal politically conservative government may use different words or terms as it engineers reform and change but it will be indebted to modernisation rather like New Labour inherited the legacy of the NPM.

Modernisation as a discourse

A lot has been said and written about modernisation in political speeches and policy documents. A critical point of this chapter is that it is essential that enough attention is dedicated to the situated activities of a range of policymakers and practitioners. There is a danger that too much emphasis is placed on state power and the privileging of system needs. It is also necessary to avoid attributing discourse and political rationalities with too much causal power. In short, the aim is to avoid reifying political and economic processes and understating the significance of agency and social action in the social construction of reality (Berger and Luckmann 1996).

There are few empirical studies explicitly evaluating the impact of politically determined modernising tendencies on the different levels of the policymaking process. The substantive chapters show that the relationship between the most powerful and authoritative structures and individuals in the policy process and other levels of the policymaking hierarchy involves varying degrees of censure, compliance and commitment. This can be gleaned from what officials may say either in formal and written statements or unwritten and informal practices. For one thing, there is no necessary correspondence between thought, word and deed. The processes implicated in the response of different agencies and agents to modernisation are more complex and multi-dimensional and not reducible to the utterances and behaviours occurring at just one level of the policymaking process.

For example, the organizational structure of the state consist of three main levels: *macro, meso and micro*. The *macro* level is where formal policies are formulated (i.e., state and government departments and other policymaking bodies: the British Home Office and the Department of Health). The *micro* level is where policies are interpreted and implemented either straightforwardly or in hybridized ways by street level bureaucrats. In between there is the *meso* level where vertical and horizontal integration occurs among policy networks, which co-ordinate systems, processes and ideas.

Thus there is a need for more research into the complex and diverse processes and structures within which practitioners and policymakers conduct themselves. There are some conceptual points worth making, though, and at this stage there are various discourses on modernisation produced internationally by the OECD (2005) and in particular countries such as the UK (e.g., Cabinet Office 1999). A discourse analysis of such documents is beyond the scope of this chapter but the general themes they address are important. Interestingly 6 and Peck (2004) carried out a search on the Internet in 2001 resulting in 5399 hits. In short, language and political discourse is significant, but not on its own. This sentiment is expressed clearly in Luckmann's (1983) statement that: 'language is the main, although not the only, medium for the constitution of social reality. It is also the most important medium for the transmission of social realities'. Jessop (1990) makes a similar point when he identifies the 'empty realist ontology' characterizing discourse analysis. Like Luckmann, Jessop partly endorses discourse theory by accepting the importance of language and discourse in shaping social reality, but suggests that 'analyses of discursive strategies and mechanisms may be one-sided but this makes them incomplete rather than wrong' (Jessop 1990).

Reinstating agency in understanding modernisation

A study of modernisation may therefore be based on various textual data sources, such as legislation, government documents and the speeches of policymakers yet these may be insufficient in themselves. The issue of modernisation and any policy response to it is not just a linguistic construction and it permeates various kinds of social action. Luckmann's (1983: 91) statement that, 'as rhetoric and a reservoir of justificatory devices, language is a partial guarantee of socially constructed normal worlds of entire societies, classes and social groups' is illuminating. The use of the word 'partial' is significant, giving a firm indication that there are other relevant factors apart from discourse. It is always possible to treat ideas and concepts as if they have a predetermined objective reality, thus negating the creative capacity of social agents as they recurrently recreate the social world as an ongoing process. However, there is also the danger of reification, which means that so much power is attributed to ideas and structures that it loses sight of the fact that constructs are continually created and recreated. A possible consequence of this is that causal powers may be attributed to ideas, such as modernisation, without due consideration of the fact that it is social agents who first make the idea meaningful. The concept of modernisation is therefore persistently made and remade by the social actors and the different organizational groups to which they belong. For example, the government's rhetoric about social problems and public policy reform may be more well-known in society and effectively cancel out other narratives, although this is not necessarily so. In other words, there are different ideas about policy problems which are understood and acted upon in different cultural, organizational and structural circumstances.

Berger and Luckmann's (1996) social constructionism is of utility for understanding the creativity of the human subject at a micro level, but the ability to change and recreate is constrained by wider macro structural properties. Social actors' ideas and perceptions are significant, but in the context of this wider social structure some individuals and groups do tend to be more persuasive and provide more influential ideas than others. Human creativity and social action is restricted because of the impositions of relatively more powerful and permanent structures in wider society. A major influence, for want of better terms, occurs at an ideological level. To clarify this Gramsci's (1971) notion of 'common sense' is helpful.

Debates about modernisation and crime are an element of policymaker's 'common sense' views of the world. Gramsci (1971) defines 'common sense' as the ambiguous, incoherent and, sometimes contradictory, assumptions, attitudes and beliefs which are part of our worldview. There is not one 'common sense', but rather the term comprises a 'multiform' and 'collective noun' (1971: 325) which does not refer to a single, unitary perspective. For this reason, Gramsci maintains that common sense does not 'constitute an intellectual order, because it cannot be reduced to unity and coherence within an individual consciousness'. Gramsci (1971: 325) expands this point:

> where one's conception of the world is not critical and coherent but disjointed and episodic, one belongs simultaneously to a multiplicity of mass human groups. The personality is strangely composite: it contains Stone Age elements and principles of a more advanced science, prejudices from all past phases of history at the level and intuitions of a future philosophy which will be that of a human race united the world over.

Gramsci's particular conception of 'common sense' is derived from one of the Karl Marx's observations outlined in the *Critique of Hegel's Philosophy of Right*, namely the necessity of articulating 'popular beliefs' with 'material forces'. In distinguishing these two phenomena, Marx's preoccupation is not with the coherence of attitudes and beliefs, rather the effects of such ways of thinking on their conduct. Even if perceptions are amorphous and inchoate they have the potential to be a force at work in the social construction of reality (Marx cited in Gramsci 1971).

To relate this to the main concerns of this chapter, there are many different representations of modernisation, which can come into conflict with each other. These diverse ideas focus on various ways of explaining interrelated economic, political and social processes. However, some ideas are more influential because certain powerful agents and institutions are in relatively privileged positions to mobilize ideologies, which in turn shape the policy response to given policy dilemmas.

Talk about modernisation is separate and autonomous from the material context with which it sometimes co-exists. Discourses tend to be unwieldy, but there are boundaries relating to what can be thought and said about modernisation. Discourses have been relatively fixed by governments, such as the New Labour regime. Consequently, there is an ideological (with a small 'i') dimension or a relatively coherent conceptual framework for understanding modernisation.

An emergent ideology of modernisation

There are two dimensions to the *coherent logics* (Hewitt 1992) of this emerging ideology, including 'continuist' and 'distinctivist' tendencies (6 and Peck 2004). On the one hand, there is managerialism (economy, effectiveness and efficiency), privatization, quasi-markets, organizational restructuring, downsizing and contracting-out. These were developed under the stewardship of successive neo-liberal governments and while these elements still exist they were combined in different ways under New Labour (6 and Peck 2004). On the other hand, there are new, more distinctive, approaches to public sector and corporate management: 'best value', for instance, with an emphasis on consultation, democratization and joined-up partnership working.

Modernisation as a method of governance

The political rationalities, discourses and an emergent ideology have culminated in three main changes in need of conceptualization: the facilitation of effective planning; reform of the policymaking process; and collaborative inter-agency working.

Facilitating effective planning

This can be seen in the type of fiscal control exercised by the government, consisting of an attempt to bring in line planning with the provision of adequate resources (e.g., the Comprehensive Spending Review, Public Service Agreements). This can sometimes go wrong, though. In the UK, at the time of writing, the Home Secretary announced the expansion of the prison estate due to overcrowding and punitive sentencing policy, but the Chancellor of the Exchequer had not made available the necessary monies. Nonetheless there is generally some commitment to planning rather than unplanned drift in the policymaking process. In spite of this policymaking is bureau-incremental rather than rational. According to Ham and Hill (1993: 84) the rational approach is a 'root method, starting with basic issues on each occasion and building from the ground up'. This approach may also be seen as revolutionary. Incrementalism is the 'branch method', beginning with a pre-existing situation, which is tweaked and modified without any fundamental changes. As such policy is serial in nature where the overarching aim is problem shifting rather than problem solving. According to Walker (1984: 71) bureau-incrementalism consists of small scale 'adjustments' to institutions which are based on 'pragmatic' considerations. Changes are minor and concerned with addressing organizational anomalies and issues relating to accountancy and financial management. Rather than resolving more fundamental problems, the 'existing structure' is conserved without unsettling the 'status quo'. Above all, policy determination is constrained by structural barriers (Walker 1984: 83), for example, the wider political economic context and the ongoing shift from a KWNS to a SWPR, as well as the drivers in global crime.

In this policymaking process, the consent of agents is secured, however passive/acquiescent they may be (Lukes 1974). Entrepreneurial agency is actively encouraged (e.g., competition, market testing) but there is the authoritarian austerity of NPM remaining as a constraint. For example, the Comprehensive Spending Review and the use of Public Service Agreements introduced in New Labour's first term in office (1997–2001) ensured there was a strong fit between planning for long-term goals in criminal justice policy and the financial resources required to achieve such ends. There may be long-term plans but these are limited to what is affordable.

Reforming the policymaking process

There are specific tools intended to produce policy outcomes. There is greater interest in creating more innovative ways of working rather than the simple measures of the attainment of policy goals. In contrast to managerialism, the modernisation of government attaches more importance to outcomes instead of simply measuring outputs. Quality in crime and public policy is, at least in principle, as important as quantity.

There is space for the creative and entrepreneurial spirit in the planning process. There is also a hunger for evidence of the impact of activities (i.e. 'what works', 'best practice'). The worst excesses of quantification are complemented with an emphasis on the qualitative, though the measures are quasi-quantifiable. However, performance targets and the ethos of 'what gets measured, gets done' are all, in the last analysis, of paramount importance, suggesting the presence of either the NPM or elements of authoritarian austerity.

Collaborative inter-agency working

Collaborative working through partnerships involving statutory, as well as private and voluntary agencies is a core component of modernisation. This is also related to David Garland's (1996, 2000) 'responsibilization strategy', which has been extended to the individuals designing and delivering crime policy who are now more responsible and accountable for the work they do. Strategies of responsibilization are also making individual citizens and the diverse communities they inhabit more and more responsible for their own day-to-day existence (a notional social contract stating that '. . . with rights come responsibilities'. It would appear that cross-departmental and joined-up thinking and working is perhaps the clearest contribution made by modernisers of government. Attempts are being made to engage more stakeholders and citizens in a more participatory form of democracy. Both of the above underpin New Labour's approach to all areas of public policy in the UK, in particular crime, health and education. Although partnerships and joined-up working are well established there is tension between, as well as within, agencies relating to ideas, principles, planning and resources. There is cultural tension too. There is also the lack of a strong fit between policy in writing and policy in action.

Conclusions

This chapter has introduced the different usages of the concept of modernisation in public policy debate. It is argued that there are two main conceptual approaches, one focusing on broadbrush social developments and the other as a governmental strategy or mode of governance. The latter has received most attention in this chapter but the Enlightenment project of modernity and all it involves is a necessary precondition for the emergence of the latter. In particular, urbanization, differentiation, geographical and social mobility, economic and technological change, individualization and loss of community remain as challenges in any attempts to modernise the state and society. Since the mid-1980s the ongoing and unfinished shift from the KWNS to an SWPR has been in progress. As part of this structural change the public sector, and the private and voluntary sectors with which it is integrated as part of a new mode of governance, is under endless pressure to reconstitute or modernise itself. Modernisation is best seen as a continuation, albeit recombination or re-articulation, of neo-liberal projects, such as responsibilization and autonomous self-government, and managerialism, in the sense that there is anxiety about the distribution of powers, responsibilities and resources between different statutory, commercial and voluntary agencies. Indeed the next chapter (Chapter 2) revisits a major element of modernisation: NPM. It is necessary for some detailed critical reflection on public policy reform as part of the welfare settlement era (1945–79), which predated the managerial society (1979–97). It is demonstrated that over the course of this 50 year period British society witnessed the development and dismantling of the Beveridgean welfare state and welfarism, which was supplanted by the managerial state and managerialist principles. Modernisation cannot be fully understood without an appreciation of these changes.

There are novel developments too, which are peculiar to governments such as New Labour in the UK, principally joined-up thinking and action sustained by a commitment to equality of opportunity and social solidarity. The structural context is important but we have argued that agency is important too.

Modernisation is an ongoing governmental project with various mutually dependent and independent trajectories, although it has certain ideal-typical features in terms of ideas, principles and practices. It is essentially a product of particular economic (structural conditions), which are fundamentally unchangeable. Modernisation has resulted in changes in the domain of public policy in terms of its structural and systemic characteristics. The policymaking processes have also changed or they are at the very least more explicitly based on governance rather than government. The workings of the core agencies in the public sector/welfare state have altered. The relationships between agencies in the statutory, private, voluntary and not-for-profit sectors have changed too The rest of this book considers the extent to which these players as groups and individuals are enlisted and participating in modernisation as a result of three key political tactics: censure, compliance or commitment.

Notes

1. 6 and Peck (2004: 6) use this term in discussing the cost implications of compliance with the recommendations of inspectorates. They also use it to show that policymakers at a local level enjoy certain freedoms and autonomy so long as they comply with central government objectives (2004: 9).
2. On 1 April 2006, the Serious and Organized Crime Agency (SOCA) replaced the National Criminal Intelligence Service (NCIS) (see Harfield 2006).
3. This can be seen through the civil renewal agenda, which is explored later on in the chapters on the police and community safety respectively.

Further reading

Driver, S. and Martell, L. (2006) *New Labour* (2nd edn). Cambridge: Polity Press.

Garland, D. (2001) *The Culture of Control*. Oxford: Oxford University Press.

Giddens, A. (1999) *The Third Way*. Cambridge: Polity Press.

Giddens, A. (2007) *Over to You, Mr Brown: How Labour Can Win Again*. Cambridge: Polity Press.

Hay, C. (1999) *The Political Economy of New Labour: Labouring Under False Pretences?* Manchester: Manchester University Press.

Young, J. (2007) *The Vertigo of Late Modernity*. London: Sage.

chapter two

From welfare to New Public Managerialism: 1945–97[1]

Chapter 1 encouraged us to begin to understand the concept of 'modernisation'. Two specific ways of exploring the modernisation debate were explored, namely: (1) the view that modernisation is a stage in social development; and (2) the idea that modernisation can be seen as a more specific governmental project. Modernisation was identified as being both an incomplete and an ongoing project. Chapter 1 acknowledged that modernisation has moved beyond the worst excesses of the free market ethos held by neo-conservatives during the 1980s and has indeed developed other value frameworks. Ideologies, policies and practices which could be subsumed under the banners of 'reforming the policymaking process' and 'collaborative inter-agency working' which were referred to in the previous chapter, certainly indicate that modernisation cannot simply be reduced to the sum parts of the New Public Management (NPM). Chapter 1 noted that NPM is still an integral part of New Labour's modernisation agenda and it cannot be overlooked. The principles of these neo-liberal reforms led by Margaret Thatcher, which were sustained by the belief in freedom of choice, natural rights and competition, were alluded to briefly whereas this chapter articulates them more fully. Specific focus is given to what was referred to previously as the 'facilitating effective planning' part of modernisation, which was characterized as being driven by what was described as the 'authoritarian austerity of NPM'. It is the contention of this chapter, that in order to fully understand what Chapter 1 implied was 'the disciplinary side to modernisation', one has to first scrutinize NPM in far more detail. This involves coming to terms with sociopolitical and economic changes which occurred during the period 1945–97.

Within this period, one can further isolate two distinctive phases, namely what Clarke and Newman (1997) refer to broadly as: (1) the welfare state settlement era (1945–79); and (2) the managerial society era (1979–97). In order to develop an understanding of this period, the chapter concentrates specifically on the following: (1) the growth and bureaucratization of the welfare state; (2) the subsequent censure (Sumner 1990, 1994) and dismantling of this welfare state; and (3) the growth of what has been referred to as 'the managerial state' which undermined and superseded many of the principles and practices associated with welfarism (Clarke and Newman 1997).

The growth and bureaucratization of the welfare state

The parliamentary parties in the UK, in the 1950s and 1960s, shared a sense of political consensus (Kerr 2002). Underpinning this consensus was a corresponding social settlement underpinned by an ethos of welfarism (Clarke and Newman 1997). During the 1950s and 1960s there was popular support for Keynesian macro-economic principles based on an advocacy of the necessity of state intervention in the free market. At the heart of the Keynesian philosophy was the belief in the pursuit of full employment. It was an expectation that the majority in employment would fund unemployment benefits and pensions by way of insurance contributions.[2]

As well as advocating economic principles, Keynesianism was characterized by an underlying moral belief that state intervention to achieve public provision represented a form of social contract. Nowhere was this belief more evident than in the Beveridge Report (1942) which insisted that the state take responsibility for attacking the 'five giants of Want, Disease, Idleness, Ignorance and Squalor', not least through the creation of a National Health Service available to all. Rose and Miller (1992: 192) pointed out that state provision was counterbalanced by the belief that there had to be an acceptance that those of able mind and body would accept a degree of individual responsibility in terms of committing themselves to employment.

Many of the assumptions, which underpinned this era, had a profound impact on the way in which public sector institutions more generally and indeed the criminal justice system more specifically, operated. The commitment both to bureaucratic administration (Weber 1978) and professionalism were characteristic of this historical period (Clarke and Newman 1997). Weber (1961) saw the growth of the rational-legal state as a better guarantee of 'equitable treatment' in terms of public provision due to the existence of a system of calculable law and administration.

By separating the bureaucratic official from the means of administration by tightly defined legal rules, a sense of neutrality and impartiality was sustained. A hierarchical chain of command meant that state officials had a clearly identifiable status position. A sense of neutrality, impartiality and professionalism, led to the growth of professional staff associations like the British Medical Association which could more easily justify their power to set standards and conditions of entry into the profession. In so doing, bodies like the BMA were demonstrating exactly the kind of 'professional expertise', identified by Weber (1978). Professionals could be left to their own devices in terms of discretion and autonomy in decision-making, and could expect to be relatively highly rewarded in economic and status terms.

The 'consensus' politics continued into the 1970s because of its underpinning by a shared value system which cut across traditional party political boundaries. 'Consultation' and 'co-operation' were the buzzwords of this era, according to Dahrendorf (1998: 194) who argued that:

> A further aspect of the value system of the 1970's was the belief that organizations which existed in society, whatever the specific interests which they represented, had to be recognized and drawn into consultation so that there should be a climate of consensus and co-operation.

Politicians like Bevan espoused a moral philosophy of social welfarism in favour of previous corrupt arrangements, which were thought to characterize the nepotistic Poor Law Boards that were responsible for welfare provision in the nineteenth century.

From the early 1970s, however, the consensus began to be challenged largely due to domestic problems set in motion by the global recession caused by the OPEC oil crisis. Clarke and Newman (1997: 8–9) commented that, 'The underlying weakness of the British economy in the context of both global recession and capital restructuring exposed public spending, particularly on social welfare, to pressures for retrenchment from the mid-1970's onwards'. The so-called 'Winter of Discontent' in 1978–9 saw rising unemployment and inflation coupled with a series of crippling strikes. After going to the International Monetary fund for guidance, the Callaghan-led Labour government were forced to reconsider some of their longstanding principles around the pursuit of full employment and how that might be achieved. This marked a watershed moment for Clarke and Newman (1997: 9), who argued that, 'The symbolic moment of a Labour government cutting back public spending at the behest of the IMF marked the exhaustion of bi-partisan political consensus on the desirability of the welfare state'. The Conservative opposition to push for a vote of no confidence in the government, prevented an attempted recovery and thus forced a general election in 1979.

The newly elected Conservative government saw the solution to these economic challenges as lying in a revival of old liberal and conservative ideologies about political economy. This was to be complemented by a reincarnation of an ethical framework based on Victorian values. In passing comment on this sense of a return to the past, Halsey (1988: 174) made the claim that:

> Mrs Thatcher is no more modern than Harriet Martineau. The arguments are fundamentally the same as those which surrounded the 1834 Poor Law. Thomas Malthus, Alex de Tocqueville, Karl Marx, the chartists and the political economists of *laissez faire* are all still alive and well. The ideas are the same; only the circumstances change.

Upon its election to government in May 1979, the 'New Right' thinkers within the Conservative party were able to question many of the taken-for-granted assumptions which had been unchallenged in social-democratic regimes throughout Western Europe and the United States since the Second World War. Many of the ideologies, policies and practices which underpinned what Clarke and Newman (1997) referred to as the post-war welfare state settlement were to be dismantled by the New Right. Halsey (1988: 185) argued that, 'Mrs Thatcher had ridden to power in 1979 on a national mood of disenchantment with the welfare state'. The policies of the first Thatcher government were underpinned by 'a new economic calculus which treated public spending as a drain on the competitive viability of individuals, corporations and nations' (Clarke and Newman 1997: 9). Professional autonomy and expertise and the administrative and bureaucratic methods which underpinned them were now presented as being inferior to markets as a means of allocating resources. The kind of state intervention characteristic of the Keynesian era was no longer seen as inevitable or even desirable. Thatcher was determined to push the Victorian values of 'thrift' and 'self-help' and this led to a questioning of the notion of welfarism not just in terms of debates around 'efficiency' but also around debates concerning its morality.

While the Conservative administration under Thatcher in 1979 advocated the supremacy of the market, they knew that on the other hand, a relatively authoritarian government would be needed to preserve this so-called free economy. This is what Andrew Gamble (1994: 35–6) referred to as, 'the doctrine of the free economy and the strong state', which is basically, 'the combination of a traditional liberal defence of the free economy with a traditional conservative defence of state authority'. There were two distinctive camps within New Right thinking. On the one hand, those that could be characterized as 'liberals', focused their energies on the establishment and sustainability of a more competitive capitalist economy. While not disagreeing with the liberals, on the other hand, those who could be labelled 'conservatives' focused much of their attention on the restoration of political and social authority in wider society. Two examples of the 'strong state' exerting its authority during the Thatcher administrations, are the central government attack on local government, the community (poll) tax and the imposition of changes in both housing and educational policies.

Those who advocated what Gamble (1994: 35–6) referred to as 'the strong state', believed that the Conservative government had to show its strength by re-exerting authority over professional public sector employees. These public sector workers were often seen as having a vested interest in the continuance of public sector bureaucracy and in some of the 'outdated' assumptions of the welfare state settlement era (Clarke and Newman 1997). To a large extent it was Thatcher who skilfully united both liberal and conservative camps by means of relatively unified political programme throughout the 1980s. In noting that the free economy and the strong state were not always compatible, Gamble (1983: 121) commented that:

> The real innovation of Thatcherism is the way it has linked traditional Conservative concern with the basis of authority in social institutions and the importance of internal order and external security, with a new emphasis upon re-establishing free markets and extending market criteria into new fields.

Rising unemployment and inflation in the late 1970s made it somewhat easier for the first Thatcher administration to popularize a monetarist economic agenda. With the assistance of the IMF,[3] monetarist policies began to be adopted in order to try to contain inflation. Expansionist demand management policies were subscribed to along with the publishing of strict money supply targets and significant cuts in programmes requiring public expenditure. Milton Friedman (1977) was one of a number of prominent thinkers who were convinced that taxes needed to be cut significantly.

Almost immediately after the election in the summer of 1979, the Conservative Chancellor, Sir Geoffrey Howe, produced a budget which doubled the rate of VAT from 8 per cent to 15 per cent. Income tax was reduced from 33 per cent to 30 per cent, while personal tax allowances were raised and the top income tax rate lowered from 83 per cent to 60 per cent. Development land tax was cut, a higher starting point for investment income announced and dividend control abolished. New money supply targets were announced along with a commitment to reduce the public sector borrowing requirement. It was aimed to cut public expenditure by £1.5 billion and annual cash limits on spending programmes were clearly defined.

A White Paper on public expenditure in November 1979 endorsed the conviction that cuts in public expenditure were a necessity in attempting to achieve long-term economic prosperity. It was planned by a variety of measures, such as new increases in prescription charges, excise duties and petrol revenue tax, to attempt to reduce public expenditure by 4 per cent before the next general election. The government set a medium-term financial strategy containing more targets for money supply growth with interest rates being increased to further tighten the money supply. In reality, however, economic conditions continued to worsen throughout 1980, with high interest rates and rising oil prices pushing up sterling by 12 per cent.

Plant closures, bankruptcies and unemployment were all too common together with inflation which peaked at 21.9 per cent in May 1980. According to Gamble (1994: 111):

> By launching a policy blitz and attacking simultaneously on so many fronts the government encouraged the belief that was bent on radical change of attitudes, institutions and policies, and that it was determined to see the policies through whatever the short-term costs.

These policy changes have to be contextualized by reference to the fact that a drastic rise in oil prices in 1979 reduced world demand and increased industrial costs, placing upward pressure on sterling. The Conservative government's fiscal policies were aimed at lowering the rate of inflation and according to Gamble (1994: 108):

> In it's first few months in office the Thatcher government made some other crucial decisions that signalled its intentions to break not only with many of the policies of the previous government, but also to dispense with several of the key institutions and agencies through which previous governments had intervened in the economy. It placed its faith in the private sector and the removal of obstacles to the working of free markets.

The effect of this shift to monetarist economics on the political climate of national governments throughout Western Europe was huge, according to Gamble (1994: 48):

> The imposition of sound money policies on national governments in the mid-1970's gave an enormous boost to those domestic lobbies who were arguing for the adoption of monetarism. The international political and financial climate was no longer favourable to national Keynesianism, and those countries – such as France after 1981 – that tried to practice it experienced a major flight of capital and an exchange crisis. Such outcomes were generally sufficient to return errant countries to the new orthodoxy.

The 'rolling back of the state' (Clarke and Newman 1997) for the liberals led to the deregulation of former public sector utilities and an agenda around privatization. This was all deemed necessary for the achievement of the number one economic priority of reducing inflation. Monetarists argued that the control of inflation was to become the main priority in terms of domestic policy, regardless of any increase in unemployment. The doctrine of the natural rate of unemployment, developed by Friedman (1977), stated that imperfections in the labour market produced a level of unemployment, which could not be reduced by government action to stimulate demand. The belief was that without 'sound money', no other objective, such as full employment or faster growth, could be achieved (Armstrong *et al.* 1984).

The originality of many ideas within the NPM agenda are called into question when one considers the fact that as well as economists, such a Friedman (1977), prominent politicians, such as Enoch Powell, had advocated such policies back in the 1960s.[4] Rose (1999: 27) went further in his appraisal of the tactics and strategies of the British Conservative government under Thatcher in the 1980s, describing them as 'contingent lash-ups of thought and action . . . in which new ways of governing were invented in a rather *ad hoc* way . . . merely dressed up in new clothes', rather than their being the realization of any systematic, coherent and uniform philosophy.

The censure and dismantling of the welfare state

This book argues that there are three main political tactics which help us to understand changes which could be subsumed under the modernisation agenda. These are, namely: (1) censure; (2) compliance; and (3) commitment. While later chapters will assess the extent to which these particular tactics were effected across a variety of criminal justice agencies, this subsection concentrates more generally on the effects of censure (Sumner 1990) across the public sector more generally.

The role of what Sumner (1990, 1994) has referred to as 'negative', 'sectional' and 'bureaucratic' vocabulary in wider political discourses was instrumental in heralding the introduction of managerial change (Long 2004). This political programme was aimed at constructing a new relationship between the state and social welfare. According to Clarke and Newman (1997: 14) 'The special contribution of the New Right in Britain was to tell a particular – and particularly effective – story about these conditions of crisis and to lay the ground for the reconstruction of the relationship between the state and social welfare'. In order that the story be believed, specific social censures were brought into being which were intended to condemn the 'old ways' of doing things and to signal the direction that change should take.

For this neo-liberal ideology to flourish, state intervention in the marketplace had to be presented as both 'unnatural' and 'unhealthy'. Limited government spending and cutbacks would not be achieved by the Conservatives under Thatcher unless specific criticisms of the welfare state would need to be generated and then sustained in political discourse.

The Thatcher regimes witnessed the generation of a censorious political discourse which was explicitly aimed at both challenging and condemning some of the assumptions of the post-war welfare settlement period (Clarke and Newman 1997). To be successful, this discourse had to be part of a wider 'coherent logic' (Hewitt 1992). This logic would be used to frame a range of different values and sources and would provide the function of legitimating specific decision-making processes and courses of action. The presentation of the negative side of bureaucracy was a fundamental and inherent part of this censorious discourse. According to Clarke and

Newman (1997: 46), this discourse linked the survival of the organization to the survival of the wider nation:

> This discourse represented large organisations as top heavy, bureaucratic and unresponsive, and as needing to change in order to survive in the marketplace. The survival and legitimacy of both nations and institutions is represented as under threat unless change is delivered.

The bureaucratic arrangements which Weber (1978) had sometimes celebrated were derided. Those who had previously been seen as 'impartial', 'hard working' public sector workers were now censured as 'bureaucrats' whose chastisement was legitimated on the grounds that they were 'self-interested' and had a propensity to hide behind 'red tape'. According to du Gay (2000: 77), 'The very identity of new wave management is constituted in opposition to bureaucratic culture. Its advocates tend to represent the bureau in language that leaves very little room for anything but a negative evaluation'. Back in the 1980s, the management guru, Tom Peters (1987: 459), implored us, 'I beg each and every one of you to develop a passionate and public hatred of bureaucracy'. Bureaucracy was critiqued as being 'impersonal' and overly procedural, based around what Reed (1992: 229) described as 'a culture of repression and control'. This was presented as being in direct opposition to the New Right's 'flexible', 'decentred' and more 'entrepreneurial' approach (Clarke and Newman 1997: 65).

This censure of bureaucracy emerged at precisely the time when the Phillips curve of trade-off between inflation and employment ceased to work and people began to lose faith in Keynesian demand management. It was a time when, according to Halsey (1988: 182), 'critics of mammoth, impersonal, inefficient, and centralized bureaucracy became widespread'.

According to du Gay (2000: 63), the condemnation of bureaucracy manifested itself at the organizational level in the following ways:

> The dominant discourses of organizational reform throughout this period all placed enormous emphasis on the development of more flexible, responsive and entrepreneurial forms of conduct which would overcome the assumed stasis, rigidity and inefficiency of 'bureaucracy'.

The bureaucrats being chastised were associated with the 'liberal establishment' which in turn, the New Right associated with the radicalism of the 1960s. The contempt for these people is apparent in the words of Paul Johnson (1980: 72), who complained of:

> the burgeoning bureaucrats of expanded local and central government; the new breed of 'administrators' who control schools and hospitals and even the arts; sociology lecturers and others on the fringe of the higher education afflatus; so-called social workers with their glib pseudo-solutions to non-problems.

According to New Right ideology, these 'empire builders' were just as self-interested as those pursuing profit in the private sector. Marquand

(1988: 163) attempted to comprehend the way in which proponents of the New Right think, by getting into their minds. For the New Right:

> The way in which bureaucrats maximise what is, for them, the equivalent of profit is to maximise their bureaus. They therefore exert an irresistible pressure for expanding government on the politicians who are nominally, but only nominally, in control of them.

In this way, 'bureaucrats' were castigated for having vested interests, which were used to legitimate further government spending programmes. From the point of view of supply side economists, 'bureaucrats' were part of the problem of the 'oversupply' of government services, which had to be addressed. This was precisely the way in which the 'New' Right were able to stigmatize those who resisted the change agenda and to simultaneously absolve themselves from any sense of guilt or moral wrongdoing. In the words of Clarke and Newman (1997: 53), 'the deployment of concepts of vested interests in such change narratives is the way in which they cast doubt on the motives of potential refusers or resisters while the change agents themselves are innocent of any taint of bad faith'.

As has already been discussed, Max Weber (1978) articulated many positives in his account of the bureau, but this was tempered (1978: Vol. 2) by a critique in terms of an account of the 'impersonalism' and 'dysfunctional hyper-rationalism' of bureaucracy. Indeed at its worst, the modern world could be by characterized as a suffocating 'iron cage' of bureaucracy.

The concept of 'charisma' was used by Weber (1964) to talk of a kind of political leadership, which had the potential to break the chains of oligarchic bureaucracy. In the context of UK politics in the 1980s, the leadership of Margaret Thatcher was the living embodiment of this kind of charismatic authority. The move towards valuing charismatic leadership required the personal touch rather than the impersonal, bureaucratic approach, as described by Kanter (1990: 280):

> In the traditional bureaucratic corporation, roles were so circumscribed that most relationships tended to be rather formal and impersonal. Narrowly defined jobs constricted by rules and procedures also tended to stifle initiative and creativity, and the atmosphere was emotionally repressive. The post-entrepreneurial corporation ('because it takes entrepreneurship a stage further'), in contrast, with its stress on teamwork and cooperation, with its building the new, brings people closer together, making the personal dimension of relationship more important.

While originating as an ideology which infused the private sector through the work of people like Tom Peters (1987), who implored us to 'thrive on chaos', the New Right were instrumental in trying to impose this ideology on the public sector.

Through the mantra of 'Thatcherism' the Prime Minister herself was presented by her supporters as being a visionary whose messages carried a quasi-religious persuasiveness. 'Visions' were a necessary precursor in terms of shaping the more practical reform process. According to du Gay (2000: 67):

> Visions come from the creator, God. They are 'given' to specially chosen charismatic figures – such as prophets – who are then seen to have the authority to demand that people learn to change their conduct. Visions are used to challenge habits and established forms of conduct. Those who 'see' them are represented as 'having power from above'.

This charismatic authority (Weber 1964) enabled the vision of Thatcher to be imbued with symbolic authority. What Ronald Moe (1994: 113–4) described as a 'theological aura', meant that Thatcher's vision was not only persuasive but that it was difficult to challenge or refute. The self-authenticating discourse of the New Right and its leader requiring compliance from 'subjects' and correspondingly enabled Thatcher to further increase her autocratic, non-consultative style, precisely because, in the words of du Gay (2000: 68), 'God does not consult people about the content of visions'. The dangers of charismatic leadership leading to autocracy are evident in the following words of Weber (1978 Vol. 1: 244). 'The only basis of legitimacy for it is personal charisma so long as it is proved; that is, as long as it receives recognition and as long as the followers and disciples prove their usefulness charismatically'.

Thatcher could be seen to be the 'prophet' of the New Right, whose divine authority it was to seek out converts and turn them into committed believers by preaching the gospel to all corners of the earth. Thatcher's management of her own cabinet was a demonstration of a passionate hatred of the kind of bureaucracy which it was felt was acting as a restraint on the pursuit and ultimate achievement of the New Right vision (Crick 1997; Heseltine 2000).

In repudiating so called 'outdated' ways of doing things, the charismatic authority displayed by Thatcher ensured that a systematic censure of the public sector could occur. Public sector employees who perhaps would have been seen as relatively selfless people, more concerned with pursuing a vocation geared towards bettering the social good rather than narrow economic profit, were redefined as 'empire builders'. This was evidenced by Pollitt (1995) who explained how the shift towards performance culture meant that there was a shift in terms of the employment of public sector workers to new disciplinary technologies (Foucault 1977), such as fixed term contracts and performance-related pay schemes.

All of the positive things which Weber (1978) identified in his account of 'the bureau', such as the distinctive ethical bearing and modes of conduct of office holders, were turned upside down. Bureaucracies were presented as being 'rigid' and 'inflexible' whose destruction was a necessity for the national survival in an ever more competitive global capitalist economy. In short, 'bureaucracy' became firmly associated with all that was 'wrong' with large public sector organizations.

Clarke and Newman (1997: 16), argued that in censuring the ideologies which underpinned existing public sector practices, the New Right displayed a distinct lack of reflexivity in failing to acknowledge their own paradoxical position:

> The identification of political 'dogma' as a problem points to a distinctive ideological paradox at the heart of the New Right. Committed as it was to the overthrow of consensus politics, the New Right created the most self consciously ideological and dogmatic politics in the post-war period. At the same time, its populist character – in particular its claim to be rooted in 'commonsense' – allowed it to speak as if others were dogmatically political.

While censuring alternative political positions on the grounds that they were 'ideological', New Right strategists either consciously or unconsciously failed to acknowledge the ideological underpinnings of their own positions.

Closely linked to the critique of bureaucracy, was the censure of the welfare state and public services as being 'monopoly providers'. This was underpinned by a New Right critique based on the argument that costs were much higher in state welfare services than in the private sector precisely because of the lack of competition. In short, monopoly provision was resulting in waste and inefficiency across the public sector. The government were keen to open up service provision to greater competition by encouraging profit-based corporations to get involved as well as the inclusion of voluntary and not-for-profit agencies. Public sector organizations were increasingly required to operate by the engagement in competitive relationships which were underpinned by contract. According to Clarke *et al.* (2000: 4):

> Aiming to overthrow the monopoly power of the old welfare producers (which treated the public as passive recipients), the New Right argued that competition between producers would create empowering conditions of 'consumer choice'.

The government's powerful and sustained attack was not limited to the public services. Legislation in the early 1980s saw trade unions were blamed for society's ills. In addition elite institutions, such as the BBC, Oxbridge and the Church of England, were reprimanded on these grounds. The association of 'monopoly' with the notion of 'corruption' was presented as the complete antithesis of the doctrine of laissez-faire.

Most notoriously in Merseyside with the case of Derek Hatton, the so-called 'loony left', were censured at local government level and in practical terms this led a large reduction in local authority control over a number of public services (Hatton 1988). Rate capping was introduced, which meant effectively that central government could target councils which it thought were overspending. Ceilings were introduced on the levels to which councils could increase local property rates. The inevitable tension between Conservative central government and a number of Labour controlled local governments, came to a head when the government managed to successfully abolish the GLC and six metropolitan councils in 1986 (Crick 1986).

As with the censure of 'bureaucracy', the New Right censure of 'monopoly' contained a paradox. The vision of an economy in which small businesses could compete freely and potentially topple the giant monopolies appeared to be the antithesis of corporatism. The paradox was that, in reality, Thatcher presided over the growth of large corporations to a greater degree in history than ever before. This is of paramount importance in acknowledging that political discourse is only one of a variety of social practices and strategies which are not always automatically consistent with one another. In the above case, the political discourse built around the censure of 'monopoly' was clearly inconsistent with the practice of monopoly actually flourishing.

At the level of political discourse, state intervention in the marketplace was censured as a 'distortion'. This was articulated by Clarke *et al.* (2000: 2–3) who argued that:

> The anti-welfarist element of the New Right treated welfare spending as economically unproductive (a drain on the 'real economy') and as socially damaging (producing a dependency culture). The anti-statist element treated the free market as the normative mechanism for allocating resources, goods and services. From this starting point, 'the state' was seen as an interference in the natural workings of market processes – a distorting intrusion.

It was immediately apparent that the Conservatives saw state intervention in the marketplace as a distortion when just two months after the 1979 election, the new government declared that the regional support budget would be cut by £233 million over the next three years.

Good governance was equated with less government with politicians exercising their power by setting policy (steering) rather than actually delivering the services (rowing) themselves (Osborne and Gaebler 1992). By rejecting exclusively governmental solutions to economic problems, New Right economists and politicians argued for market solutions. The Keynesian economic policies, referred to earlier in this chapter, which were part and parcel of a welfare state settlement, which in turn saw state intervention as being healthy, were censured as a distortion on the grounds that they could prove to be inflationary (Clarke and Newman 1997). The 1944 White Paper on employment policy (Joseph 1944) had spoken of the pursuit of 'a high and stable level of employment' and this was effectively thrown into the dustbin by the New Right. Individual enterprise was the way forward in sustaining wealth creation with the government turning its back on fiscal strategies aimed at greater social equality. This laissez-faire approach was underpinned by the belief that men and women, acting as rational actors in pursuit of their own self-interests, could only realize their aspirations when free from the 'interference' of others (Smith 1776). Examples of the effect which this critique had in practice were the fact that the National Enterprise Board was forced to sell assets worth £100 million and the British Steel Corporation was forced into the closure of the works at Corby.

According to Marquand (1988: 160) the idea of the 'minimal state' and the subsequent disapproval of state intervention in the marketplace was dependent upon the New Right telling a story of 'apparent national decline', in the context of overwhelming global pressures, whereby Britain had been affected by political decisions made by the oil producing states. Marquand (1988: 163) argued that minimal state intervention was favourable to the New Right because they didn't want a situation to develop whereby the public would put the government under more pressure to meet 'exaggerated' demands. The condemnation of state intervention as a 'distortion' led to a rejection of the type of planning, tripartism and quasi-corporatism (involving co-operation between government, trade unions and employers' associations) which was characteristic of the 1960s and 1970s. The clear message, according to Marquand (1988: 162) was that, 'government failure is more likely than market failure'. 'Big government' had failed back in the 1970s when governments had attempted to adjust to the oil crisis and the message was 'if it didn't work then, it won't work now'.

High levels of personal and corporate taxation were criticized as being 'excessive' and an 'inhibition' to market competition and enterprise. New Right thinkers followed the logic that high earning individuals would work much harder if taxes were lowered meaning that the economy would be generally far more prosperous. This was consistent with the conviction that governments were powerless to affect real aggregate demand through Keynesian-style policies of tax and spend. The redefined role of government was the encouragement of entrepreneurship and the creation of wealth by changing incentives through tax policy. In fact more extreme neo-liberal economists went much further than this in referring to taxation as 'theft' by the state. One such economist was F.A. Hayek, whose *The Road to Serfdom* (1944) conveys the sentiment that government intervention in the marketplace was not only thought to be economically inefficient but moreover, in moral terms, was thought to be a restriction on individual liberty. This was part and parcel of a much broader ideology that there could be no moral basis for redistribution. This remoralization of public policy was inherent in the work of Robert Nozick (1974). In his writings, Nozick defended the notion of existing private property rights, arguing that there could be no moral basis for redistributing property against the consent of the owner. Critics argued that his argument was fallacious in that he made the naive assumption that all property had been originally acquired without coercion. While retaining some notion of a minimal state in order to offer protection to the lives and property of its citizens, these writers argued that absolutely nothing beyond the minimal state should be guaranteed.

This type of libertarianism when taken to its extreme, meant some even argued against the notion of a minimal state on the grounds that not everyone was able or willing to pay for protection of life and property by state agencies. While not aligning herself with this view, Margaret Thatcher perpetuated the belief that high levels of taxation were 'inhibitive' and 'excessive' in her rejection of the type of 'bourgeois guilt' referred to by Minogue (1988: 126). Thatcher herself (1977: 4) defined this accordingly as 'that sense of guilt and self-criticism that affects those, not only the very rich, who cling to a relatively comfortable life while feeling a troublesome pang of conscience because there are others less well off'.

Again the difference between ideology and practice is evident when one considers that in the period of the first Thatcher administration, between 1979 and 1981, due to the fight against inflation, taxes were actually raised in the 1981 budget. Despite this temporary measure and the fact that the tax burden was shifted away from income and personal taxation, rather than reduced, the censure of high levels of taxation as being 'excessive' and 'inhibitive' was an ideological one. It was ideological in the sense that it was inextricably linked to the New Right's moral conviction of taking the state 'off the backs' of the hard working and industrious people in society.

The struggle for the maintenance of employment rights, which were once part of the post-war welfare settlement (Clarke and Newman 1997) were now presented as being 'unreasonable'. The industrial action of the 1970s was seen to be pure 'evil' under a neo-liberal diagnosis. Trade union practices were not only in need of reform but the unions themselves were associated with a 'dangerous' militant tendency which was perceived to have an interest in subverting the 'national interest' (Crick 1986). Unions were condemned as representing sectional interests rather than the national interest, and the case was presented that they were prepared to 'blackmail' both government and general public in order to obtain unjust privileges. Trade unions had to be castigated because of their history of exerting continual pressure for collectivist policies and government intervention in free markets. Union power had to be restricted in order to prevent 'interference' with management's 'right' to manage (Routledge 1994). The practical effect of this was realized in legislation which effectively paved the way for the abolition of trade union legal immunities. Two major acts introduced by Norman Tebbitt were effective in censuring industrial unrest due to their altering of the relative financial costs of strikes to firms and unions. Trade union immunities were removed from common law tort action for damages, except for 'primary' strikes sanctioned by a majority in secret ballot.

The market notion of 'incentive' was used to make it tougher to access benefits and welfare services and such provision began to be condemned as a 'disincentive' to an individual pursuing paid employment. It was judged that the expectation for the provision of state handouts was simply incompatible with the new found requirements of a disciplined market order. Those who expected the state to continue to provide them with welfare and benefits were demonized as 'scroungers'. People were to be encouraged to fend for themselves rather than relying on state support in the form of a system of redistribution, censured by Thatcher as the 'nanny state' (Brittan and Lilley 1977). The principles of 'cradle to grave' support enshrined in the Beveridge Report (1942) were further undermined by Lord Young's 'Restart' programme. Benefit withdrawal was the ultimate sanction for those who were deemed to fail this work test. The censure of welfare benefits as being a 'disincentive' to work was inherently moral in the sense that while offering positive help to those who could prove that they were actively seeking employment, programmes like Restart clearly defined their obligations in return for the provision of welfare support. The balance of responsibility was clearly shifting from the individual to the state. According to Clarke and Newman (1997), the censure of the 'scrounger' cannot be dissociated from the blaming of others so labelled as 'dependants', including the supposedly sexually promiscuous single parents and the feckless and undeserving 'underclass' who were beyond redemption.

In order for the censure of 'the scrounger' to be effectively sustained, Thatcher herself had to ensure that those in her own Cabinet who were seen to display sympathies with certain policies around the pursuit of full employment, which were associated with the welfare state settlement, were dismissed as being 'wets'. Anthony King (1998: 57–8), writing in the late 1980s, argued that this was due to the kind of charismatic authority referred to earlier in this chapter which was displayed by Thatcher:

> Mrs Thatcher has a formidable personality, and she is capable of hectoring, cajoling, threatening, wrong-footing, bullying, embarrassing and even humiliating her ministers and officials. She is, in this respect, the Lyndon Johnson of modern British politics . . . She puts the fear of God into people, and they usually respond well.

High profile ministers, such as Jim Pryor and John Biffen, were among a number who were removed from the Cabinet for allegedly 'stepping out of line' drawn by Thatcher.[5]

The fact that the Thatcherite project was characterized by a number of paradoxes and apparent contradictions has been a consistent theme throughout this chapter. This is of utmost importance in explaining how censures are as much to do with the exertion of a moral and moralizing effect as well as being driven by a purely economic agenda. The criticism that government intervention in the marketplace was a 'distortion', for example, has to be seen as a moral censure rather than one which was driven purely by a 'rational' economic approach. This was precisely because by the end of Thatcher's second term in office, public expenditure was in fact slightly higher than it was when the government actually came into office.[6] Another example was that subsidies to the nationalized industries had to be increased and as unemployment rose, so did the corresponding amount of spending on social security.

At face value these facts do not seem to square with the New Right's ideological assertion that state intervention in the marketplace was a 'distortion'. This again reinforces the difference between political discourse on the one hand, and practice on the other. Discourse does not simply filter down and automatically translate into practice and there are tensions, inconsistencies and contradictions. These examples highlight the point made in Chapter 1, in terms of the necessity of distinguishing between the 'real' and the 'symbolic' effects of censure. Later chapters explore the extent to which real and symbolic censures have been effected across a range of criminal justice agencies by asking questions such as: Was and is compliance characterized by active or passive consent? To what extent does the appearance of co-operation with the requirements of the modernisation agenda reflect genuine commitment? How are the demands of the modernisation agenda resisted by the social practices of the agents who work at both strategic and operational levels within the criminal justice system?

The managerial society

In practice, practical reform of the public sector was predominant during the third Thatcher administration post the general election of 1987. Gamble (1994: 135) argued that 'Having got the economy right, as they believed, and having won a third successive popular endorsement, the Thatcherites saw the reconstruction of the public services as a key task in refashioning the British state and British civil society'. Clarke and Newman (1997) distinguished earlier from more later phases in the reform process. The 'early' phase of managerial reform concentrated upon improving the 'efficiency' of public services within an existing 'planning' framework. For example, the introduction of devolved budgeting and management in the Civil Service; rate capping in local authorities; and the introduction of general management in the NHS. The 'later' phase was characterized by 'market-based phases of reform', examples of which included direct privatization; the contracting out of selected services; and the introduction of charging for services.

The political and organizational censures, referred to above, were ideological in the sense that they served as legitimators for certain types of managerial change. Legitimation is one of the major social functions of ideologies and likewise, 'legitimation is a prominent function of language use and discourse' (van Dijk 1998: 255). The effect of this discourse was to sustain a belief that in order to survive into the twenty-first century, organizations must be prepared to 'reinvent' themselves in ways which may be uncomfortable. According to Clarke and Newman (1997: 38), a 'transformation' agenda was intended to be effected across the public sector. 'The "reinvention" case is that in order to respond creatively to problems, such as crime, failing schools and the health crisis, a fundamental transformation in ways of thinking about the role of government is required'.

The censures articulated above, highlight the success of the Thatcher regimes in establishing a binary discourse, which was reliant on the creation of dualities and oppositions. The 'new' managerial agenda could quite simply constitute the social world as being divided between 'old' and 'new'. Clarke and Newman (1997: 49) add further insight into this process with their argument that 'Prescriptions for change are set out through such structured sets of oppositions in which the "bad" old days are contrasted with the new, flexible, responsive and above all, managerial future'.

The censorious discourse sustained by the 'New' Right, was both dictatorial and evangelical. In arguing that contemporary managerial discourse derives many of its characteristics from Christian theology, du Gay (2000: 67) points out that 'one of the most remarkable features of contemporary managerial discourse is the prevalence of religious language and metaphors, especially those derived from apocalyptic, millenarian Christianity' and furthermore that 'it is difficult to think of a recent period in which the religious language of "visions", "missions" and the like has enjoyed such widespread currency in the ostensibly banal domain of management'. Indeed, the notion of a corporate 'vision' in contemporary discourses about organizations is derived from the Judaeo-Christian tradition of 'war against evil', according to Pattison (1997: 71). The censures, which have been examined above, had a quasi-religious like zeal in the sense that they preached about the 'evils' of 'inefficiency', 'ineffectiveness', being 'unaccountable', and so on.

Through a discourse built around, 'the vilification of the old and the idealization of the new' (Clarke and Newman 1997: 65), the status, power and, more importantly, the autonomy of the professional, was open to attack. McLaughlin *et al.* (2001: 303), referred to this process as, 'a fundamental assault on the professional cultures and discourses, and power relations embedded in the public sector'. Teachers could no longer say, 'We know best, we teach students'. Nurses could no longer say, 'We know best, we treat patients' and police officers could no longer say, 'We know best, we deal with the public'. Claims to self-regulation and autonomy could no longer be sustained by the professionals themselves. This social process was referred to by van Dijk (1998: 258) as 'the delegitimation of internal dissidence'. This censorious discourse energized the change agenda, according to Clarke and Newman (1997: 39), so that:

> the unthinkable became thinkable; the unspeakable became speakable; and things which at first appeared to be terrifying inversions of older certainties came to be a normal part of everyday practice. Management has not just been the means through which change is to

> be delivered: managerialism as a discourse has energised the very process of change.

Change was presented as being 'inevitable', 'necessary' and 'desirable' and in this way, vocabularies of opposition were rendered as being 'regressive' or more simply, 'irrelevant'. According to van Dijk (1998: 262), 'If dissident or opponent discourse is delegitimated, and hence the "normal" processes of communication and persuasion are impaired, also the construction of alternative ideologies is made more difficult'.

Chapter 1 noted how one aspect of the modernisation project has involved the subordination of social policy to the requirements of economic policy. More specifically, mention was made of how part of the ongoing modernisation project involved: (1) the devolution of responsibility (especially budgetary); (2) the delivery of services more economically, effectively and efficiently; and (3) the increased targeting of resources. Later chapters will explore the extent to which the NPM reform agenda impacted on specific criminal justice agencies. It would be a massive mistake to assume that managerial reform was introduced across the criminal justice sector uniformly because this naively underestimates local variations, patterns of resistance to change and political motivations for targeting certain institutions for reform at particular historical moments. As well as variation between different agencies within the UK, in addition to this, one cannot simply relegate the rise of NPM to an automatic response to 'globalization' according to Clarke and Newman (1997), who suggest that:

> It is possible to *overread* the logic of change, seeing forces such as globalisation, institutional fragmentation, the adoption of business ideas and practices in public service delivery, as cascading down from the global level of new economic pressures to the world of individual experience and action in a way which suggests simple and linear sequences of cause and effect.

Despite acknowledging the existence of the differential impact of managerial reform between different countries and between different institutions within individual countries, many commentators choose to identify, 'international similarities of reforms' (Schedler and Proeller 2002: 176). They point to the fact that with the exception of France, a number of European countries, such as the Netherlands, Germany, Switzerland and Spain, have all pursued 'new' managerial reform programmes to a greater or lesser extent. McCourt (2002: 234) points to the experience of so-called 'developing countries', making specific reference to Ghana, Jamaica, Singapore, Tanzania and Uganda to argue that 'there are significant instances of NPM implementation'. This leads one to conclude that to simply assume that NPM has been applied uniformly across the globe would be utter nonsense. However, one can say with some certainty that there are some consistencies and continuities which do not make the experience of the United Kingdom unique.

Having accounted for (1) the growth and bureaucratization of the welfare state, (2) the censure and dismantling of the welfare state and (3) the managerial society. Chapter 3 goes on to explore in greater detail the key features of NPM. It goes beyond the remit of this chapter by beginning to explore the more specific impact of the managerial project on the criminal justice sector. The distinctive manifestations of managerialism are located within the much broader context of the 'New' Labour modernisation agenda post-1997. Further attempts to theorize the nature of both managerial and modernist governance are made with reference to the work of Rhodes (1997). Key questions are asked in order to interrogate the modernisation agenda: What has been the impact of privatization and marketization on the criminal justice sector? What is the distinctive nature of corporate management and regulation in the criminal justice context? How does the appearance of decentralization fit with greater political control across a range of criminal justice institutions? By attempting to answer these questions, Chapter 3 sets up the opportunity for the rest of this book to concentrate on the differences between specific criminal justice agencies in terms of whether they can be characterized as vulnerable to reform, resistant to reform or whether they are able to actively embrace and even celebrate reform in a genuinely transformative way.

Notes

1 An earlier version of this chapter appeared in Long, M. (2004) Naming, shaming and the politics of blaming: police middle management perceptions of the impact of best value. Unpublished PhD thesis, University of East London.
2 See Williams, F. (1994) Social relations, welfare and the post-Fordism debate, in R. Burrows and B. Loader (eds) *Towards a Post-Fordist Welfare State?* London: Routledge.
3 International Monetary Fund.
4 It is important perhaps to acknowledge when speaking of the 'New Right', that there were internal debates and disagreements between those who publicly advocated monetarist policies. F.A. Hayek, for instance, criticized many monetarists for what he saw as the all too slow way of pushing inflation out of the economy. He suggested abolishing inflation immediately by introducing a complete reform of currency as had occurred in Germany in 1923.
5 Other names could include Francis Pym, Sir Ian Gilmour, Lord Soames and Mark Carlisle.
6 Skidelsky (1988: 159). They point to economic, demographic and technological changes which ensured that overall spending did not fall.

Further reading

Clarke, J. and Newman, J. (1997) *The Managerial State: Power, Politics and Ideology in the Remaking of Social Welfare*. London: Sage.

Clarke, J., Gerwittz, S. and McLaughlin, E. (2000) *New Managerialism: New Welfare*. London: Sage.

Gamble, A. (1994) *The Free Economy and The Strong State: The Politics of Thatcherism*, 2nd edn. London: Macmillan.

McLaughlin, E., Muncie, J. and Hughes, G. (2001) The permanent revolution: New Labour, public management and the modernisation of criminal justice, *Criminal Justice*, 1(3): 301–18.

Pollitt, C. (1993) *Managerialism and the Public Services: Cuts of Cultural Change in the 1990s?* 2nd edn. Oxford: Blackwell.

Skidelsky, R. (ed.) (1988) *Thatcherism*. London: Chatto and Windus.

Smith, A. (1776) *An Inquiry into the Nature and Causes of the Wealth of Nations*. New York: The Modern Library, Random House.

chapter three

Understanding the modernisation policy process

Introduction

The first two chapters have constructed the scaffolding which shapes the notion of modernisation in both its macro and micro manifestations, and then sketched the climate in which ideas of new public management (NPM) first appeared on the political agenda in the 1980s and 1990s to be taken up and reshaped by New Labour. The final chapter in this section is concerned to unpack in more detail the ideas underpinning NPM with three underlying purposes. First, to discern some conceptual clarity about the concept itself and erect some building blocks to describe and apply the concepts. Second, and as a consequence of the first activity, to begin to explore the distinctive manifestations of manageralism contained in the New Labour notion of modernisation and to begin to raise questions about the degree to which it represents distinctiveness, innovation and change. The third element brings the analysis into the criminal justice domain to identify the ways in which these tenets of NPM and modernisation began to translate into the criminal justice sector and in so doing to see the varied ways in which the concepts impacted. This chapter will conclude by constructing a conceptual framework, drawn from all the opening chapters, which will then form the blueprint to be tested in the chapters in Part Two, focused on the key agencies in the criminal justice sector. This framework will help test the tenets for their robustness and applicability both within England, Wales and beyond.

In seeking to create some conceptual clarity concerning the key tenets of new public management and its New Labour variant – modernisation – the intention is not to impose a spurious, neatly packaged consistency. NPM does not represent a single theoretical approach (Pollitt 1993; Rhodes 1997; Newman 2001) but a set of managerial and governance responses to the changing political and economic climate in the later part of the twentieth century. As Rhodes contends the 'distinctiveness lies in the package not in the parts but there is no uniform, agreed package'. However, any listing of NPM will reproduce similar aspects. There is little disagreement that at a general level the trends associated with new public management, as highlighted in Chapter 2, can be identified as indicating a:

- shift to dissaggregation of units, including the creation of Next Steps agencies and the growth of regulatory bodies;
- de-professionalization and de-privileging staff groups seeking to reduce the control over policy and practice of the 'expert';
- hands-on professional management, but often creating responsibility without authority;
- explicit standards, procedures and measures of performance management;
- greater emphasis on output controls and managing by results;
- shift to greater competition;
- stress on private sector styles of management practice;
- stress on greater discipline and parsimony in resource use using mechanisms, such as value for money regimes, and cost-cutting mechanisms, such as cash limits and formula funding.

At this level of abstraction these trends can be discerned operating in a range of ways across different parts of the public sector (Newburn 2002; Raine 2002; 6 2004). These trends also appear to have some resonance across the world (Christensen and Lægreid 2005). Claims for NPM as a global phenomenon are, however, hotly disputed as Rhodes claims 'the case for NPM as a global paradigm was overstated' (Rhodes 1997). But, as we shall see as this book progresses, such techniques are impacting upon criminal justice systems in a variety of international jurisdictions.

NPM is certainly observable in the criminal justice sector as highlighted by a range of commentators (McLaughlin *et al.* 2001; Newburn 2002; Raine 2002) and experienced by agency personnel, although the impact of these processes appeared somewhat later in time than in the rest of the public sector. This is in part due to an incoming Thatcher government's strong commitment to law and order in 1979 which militated against the urgent application of such techniques in the sector. Though another early trend can be noticed here and that is that even within a single sector, such as the criminal justice sector, the impact of NPM occurred at different rates across the different agencies and this suggests the need to consider what orientation to reform and change might determine the pace, the acceptability and the shape of alignment to these modernising tendencies.

During the 1990s there was a gradual imposition of such techniques, even within the criminal justice sector, as the last chapter highlighted. These changes were conducted in a censorious and coercive atmosphere in the context of market-driven ideologies of governance. Chapter 2 traced how the public sphere became fragmented with large scale dismantling of state bureaucracies and privatization of key industries. Janet Newman (2001) argues that at the level of discourse, the continued implementation of the tenets of NPM took place under New Labour within a Third Way ideology of networks but that traces of market-driven mechanisms were not entirely removed, thus creating a political environment in which different philosophies helped shape the patterns of change. As she writes, 'different elements of new and old are packaged and repackaged as different modes of governance are overlaid on each other' (Newman 2001: 4). This chapter will trace how the censure, so redolent of Thatcher, began to be supplanted by organizations which showed a willingness to comply with the demands of NPM and some, sensing new opportunities for advancement, expressed a strong commitment to these changes. But first a template for identifying the key features of NPM, as remoulded by New Labour in the twenty-first century is needed.

Even if we regard the attempt to construct a single framework from NPM as a flawed enterprise with many commentators referring to the malleability of the idea, we can see that the trends highlighted above can be formed into a framework for analysis. This has been attempted by Rhodes in his examination of the Civil Service. This offers us a heuristic device for analysis. This chapter will utilize Rhodes (2000a) attempt at a division of NPM into six dimensions – *privatization, marketization, corporate management, regulation, decentralization and political control* – to explore how these dimensions have rolled out in the criminal justice sector and the way those dimensions have altered or developed under the modernisation agenda of New Labour. This will help in creating some conceptual clarity and contribute to our conceptual map at the end of this chapter.

Privatization

In the 1980s any moves towards privatization were fought on ideological grounds with strong moral concerns about any aspect of the public sector being administered by the private sector. This was particularly the case in the criminal justice sector. The resistance to the possible introduction of private prisons was hard fought. The prison service, since the nineteenth century, had grown up as a public service with strong centralized management (Nash and Ryan 2003). In the 1990s the Conservative government, championing NPM techniques, began to create the agenda for change. But while agency status and private management techniques might be acceptable, the introduction of the private prison was not:

> The Prison Officers Association strongly opposed prison privatization, believing that it would cost its members their jobs or, at the very least, reduce their conditions of service. Penal lobby groups such as the Howard League and the Prison Reform Trust were almost unanimous in their opinion that handing over the delicate business of punishing people to companies like Group 4 was a privatization too far.
>
> (Nash and Ryan 2003: 159)

The resistances were related to the very concept of privatization itself. Working in the public sector had been seen as a vocation and a lifelong commitment which could not be sustained when the profit motive became part of the package. Even a government with a strong majority had to overcome the resistances associated with this idea. The introduction of the powers to appoint private contractors to build and manage prisons was only reluctantly conceded. Penal lobby groups, public sector unions, such as POA and Napo, and opposition politicians were all united against the very notion of private provision in the criminal justice sector. Despite this seemingly massed resistance this battlefield increasingly represented an arena where ground was constantly being ceded – private prisons were quickly followed by court escort work, electronic surveillance and private policing.

Indeed by the time the conservatives lost power in 1997, there were few organizations resisting privatization on moral or ideological grounds alone. Significantly politicians keen to import the role of the private sector into the criminal justice sector chose new or less contested areas of new provision. Nowhere was this better illustrated in the introduction of electronic surveillance. Strong ideologically motivated opposition to 'tagging' was expressed by the public sector, most notably the Probation Service. Napo expressed its opposition to this development in its entirety challenging it as a programme of community sentencing on the grounds of both ethics and practicality. In addition the Probation Service and the police did not see themselves as the natural home for delivering such services and this facilitated the government looking to another sector for its delivery. Given that electronic surveillance required new and innovative technologies, not yet employed in the public sector, this gave a licence to new agencies to make a mark. So the private sector, often with American sponsorship, gained the kind of foothold in service provision which has been hard to resist in more recent times (Nellis 2004). It should be noted this was not a necessary consequence of this change as in Sweden, for example, the public sector, led by the police, has led on electronic surveillance.

If NPM can be identified as committed to privatization in the 1980s and 1990s this principle was not to be unravelled by a new government despite its own historic opposition to privatization. Indeed New Labour have shown no inclination to unravel the involvement of the private sector and in fact their role has been encouraged and enhanced under new arrangements. However, the goal in current policies appears not to be privatization *per se*. Rather we have seen a government intent on a policy which seeks a service delivery sector that comprises the public sector and the voluntary and community sector as well as the private sector. This 'mixed economy of provision' prominent in current commissioning processes under the National Offender Management Service is the constant refrain of government officials. What we have seen, therefore, is a refining of the concept of privatization under the modernisation agenda such that private sector involvement is welcomed, not because of a commitment *per se* to the private sector but as an option in the commissioning process. New Labour did not dismantle the privatization thrust of early NPM reforms, rather they accepted this as a reality but widened the goal to a mixed economy.

Marketization

This Rhodes refers to as 'the use of market mechanisms in the delivery of public services' (Rhodes 2000a: 152). Consistent with the concerns expressed above about privatization, the market testing of criminal justice services was hardly to be welcomed in the 1980s and 1990s. The initial protection of the sector against this approach was in part due to the dependence on the police to support the law and order approach in which Thatcher had come to power (Savage 2003). This allowed a resistance to such changes to be pursued. This resistance was at its strongest in relation to the police and it was post-Sheehy before significant inroads into the management style and the reduction of the influence of local authorities that NPM began to bite even in policing.

Marketization was first tested with private prisons. The conventional wisdom today is to regard the introduction of private prisons as a core example of the success of market testing. As Martin Narey said, while head of the new NOMS organization in 2003:

> The experience of private sector involvement in the provision and operation of prisons has been a great success. Not only have the private sector providers demonstrated they can run prisons which are

> among the best in this country, but the introduction of competition has been a key catalyst for change in the wider prison service.
>
> The private sector has demonstrated a long-term commitment to raising standards of prisoner care through decent and constructive regimes. They have set high standards of mutual respect between prisoners and staff which is so necessary for healthy, orderly and safe prisons.
>
> There is no doubt that competition between providers, public and private, has improved performance, reduced costs and overcome resistance to change across the service as a whole.
>
> (Narey 2003)

The benefits of a mixed economy are seen as self-evident following this experiment. But there is always scope for further progress. As the market matures, private providers face the twin challenges of maintaining innovation and reducing their reliance on imports from the public sector to fill senior posts and give them an edge. The transformation of the public sector provision on the back of losing some prisons to the private sector is championed as evidence of how this approach works. Indeed coterminously with the introduction of private prisons, the mechanisms of NPM impacted upon the management and organization of the prison sector as a whole. Whether spurred on by the growth and threat of the private sector or the performance management culture *per se*, another innovation of NPM, public sector prisons did improve and to such an extent that they were able to regain control of two prisons previously lost to the private sector.

With marketization established in the 1990s, the modernisation agenda had a mechanism which could allow them to introduce and support greater diversity in provision across the criminal justice sector. New Labour have coined a new term to describe this process. The use of the term *contestability* seems, in principle if not quite in practice, to signal a slight change in orientation from the concept of marketization. Its rhetoric is about creating the possibility of competition, not insisting on the outcome being of a particular hue. The determination that prisons would have a degree of privatization, which became the object and goal of market testing supported at a political level under the neo-liberal reforms of Thatcherism, is recast under New Labour. The theory of contestability is that service delivery should be open to competition without prejudice to the outcome. Narey again, interviewed by Jeremy Paxman on BBC stated, 'Contestability is about letting the public sector compete against the private sector. We choose the best' (http://news.bbc.co.uk/1/hi/programmes/newsnight/3707323.stm). Contestability is said to open up the possibilities for all the relevant sectors to apply – be it the public sector, the private sector or the voluntary sector. Currently service delivery of community sentences is about to be subject to contestability processes which many fear (although some welcome) will produce a rump of a Probation Service having to compete for services which, ironically under other modernising criteria, for example, performance management have been seen to be successful in recent years.

Corporate management

Rhodes here refers to 'introducing private sector management approaches in the public sector' (2000a: 152). The hollowing out of the state, which was regarded as a feature of NPM reforms, has progressively led to modes of governance which are more diffuse and decentralized while, it must be noted, often paradoxically retaining central control. The origins of these changes were highlighted in the last chapter with the attack upon and subsequent dismantling of the welfare state by Conservative governments in the 1980s and 1990s. It was argued that the public sector were unresponsive to the needs of the public and had created self-serving bureaucracies, inefficient systems and self-serving professional elites. The yardstick used by the neo-liberals was adoption of the 3Es – efficiency, economy and effectiveness. This value for money approach was to impact across the sector. Local authorities were cash limited, which impacted on their ability to deliver public services and all departments were required to demonstrate value for money. Thus the major institutions of the state – education, health and social services – were subject to new controls and continuous economizing. This was accompanied by new modes of governance which devolved power, for example, through local management of schools or development of NHS Trusts.

Again we can see these processes at work in the criminal justice sector though again somewhat later in its timing particularly with the police and to a lesser extent the courts (Raine 2001; Creaton 2003). The creation of the Prison Service as a Next Steps agency removed the day-to-day management of the prison service from government, and indeed upon its creation also appointed a private sector manager to be its first director (Lewis 1997). The Probation Service was not to become a single national agency until 2001 and amalgamation of the Police Service remains a task too far, though regional mergers were being pursued until successfully resisted in 2006.

Alongside such institutional changes was the use of performance management as the tool to audit and assess performance in the public sector in general and in all the criminal justice agencies. By far the biggest practical legacy of NPM reforms is this attention to standards, target settings and output controls. To take the Probation Service as an example, we can see national standards first introduced in 1992 with subsequent versions in 1995, 2000 and 2002 tightening the targets. Indeed performance management tools have been an element of NPM which New Labour have continued and then enhanced, as we shall see in detail in Part Two.

We can see the governance agenda changing and reshaping under modernisation with best value regimes replacing value for money and with attempts to introduce outcome measures as well as output measures. This appears to have been a change of degree rather than direction. However, guiding the performance management process has been an increased adoption of evidence-based policies captured in the criminal justice networks as 'what works'. This orientation has introduced a feature not given prominence in the previous regime. Support for 'what works' became an ideological battle cry for professionals under pressure. Introduced in the Probation Service, with evangelical zeal, it has had a marked influence on the quality indicators developed for managing service delivery though has recently come under critical scrutiny (Mair 2004).

Regulation

NPM has been driven by economic concerns and it is no surprise that accompanying this orientation is an economists favourite tool of audit. As Rhodes notes 'the "audit explosion" refers to all forms of internal and external regulation' (Rhodes 2000a: 153). The audit culture has increasingly had an impact on how public services are perceived and what policies need to be developed to respond to the analyses of the various audit bodies, such as the Audit Commission. Examples of major reports abound across the public sector and in criminal justice. *Misspent Youth* had a profound effect on New Labour's agenda for youth justice which was its first urgent legislation via the Crime and Disorder Act 1998 (Audit Commission 1996).

This audit culture has developed at the same time that criminological thinking has sought to use similar tools. Actuarial criminology (Feeley and Simon 1994) with its focus on risk assessment and risk management is redolent of the concern to measure and generalize responses to crime problems. Judgements of agency performance are based on measurable and accountable elements of service delivery. What gets measured is what counts. These performance indicators were clearly borrowed from the private sector, another example of the influence of that sector on the management of public sector provision.

A classic example of the way service delivery was changed because of this approach was the demise of the bail information schemes of the 1980s. At this time the Probation Service was required to make cuts and in looking at their current provision it was noted that no targets were set for reducing the numbers remanded into custody. As a direct result of this the Probation Service throughout the country withdrew from such schemes and at a single stroke withdrew from an important and well respected area of service delivery. It is only in 2006 that such schemes are reappearing on the agenda often inspired by Third Sector involvement.

Audit reports are an occasional device used to measure progress; what was needed in addition was more focused and available analyses on the day-to-day operations of the various agencies. This brought the Inspection Services to the forefront. We will trace in Part Two the impact that the

Inspectorate has made among the different agencies. Suffice is to recognize at this point that their role in supporting accountable and auditable services has been progressively increased under New Labour. Janet Newman points to how this focus on regulation has altered the political imperative under New Labour, 'standards and norms become incorporated into the practices through which staff are recruited, trained and appraised' (Newman 2001: 95).

Decentralization

At the rhetorical heart of neo-liberal changes was their view that the state was too directly involved in the management of criminal justice services, indeed of the public sector in general. However, the apparent decentralization singled by Next Steps agencies and the injunction to managers to manage their own practices was often done through an agreed set of centralized requirements (PSIs), targets and performance measures, as discussed above. The introduction of national standards in the Probation Service was the biggest single factor in controlling the historic autonomy so beloved of probation officers and ensuring that they focused in those areas deemed to be important by the policymakers. Each successive change to these standards tightened up on the discretion experienced by practitioners. So there is a centralizing imperative at the heart of any policy to decentralize and give more responsibility to local management. This responsibility was often without authority and a tight rein on spending, policy and performance, and standards was a feature of growing significance in all sectors and certainly in criminal justice.

How this has begun to unfold in this sector will be developed in Part Two but three trends can be identified: decentralization, deconcentration and regionalization. Each of these elements can be observed in the sector. The growth of local projects in crime prevention and crime reduction has grown rapidly since 1997. The setting up of Crime Reduction Partnerships and the crime reduction potential of Neighbourhood Renewal projects, and the investment from European Social Funds in supporting local crime projects are a rich source of crime reduction activities. This will be developed in Chapter 6.

Deconcentration refers to the process whereby central government releases control to a local level. While there are examples of this it is always in the context of maintaining oversight via central targets. The growth of units of responsibility in the police via the introduction of Basic Command Units and a recent thrust towards neighbourhood policing are examples of this deconcentration process. The contradictions, however, remain crucial. Even if neighbourhood policing is pursued, the merging of large police forces will produce a concentration on central decision-making. New Labour have at the same time as introducing deconcentration recrafted the central–local relations around issues of regionalization.

Regionalization has become a distinctive feature of the modernisation agenda. This has not been without its critics and remains an unfinished and uncertain project. The position of central government was arguably strengthened in the regions through the setting up of Regional Development Agencies, Government Offices and assemblies. This was illustrated by the way the Street Crime Initiative, rapidly introduced by Blunkett, cut across previously established local priorities.

The Police Service were to merge into larger units, though some services have resisted this tendency and this has now receded from political view. The Probation Service will follow any police reorganization even though it has already reduced the number of areas in recent years to 42. Coterminosity across the criminal justice sector is a desired goal and as the Police Service is the biggest agency its final structure will be copied by probation, courts and the CPS. The development of NOMS and the Regional Offender Managers in nine regions, plus Wales, will form the central point for the contestability and commissioning processes of both custodial and community sentencing. This process is still in its infancy and acts as an opposite trend to the decentralization and deconcentration previously discussed.

Political control

The growth of political power against agency control has nowhere been more evident than in the criminal justice sector. The deprofessionalization of the public sector was a central tenet of NPM as introduced by Thatcher. The censure of the public sector, discussed in detail in the previous chapter, formed the basis for the deconstruction of the centrality of experts who had previously enjoyed control over how services developed. Successive Home Secretaries under Thatcher and Major charged the criminal justice system with being idiosyncratic and unaccountable. Rhodes discusses how this impacted at the level of the Civil Service and notes how political advisors became a key feature of governance under New Labour. But political control also involved centralizing what was considered good policy and practice which impacted upon professional discretion, for example, in the development of offending behaviour programmes with a nationally determined and accredited provision (Mair 2004).

This can be further illustrated here with reference to the staffing of the Probation Service. The growth of non-professionally trained staff began to grow in the 1990s and the attack by Michael Howard on the training and social work orientation of probation officers was a significant interference in professional power and influence. A change of government in 1997 brought a reprieve for professional training which remained partly in higher education but moved away from the social work profession. Training has continued to be a battleground for changing the standpoint of agency staff and ensuring that political control is maintained and enhanced. The role of sector skills councils, such as Skills for Justice, will continue to unfold in the next few years.

One of the consequences of political engagement in criminal justice is that it ceased to be seen as a bipartisan politically neutral activity. This process had begun in the 1970s and explicitly was championed by Thatcher in her approach to law and order. Labour failed to capture this agenda in three successive elections until, as part of the New Labour modernisation agenda, its own version of law and order politics under the now famous maxim of Tony Blair, '*tough on crime, tough on the causes of crime*', took hold. This penal populism (Pratt 2007) and stress on public protection is redolent of the drivers for global crime of late modernity highlighted in our opening chapter and support for this sound bite helped steal the issue from the Conservatives when political power was transferred in 1997. As we shall see as we look at distinctive aspects of the modernisation agenda, this element could challenge commitments elsewhere.

From New Public Management to modernisation

Having drawn on the elements of NPM, highlighted by Rhodes's writing in 2000, we have seen how those elements have been utilized and on occasions repackaged in the modernisation agenda. The driving force to the initial changes in the 1980s and early 1990s was strong central government conducting business in an atmosphere of censure and blame, as the previous chapter discussed. What we have seen, albeit in an uneven and uncertain way, are these basic concepts built upon and altered by the modernisation agenda. New Labour's version of NPM is more collaborative, joined-up, inclusive and involves citizens and communities in partnerships and alliances at least at the level of discourse. This reflects the move to network governance, highlighted in Chapter 1. The changes are summarized in Table 3.1. The political tactics have become more sophisticated to seek both compliance to these changes and at its best commitment to change and innovation. As we unpack this process in Part Two we will be able to chart more clearly the way in which agencies have been able to

Table 3.1 Changes in NPM under New Labour: a summary

Rhodes's dimensions reflecting initial development of NPM under neo-liberalism	New Labour modernisation of criminal justice using Third Way principles
Privatization	Mixed economy of provision
Marketization	Contestability
Corporate management	Performance management
Decentralization	Deconcentration and regionalization
Regulation	Audit and inspection
Political control	Penal populism and risk management

accommodate such changes and remain consistent with their own internal priorities.

There are however three additional areas which can be seen as distinctive features of the modernisation agenda as it unfolds under New Labour, and we finish this section of the chapter by discussing these features. They are the dimensions of *pluralization*, *joined-up justice* and *responsibilization*. It is certainly the case that elements of all these features were beginning to emerge in the 1990s but not only have they become core features of the modernisation agenda they most typify the distinctive agenda shaping altered modes of governance under New Labour's Third Way.

Pluralization

A consequence of the denigration of professionals by Thatcher, when joined-up with cost-effectiveness, brought a radical rethinking of what was required to deliver any particular service. The generic professional who was seen to be expensively trained and was, alone, allowed to undertake many key tasks, was seen as encapsulating the preciousness and publicly unaccountable domain of the professional expert. Gradually at first agencies appointed assistants to complement the work of the professionally trained staff, should they be teachers, social workers, probation officers or police officers. Distinctive roles began to be developed for these staff members. As the combination of financial austerity and public disquiet about the role of the professionals gained ground, more tasks began to be reassigned to such assistants.

An example from the Probation Service indicates this. This was a service that until late 1980s was dominated by probation officers – the qualified grade. First tentatively and more recently in huge numbers the balance between grades has changed. As a direct result of this, many roles previously seen as the preserve of the probation officer are now undertaken by other staff. This is replicated across the criminal justice sector, for instance, in relation to policing encapsulated in the phrase police family or plural policing. This trend is not unique to the New Labour agenda but certainly has intensified since 1997. The probation officer training under threat from Michael Howard was retained but the growth of other staff in the Probation Service continued and now far exceeds probation officer grades. This raises all sorts of issues about the relationship between elements of the modernisation agenda including how far employing cheaper, less well trained staff accords with principles of good practice, and what risks this might entail for a government who has also put risk management at the top of the agenda.

Joined-up justice

A focus on modernisation, as joined-up government has been seen, is a reaction to a lack of central strategic capability, with one impact of neo-liberal reforms being a fragmentation of provision and a 'silo' mentality. Partnership working has been strongly promoted by New Labour. Again it featured as a muted theme under neo-liberal conservatives with public/private partnerships, SRB funding and the impetus provided by the Morgan Report (1991), but it has gained considerable ground under New Labour and has been a particularly resonant theme from successive Home Secretaries in neighbourhood renewal, social inclusion projects and community safety. Integration has been attempted as both a horizontal and vertical measure bringing together a mixed group of providers or seeking to combine the local with the central, as in the Street Crime Initiative.

On the one hand, a commitment to partnership shares all the features of a penal measure which should be supported. It reduces fragmentation of provision, a criticism levelled at early NPM changes; it supports integration; it provides holistic provision; it makes the best use of shared expertise; it evokes a systemic imagery; but it can come with a price. Issues such as accountability, pragmatism, flexibility and sustainability all impact upon success. As Newman comments, 'the inclusive and participative activities which help build sustainability are precisely those which may be sidelined under pressure to deliver a bid or an outcome to a tight deadline' (Newman 2001: 114).

Who leads in partnership projects is a question that has bedevilled good practice. Power relationships are key, particularly when considering potential cultural dissonance between partners. Examples abound in illustration. The relationship between the police and local authorities in CDRPs has not been an easy one (Hicks 2002). The role of the voluntary and community sector receiving so-called 'partnership' monies from the Probation Service all raise difficulties (Senior *et al.* 2005). A tension between best practice or what works and cost-effective delivery in an environment where competition and contestability determine contracts threatens the openness and sharing invoked by notions of partnership working.

Responsibilization

According to Garland (2001) responsibilization is an attempt to increase the influence of state agencies on crime policy by 'shedding' and giving more responsibility to non-state agencies in the private and voluntary sectors as well as communities. In a nutshell, 'the state alone is not, and cannot be, responsible for preventing and controlling crime' (Garland 2001: 126). In other words, the state no longer acts as a sovereign power influencing crime policy in a top–down way. The new form of rule is, in Foucauldian terms, 'governmentality', a method used to win the support of other agencies and to create new alliances and partnerships. For example, criminal justice agencies can publicize via media initiatives, such as Neighbourhood Watch, to secure the commitment of communities. In addition to this, successive governments have set up quasi-governmental organizations (e.g., Crime Concern, National Crime Prevention Council) where there is a strong emphasis on partnerships and inter-agency working. Under New Labour there is also more cross-departmental working where departments who once had no contact with crime issues now must deal with crime and disorder. For example, the central importance of work in enhancing citizenship has not only changed the emphasis within prison and probation work with a strong ETE (education, training and employment) and Basic Skills focus but has engaged the Learning and Skills Council through the Offender Learning and Skills Service (OLASS) and Job Centre Plus.

How does the above relate to the tactics of modernisation? In contrast to the command and control policymaking of neo-liberalism, backed up by the coercive and censorious powers of the state, social actors in all walks of life are being persuaded to recognize and commit themselves to controlling crime. From time to time attempts may be made to ensure compliance, for example, the manufacturers of stealable products may be pressured to do more to reduce the stealability of items. This also draws down to the individual citizen where they are made responsible for ensuring items are not stolen from their cars vis-à-vis the magpie adverts or the focus on parenting orders as a measure to encourage parental responsibility for anti-social behaviour. The citizen focus, which began under John Major, has intensified with New Labour. As Newman (2001: 127) argues, 'the development of a plural and differentiated set of connections between state, service deliverers, users, citizens and other stakeholder'. This focus is built on neo-liberal reforms which had identified the need for more responsive public services. New Labour wanted, at least ideologically, to build social capital while overcoming social exclusion and to do this in ways which would exert greater pressure on public sector managers and professional workers. Newman identifies the importance of this strategy of 'deliberative democracy' when she writes that, 'the transformative possibilities of deliberation and the "responsibilization" flowing from collective processes of decision-making are viewed as major benefits' (Newman 2001: 132). However, the cautionary note she adopts warns against any simplistic solution concerning the capacity of equality of access to representation. This can be seen in criminal justice where particular public groups dominate the emotional tone of policymaking at the expense of other groups and this can be seen in responses to hate crime, domestic violence and the current hysteria about anti-social behaviour. Responsibilization demands a consensual image of community relations where a shared sense of responsibilities in relation to work, family and community are demanded to achieve social inclusion, 'the inclusive and consensual imagery of community and "the people" served to mask exclusions, with clear limits to how far communities of identity – of "race", of culture, of sexuality – could be incorporated' (Newman 2001: 157).

It is a political tactic with wide ramifications for modernising processes. In Garland's (2001: 127) words:

The motivation behind these responsibilising developments is not merely the off-loading of troublesome state functions, though the sharing of responsibility is clearly an attractive strategy for criminal justice executives hoping to avoid being blamed for the shortcomings of their organisations. Nor is it simply the 'hiving off' or the 'privatisation' of crime control, although the desire to reduce staff costs is certainly a factor, and one of the effects of the strategy has been to further stimulate the already growing market for private security. Rather, it is a new conception of how to exercise power in the crime control field, a new form of 'governing at a distance' that introduces principles and techniques of government that are by now quite well established in other areas of social and economic policy.

Towards a framework for analysis

Setting the context

This final section brings together the developing thinking of the first three chapters. Chapter 1 identified the larger debate around late modernity drawing on Giddens (1999) and Bauman (2000) to indicate some of the systemic changes in modernisation which occurred in the later part of the twentieth century. These global paradigmatic features are represented in Figure 3.1 on the outer edges of the diagram. Any discussion of the development of modernisation takes place and is in turn influenced by this wider context. In subsequent chapters, therefore, the context within which change takes place within each organization will need to be carefully drawn. Whatever the particular ways in which the modernisation (2) agenda impacts upon each agency it does so informed and shaped by the agenda of modernisation (1). This can help put into context apparent contradictions and paradoxes which abound in current crime policy and practices. Chapter 1 went on to identify the drivers of global crime which have been identified in late modernity (Garland 2001). These trends impact upon the way crime and attitude to crime is exemplified and the public and policy responses. While each country will react to such changes in a particular manner, the trends are part of the context within which change occurs in each criminal justice agency.

The permanence of paradox

One feature which will emerge as a constant in the detailed analysis of any agency is the presence of conflicting and contested interpretations of all the tenets identified. This is a consequence of no system of governance being hermetically sealed from another. Elements of the traditional Westminster model persists, as does the market-driven changes of neo-liberals. No matter how far New Labour can translate a network mode of governance from rhetoric to reality it co-exists alongside competing systems.

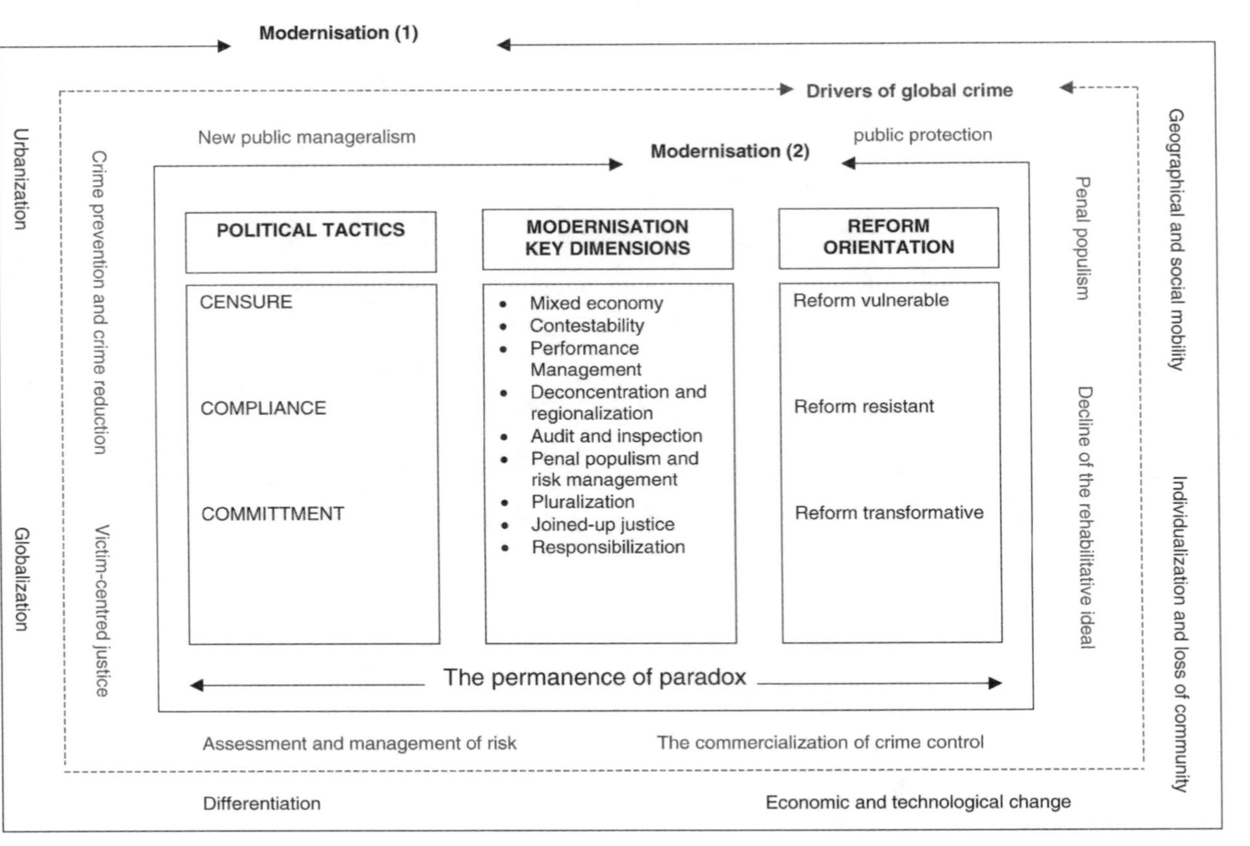

Figure 3.1 A conceptual framework for analysing the criminal justice sector under the modernisation agenda

In addition the factors identified as features of modernising criminal justice themselves exist in tension with each other. A series of polarities at the heart of modernisation illustrate the dilemmas and paradoxes of policy implementation:

- centralizing policy – liberalizing operational and regionalizing responsibility;
- doing justice more openly (better) – cost-effectiveness, speed, efficiency (faster);
- dynamic, modern – vested interests and 'forces of conservatism';
- reform-resistant – reform-vulnerable;
- interfere and control more – govern less;
- cross-cutting targets – agency-driven targets;
- freedom to manage – national standards;
- outputs – evidence-based policy;
- managerial oversight – professional self-regulation.

We shall see that such paradoxes are a constant and permanent feature of criminal justice policymaking and in attempting to make sense of policy changes, failures or successes the complex interplay between such factors must be accounted for.

Political tactics

We saw in Chapter 2 that the preferred way in which neo-liberal conservatives, such as Thatcher, Major and Howard, imposed their market-driven agenda was through a process of censure, coercion and blame. However, this strategy which bullied some agencies into submission could not be a long-term approach. Since 1997, driven by principles dubbed the 'Third Way', two other tactics have been employed to build upon change in a less censorious but no less effective manner. These have been termed 'compliance and commitment'. Newman comments: 'Oscillations between commitment-building and control-based approaches to the management of change characterized its strategies for public service reform' (Newman 2001: 95). Newman goes on to discuss the concept of trust in public sector reform. She argues that the 'eclectic mix' of instruments used by New Labour involved different modes of trust which she identifies as calculus-based, knowledge-based and identification-based. The first two are redolent of the concept of compliance used here, 'the programme of incentives and threats tended to produce a focus on game playing, information management and presentation rather than the delivery of sustainable outcomes' (Newman 2001: 101).

Identity-based trust has been eroded by new public management and its underlying censure. New Labour through oscillating strategies of pressure and support do seek to regain the commitment of its deliverers in ways which hark back to the 'collegial, professional and corporate forms of trust which characterized the post-war public sector' (Newman 2001: 100).

Compliance is still a control-based strategy, but its focus is a performance management process which challenges agencies to compete against each other and gain rewards from achieving goals. The performance improvements generated in those services enable government to demonstrate progress at least on the targets it sets. In turn the agencies both survive and, under the watchful eye of government, prosper if only in the image that government desires. Since 1997 compliance strategies have been accepted as a feature of running prisons, Probation Services, police and court systems. Often there is a sense that the wrong targets are set or adhered to but with a reluctant acceptance that such monitoring informs good practice and quality assurance. Compliance is centrally a tactic adopted by managers and a management discourse which brought about culture change in organizations. Such managers tend to occupy a more neutral ideological space, as they see their job as delivering quality services as demanded by government standards, targets and directives. Compliance under New Labour has been closely linked to the development of evidence-based policy, measurement and audit, which are key features of the modernisation agenda.

For a minority of players in the criminal justice system, performance management has been more enthusiastically welcomed and *commitment* has been engineered. This is so for the private sector which has had many opportunities to prosper under contestability regimes. The voluntary and community sector too have seen areas of expansion which have encouraged them to become more business-oriented in order to win contracts in place of or in partnership with the public and private sector. Even in parts of the public sector some senior managers have embraced the new management practices with more commitment than that of simple compliance. In this atmosphere it becomes less necessary to censure such agencies and commitment acts as a stage towards the transformation of the agency role.

Political tactics have thus become tempered and shaped to seek greater buy-in to the philosophy of modernisation, though the extent of change engendered will depend on an organization's capacity and orientation to reform and change.

Reform orientation

In addressing change in the criminal justice sector, we can see at least three distinctive orientations to reform and change. Although organizations will not simply reform in one particular way, there is sufficient differentiation between agencies to be confident of examining the extent of change through the lens of reform vulnerability; reform resistance or reform transformation.

Reform vulnerability applies to those agencies whose own structural position is weakened by censure and without public support or where its capacity to resist change is weak, which makes it easier for government to impose change using it as a forerunner for other agency change. As we shall see in Part Two, the Probation Service has been the subject of continuous change since 1990. Never organized enough to resist such change, it was often used to test out new approaches.

Reform resistance is typically seen in agencies whose structural position, in relation to the government, is more secure by dint of their size and referential power or by their usefulness for the government agenda. The Police Service fits this image on both accounts. Needed by Thatcher for her approach to law and order the first round of NPM hardly touched police reform. Since that time attempts by successive Home Secretaries to reform the police have faced the often organized and steadfast resistance of independent and powerful chief constables. Notwithstanding this orientation and the consequent failure of attempts to censure the Police Service, government has succeeded in a tactic of compliance to slowly induce change. This will be developed in Chapter 8.

Reform transformative agencies are those which, driven by commitment to the government agenda, begin to transform their own agencies to be in a prime position to benefit from change. In this sense the private sector, through a combination of financial power and an ability to attract key public and voluntary sector personnel, have gained a real foothold in criminal justice business. The voluntary sector too has transformed its operation to take on board new demands and new responsibilities.

The complexity which reform has demonstrated and generated is nowhere better illustrated than in relation to the voluntary and community sector (VCS). This will be developed in detail in Chapter 9. However, it can be seen that some of the smaller agencies have been reform vulnerable in contracting situations where regional bidding becomes the norm. Their very survival is threatened by such contract innovations. At the same time some of the well established VCSs, who are established outside of the concerns of criminal justice, will resist the temptation to change their basic philosophy to become more user-friendly for the government agenda. Yet a third group sensing increased funding at a time when other funding streams, such as ESF and SRB funding, are coming to an end and are prepared to alter their practices to conform to such needs. The VCS is in its sheer variety demonstrating reform orientations across the spectrum.

Further reading

Cook, D. (2006) *Criminal and Social Justice*. London: Sage.

McLaughlin, E. *et al.* (2001) The permanent revolution: New Labour, public management and the modernisation of criminal justice, *Criminal Justice*, 1(3): 301–18.

Newman, J. (2001) *Modernising Governance: New Labour, Policy and Society*. London: Sage.

Pratt, J. (2007) *Penal Populism*. London: Routledge.

Ryan, M., Savage, S.P. and Wall, D.S. (eds) (2000) *Policy Networks in Criminal Justice*. Basingstoke: Palgrave Macmillan.

Part Two

chapter four

Modernisation and youth justice

Introduction

Since the mid-1980s, youth justice services have been lauded by government as an example of 'delinquency management' which is to be copied. This 'success story' will be traced through an examination of the delinquency management policies of the 1980s and its impact on the 1991 Criminal Justice Act. The support for a managed approach, for a while, appeared to unite those on the political left and right. However, the subsequent troubles youth justice experienced in delivering on a Tory agenda suggests a caution which needs interrogating. This chapter will then focus closely on its reincarnation as a kitemarked service under New Labour. New Labour's first major criminal justice project was youth justice and many of the ideas and tactics underpinning modernisation were first developed here, including the criticism and censure of existing youth justice services as a prelude to wholesale changes in 1997. Its 'success' will be put under a critical lens and its modernisation features will be critically addressed and evaluated.

Contextual outline

> As might be expected, the large majority of youthful criminals are drawn from the ranks of the youths who spend idle and vicious days in the least reputable districts of great centres of population, and these youths again have commonly been reared by feckless parents in the very poorest circumstances
>
> (Russell 1910)

Whatever else new governments tackle the issues of youth delinquency and its prevention are always prime candidates for new ideas and approaches although as the quote illustrates and Pearson (1983) demonstrated, the responses to young people are often recycled by successive generations. In 1997, the incoming Home Secretary, Jack Straw, explicitly staked his reputation on the success of his new vision for this group of offenders. Throughout legislative and policy history there has been an undercurrent of contradictions generated by differing perceptions of the place of young people in modern society, mediated by public perceptions and media-fuelled controversies. Crude characterizations of young people as both society's collective future and as a social problem to be dealt with has generated a dualism in social policy for young people which has had a central effect on the development of youth justice policies.

This dualism is evident in a plethora of policy changes – young people are sometimes seen as fully responsible for their actions and therefore punishment should reflect such personal culpability or, in stark contrast, in need of help or welfare. This contradiction is often expressed as a pendulum swinging between policies focused on the welfare of young people and those focused on punishment and personal responsibility. In addition, this pendulum often swings wildly, according to pressures exerted by individual events such as the disproportionate effect of the James Bulger murder in 1993 on subsequent youth and arguably adult policies. Moral panics about young people, like this one in the 1990s, offer a perfect policy example of Cohen's thesis (Cohen 2002).

Legalization has always grappled with this dualism of care/control and welfare/punishment. Although the 1969 Children and Young Persons

Act is generally seen as the high point of welfarist policies, such a crude polarization does not do justice to the competing punitive strands which remained on statute and crucially influenced developments in the 1970s. Indeed policies which sought to protect young people were capable of yielding punitive results as the misuse of the 7(7) Care Order (CYP Act 1969) illustrated in that era (Thorpe *et al.* 1980). This was where social workers took young people to court and sought such an order in criminal proceedings, as the proof of care needed was less onerous than that demanded for Care Orders in civil proceedings. This meant that large numbers of young people were placed in care on a minor offence and could stay in care until they were 19 (Thorpe *et al.* 1980). In fact the defining feature of this dualism in social policy is, in practice, their actual co-existence. How those options have been played out in the practices of the police, courts and supervisory services during the last 30 years will help us understand how the modernising impulse will emerge in practice. The contradictions run deep. Ideological support for welfarist policies can still obscure the moral agenda which is implicit in, for example, child protection policies and can lead to very restrictive and punitive outcomes.

Political pragmatism can produce responses which owe more to satisfying penal politics than their inherent benefit for young people. The consequences of bartering on pragmatic managerialist grounds against more punitive solutions can result in a failure to do justice to the integrity of one's own philosophy. Social work interventions in the 1970s became the object of criticism from the left and from the right. This led to a systems disaster whereby young people brought into the system on welfare grounds found themselves accelerated into care or custody and experiencing the punitive end of the system early in their offending careers.

Individual practitioners accompanied by left wing lawyers and radical academics did begin to identify the kind of practices which were to have such a success in the 1980s (Morris and Giller 1987). Clearer targeting of particular offenders who could benefit from intervention, high quality groupwork practices using social skills and cognitive behavioural methodologies and some systems co-ordination, led to isolated success stories. By the end of the decade, the interest in the child as the object of intervention was decidedly on the wane and the 1982 Act was no longer legislation in the interests of children and young persons but a criminal justice act. Responsibility was being firmly rooted in individual and parental culpability and the justice model offered a rationale apparently suiting all strands of political and public thinking. It also suited, if not also demonstrating an early case study, a growing interest in new public management (NPM).

Talking to youth justice workers in the 1980s one found a bullish attitude. Juvenile justice workers proudly declared themselves as 'justice oriented' in philosophy and smugly revealed how successful their interventions had become. These developments were characterized by:

- A set of principles which were designed to govern intervention (Morris and Giller 1987).
- A 'systems or delinquency management' schema pioneered initially at the Centre for Youth, Crime and Community at Lancaster University linking risk-based assessments to interventions.
- An approach to group work programmes (Denman 1982) which appeared to show some success in outcomes – early evidence of cognitive behavourial interventions.
- Greater co-ordination of policies and practice, early joined-up justice, across agencies particularly in relation to crime prevention and diversion from court through cautioning and bail support.
- Restriction on the powers of the magistracy through sentencing guidelines which foreshadowed the sentencing approach to the 1991 Criminal Justice Act echoed more recently with the intentions of the Carter Review (2003).
- A supportive government: despite carrying a 'law and order' platform was in the first instance very supportive of this approach.

As Eadie and Canton observe:

> Systems management was needed, where the processes had to be understood and then manipulated. This in turn entailed targeting and gatekeeping, bringing constraints on professional autonomy, together with increased oversight and accountability. There was no room for idiosyncrasy in the new management of systems.
>
> (Eadie and Canton 2002)

Conferences and publications proclaimed the success of these strategies and indeed in the lead up to the 1991 Act, the government White Paper confirmed that new measures would draw heavily on the perceived success of this period (Home Office 1990b). Indeed the creation of the Youth Court under the 1991 Act was an explicit attempt to engage older youths in the perceived success of the juvenile justice system.

From juvenile justice workers through the liberal arm of the legal profession to the New Right of Thatcher, there was apparent consensus that the principles of a justice approach – proportionality in sentencing, focusing on the deed not the need, fair and open procedures, minimum intervention and using least restrictive alternatives – gelled well with the government mantra of personal responsibility for criminal behaviour. Social work intervention in the 1970s, on the basis of need, stood accused of being responsible for the rising use of care and custody. Rebadged as juvenile justice in the 1980s it was deemed to be radical, innovative, just and fair and, with a surprising lack of discomfort, government support was the proof that things worked and not the problem to be wary of. This looked like a precursor to joined-up thinking and practice!

There is no doubt that the dramatic drop in the use of care and custody was the result of a systematic and targeted attempt to tackle juvenile offending imbued with a clear set of principles. The trumpeted discontinuity from the 1970s obscured the fact that much which had developed had begun to emerge in that earlier era but had lacked funding support and the initial benefit of a lower birth rate.

Crucially too, system deficiencies remained. Justice by geography, where you lived was as important as what you did, did not disappear. Custody-free zones heralded in one borough were a distant prospect down the road in the next. A further problem related to threshold issues. To gain 'justice credibility' the prospects of net widening were minimized and the problems of net strengthening were ignored (Cohen 1985; Hudson 1993). Justice proponents concern with consistency and fairness in sentencing obscured problems of severity of sentence. This fostered co-option from the New Right and its punitive law and order bandwagon. Systems management focused on proportionality, ensuring that different categories of offenders received similar sentences. However, sentencers could act consistently but severely. Juvenile justice workers seemed strangely silent about the severity of sentencing and ever more intrusive interventions, such as tracking, the precursor to tagging, and conditional bail, began to appear.

The sense of discomfort among some social workers and commentators at the transient nature of this success was not commonly heard by those in control of the politics and practices of juvenile crime. Managing the system without getting fundamental agreement as to what system you desire means you are increasingly subject to the changing political landscape. This is precisely what began to unfold in the early 1990s as Thatcherite law and order under Major, Clarke and eventually Michael Howard reasserted its authority and distanced itself quickly from identification with social work.

Between the summer of 1991 and immediately post-Bulger in the summer of 1993 a series of events, real and constructed, tilted the government towards a punitive approach which, in the following five years before losing power, resulted in the development of an array of punitive policy outcomes with a growing application of new public management which Jack Straw reshaped but fundamentally followed as New Labour's modernisation agenda took over in 1997. The political dye was cast in the public's mind with the demonization of young offenders, and young male offenders in particular.

The Secure Training Centre dreamed up as a soundbite by Kenneth Clarke was put on the statute books in 1994, thus creating a new era of child jails to which the new folk devils of persistent young offenders were to be housed. As we shall see below, the principled objection of Social Services to managing this 'innovation' brought the private sector into provision for young people – a monopoly they still hold on such centres. Other punitive ideas began to be touted. Boot camps or more euphemistically, 'high impact incarceration', another American import, was muted as the latest short, sharp shock and a Colchester military correction centre was to be utilized to develop this idea. The coercive tilt of policy left the youth justice services intact and still with many of its original clientele but the cost was an ever expanding penal estate and punitive community measures which served to reshape the landscape once again.

It is in this climate that the Labour government came into power in 1997. Jack Straw indicated that new directions in youth justice policy would be the hallmark of his tenure as Home Secretary. A series of discussion papers were produced, almost immediately followed up by a White Paper (Home Office 1997) while his task force on youth offenders gathered their own evidence. Without any meaningful time for consultation he brought forward measures in the Crime and Disorder Bill which codified his aims for the youth justice system.

It is beyond the scope of this chapter to summarize in detail the particular measures Straw proposed but, as Pitts identified, the changes seem to fall into four categories:

- '*The anticipation of future criminality and early intervention*, via child safety, anti-social behaviour, child curfew and parenting orders'.
- '*The dejuvenilization of the youth justice system* by the abandonment of the principles of *doli incapax*, allowing some naming and shaming, and reducing the age at which a lone juvenile may be tried in an adult court'.
- '*Earlier intervention* via final warnings backed up by programmes of restorative justice, cognitive/behavioural change and parental education, and more robust mid-tariff interventions in the form of an action plan order and a revamped supervision order'.
- '*Extending the powers of the bench* to remand youngsters to security and paying no additional legal or administrative constraints upon the powers to sentence to custody'.

(Pitts 2001a)

Early intervention always has seductive force. This is often based on crude positivist principles – if only the right identification on problem children can be made then preventative measures can 'nip criminality in the bud'. While the sentiment is unimpeachable the actual practice remains deeply flawed. Three key concerns have never been resolved:

- *Accurate prediction* – how can selection of 'pre-delinquents' ensure that those highlighted for early intervention would have gone on to offend – this is the challenge that actuarial justice and risk assessment took on. The risk of false positives as well as false negatives impact upon this field (Bottoms 1977).
- *The avoidance of counter-productive intervention* – the impact of labelling (Becker 1963) on future criminality, where young people have been on schemes run by youth justice services find that any minor offending subsequently becomes evidence of the need for more intervention – young women have particularly suffered from this type of inclusion and

now those on anti-social behaviour orders are likely to be escalated up the system in a similar manner.

- *The need to locate actions in wider social policies* – early intervention must be located in wider policies for youth not within the particular concerns of the youth justice arena.

The series of measures supported by New Labour are all predicated on a punitive climate as, in the event of failure, they run the risk of accelerating individual young people through the system. The annexation of 17-year-olds to the Youth Court via the 1991 Act can now be seen as a paradox. Although offering the prospect for young people to be treated on the basis of their level of maturity, however difficult to define, what it encouraged was the seeping into the court procedures of interventions previously available only in the adult courts. So Community Service Orders were extended, probation orders were reintroduced into the arena, and probation services were firmly re-engaged in plans for youth justice services.

Reforming youth justice

Services for young people are frequently the object of criticism and censure and each major change, briefly outlined above, has resulted in criticism of the previous arrangements. By the time New Labour had come to power the job of censure had been done by the Conservatives. Their critique, which had gathered pace following the Bulger murder and fuelled by images of 'rat boys' and 'bail bandits' had sought to downgrade the professional contribution to the extent that we began to see under the NPM critique of deprofessionalization a threat to the professional identity of such workers. In addition the Audit Commission report *Misspent Youth* (1996) condemned the work of the juvenile justice system by pointing to a lack of achievement and failures in co-ordination. Both welfare and justice philosophies were in retreat and the new arrangements setting up the Youth Justice Board and the locally run Youth Offending Teams and juvenile secure estate was built on the principle of 'preventing reoffending'. This guiding aim was driven by a government appointee, Lord Warner, who as chair of the Board set about imposing a style of operation which was forward looking, refusing to look back at any prior practice and dynamically marketed to push through new ideas and processes.

Given the new configuration of the Youth Offending Team (YOT) it was hard for change to be resisted and it was felt that engagement as a YOT worker or manager with a host of other agencies had the potential to transform practice. How far this was echoed on the ground in day-to-day actions is less clear and will be debated below. The obvious punitive intent of the legislation was also masked by an apparent commitment to restorative justice, which was in fact much more muted in legislation and action until the turn of the century. But as a rallying call to gain compliance and even commitment, the promise of positive measures around concepts of restorative justice fostered support for changes and it provided a positive gloss to the work of this new corps of youth justice workers.

The next section focuses on the detailed dimensions of modernisation which accompany the modernising agenda of New Labour and helped shaped the way in which youth justice has been delivered under the current government.

Key dimensions of modernisation

Mixed economy of provision

By the nature of the way the legislation was constructed, the YOTs exemplify one approach to a mixed economy of provision, though rather different relationships between the public, voluntary and private sectors are set up as a result of the particular structural configuration of the new system. Setting up a multi-agency team which statutorily required workers from social services, probation, police, health and education (1998 Crime and Disorder Act) ensured that differing perspectives would be enabled to influence local practice, though as we shall see, this was increasingly guided by central direction about the nature of the work. This configuration into YOTs was not, however, predicated on competitive bidding for work and the voluntary and community sector and the private sector were only able to compete as providers for services contracted out by the YOTs. The YOTs were not themselves set up as a competitive project and were managed by local authorities through the edicts of the Youth Justice Board.

The private sector have, however, got involved in provision particularly in those areas where the public services were not keen to be involved. So, as in the adult sector, electronic surveillance was managed by the security firms and, as we saw earlier, the Secure Training Centres continued to be administered by the private sector. Pitts characterizes this approach to provision as follows:

> YJB's uncritical enthusiasm for the 'internal market', it has initiated purchaser–provider relationships with secure and penal institutions. This has meant that the Board has relinquished direct managerial control, relying instead on a variety of inspection regimes, and financial and other penalties for non-compliance with quantitative contractual obligations or unfulfilled targets.
>
> (Pitts 2003)

YOTs themselves competed with each other for funds to develop showcase projects and funding roll-out only followed projects which were seen as successes, for example, Youth Inclusion Programmes and Intensive Supervision and Surveillance Programmes. The voluntary sector became partners in many pieces of project work in drug and alcohol counselling, in education, in health, etc., and various models developed around the location of the delivery with some VCS sharing office space with the YOTs, others delivering more at a distance. Again Pitts notes:

> 'The rise of "contract culture" has meant that voluntary sector organisations are under immense pressure to act as low-cost providers of mainstream public services rather than exemplars of innovative practice or advocates for young people in trouble with the law'
>
> (Pitts 2001b).

Contestability

Despite this notion being so central to the adult correctional services, as discussed below in Chapter 5, this has been much less an issue for the provision of services in youth justice. Indeed there seems no political desire to contract out YOT services from this statutory provider. Rather, as highlighted above, in most respects the commissioner has been at a national level, the YJB or when resources are available, the YOTs themselves with the latter encouraged to develop their own partnerships.

Partnership working has some extended history in this area. Voluntary sector agencies were involved in intermediate treatment schemes in the 1980s and the early development of cautioning owes much to a productive partnership between police and Social Services. This lack of an explicit politically inspired competitive framework tends to demonstrate that contestability is not the only model of market testing and marketization utilized by the current government.

Since 2000 the YJB has acted as the commissioner for the juvenile secure estate. This covers young offender institutions (YOIs), secure training centres (STCs) and secure children's homes. There have been difficulties in creating a model of contestability here. Indeed the Chief Executive of the YJB herself summed up the situation for youth justice services:

> We have learnt that the diverse nature of the sectors we inherited limit the degree to which we can sensibly use pure contestability and market mechanisms to drive improvement. Our experience has taught us that, despite the clarity of the model underlying it, commissioning in the public sector is a complicated process and needs to be recognised as such.
>
> (Roy *YJB News Issue 33* 2006)

She goes on to say that their experience has taken them down a different route:

> At the YJB we have learnt that in order to mitigate the potential problems we need to adopt a strategic partnership approach to

> commissioning. We recognise the need for a strong working relationship with providers, albeit within a contracting environment, which is geared towards delivery of improved services that are fit for purpose.
> (Roy *YJB News Issue 33* 2006)

It is their quality and standards framework which drives the YJB approach to control performance rather than overt contestability regimes.

Performance management

Target setting has governed the development of youth justice at all levels since 1997. New Labour's White Paper, *No More Excuses* majored on delays in processing offenders through the courts, 'They impede justice, frustrate victims and bring the law into disrepute. And delays do no favours to young offenders themselves: they increase the risk of offending on bail and they postpone intervention to address offending behaviour' (Home Office 1997: para. 7.3).

The focus on key targets, as a mark of government progress, has been a constant feature of youth justice performance management. It is clear that such targets have not always been met and targets at a national level have sometimes had to shift to respond to other changes in the system. This approach to target setting has been at the forefront of the YJBs approach to performance management as Brown comments, 'performance' is increasingly measured in terms of deliverables: deliverables not being overarching successes such as real reductions in harmful behaviour but rather measurable, target-output achievement' (Brown 2005: 97).

The development of performance targets and thus the management process itself is heavily centralized as a result. Smith (2003) notes that the tight control over the preparation of local youth justice plans by the YJB leads to the production of objectives which meet national concerns such as those of swift administration of justice, responsibility of parents, effective practice precepts and victim/offender restorative justice. The key issue here for Smith is how far these plans appear then to exclude elements which local practitioners might see as also crucial to good practice. On reflecting on local plans he notes there is little about, 'promoting anti-discriminatory practice or protecting the rights of young people in any other way; there is nothing about addressing welfare needs . . . [or] . . . promoting opportunities for young people through education . . .' (Smith 2003: 84).

There is a rationalism about this approach which reaches its apotheosis with the directives for practice. The ways in which assessing and delivering performance will be conducted is via the YJBs 'Key elements of effective practice and its structure for assessment, planning, interventions and supervision' (*YJB News Issue* 2002). This problem-solving approach – assessment, evaluate issues, apply guidance and evaluate outcomes – assumes that best practice can be captured by an analysis of the criminological literature and guidance reliably developed from it. This capture of evidence-based practices lessens the need for professional training and knowledge of the 15 KEEP booklets (Key Elements of Effective Practice, YJB) becomes the accepted wisdom. The thinking for your practice has been catalogued neatly. The tendency yet again to see young people in clusters rather than as individuals directs the approach taken. Pitts points to the issue for criminologists and for practitioners:

> In these circumstances governments have utilised criminology pragmatically, incorporating those scientific discourses which articulate most closely with their policy objectives, and so it is seldom clear whether criminological science is serving as a source of intellectual illumination or political legitimation.
>
> (Pitts 2003: 6)

National Standards, although coming later to Youth Justice than to the Probation Service, also contain the usual array of process requirements which give measurable outputs if not processes which can get in the way of positive outcomes. The year 2008 will see a further tackling of these issues with risk-based National Standards promised, new end to end operational guidance on case management; revised Key Elements of Effective Practice and training for YJB practitioners (Monk 2007). Training takes on an interesting perspective here. This is about ensuring a particular approach, desired by the centre, is followed by each of the 155 YOTs. This is redolent of the discussions and concerns about 'bespoke training' to be had below in the chapter on correctional services.

Deconcentration and regionalization

Local delivery through the 155 YOTs is the key feature of youth justice delivery and this was structured into the system in 1997. However the relationship with the YJB as major funder of services and setter of targets and direction, which has been extensively discussed above, makes the relationship between the local and the centre a contested one. There is now also a regional component in that regional managers were appointed (by the YJB not by the local YOTs) as a focus for the YJB in the areas. The training function delivered in the last four years to create a 'licence for practice' was also administered at a regional level though mediated through a national private consultancy, ECOTEC. All YOTs are required to send annual plans for approval and as we shall see below the inspection regimes closely monitor the work of each YOT. John Pitts reflecting on the relationships between locality and the centre suggests, 'Indeed, the "New Youth Justice" marks the advent of what we might call "top-down corporate correctionalism"' (Pitts: 2003: 6). This feels a very apt description of this uneasy relationship. National boundaries are set in such a way that it is hard for the local areas not to pursue, in general terms, and operate in a fashion directed by the centre. The strategic use of funding to achieve these goals is a significant feature of this process:

> The Youth Justice Board has, it seems, used its distribution of funds to develop a strategy for youth justice that appears to rely heavily on targeting specific groups, at all stages of the process, and increasing the levels of intrusion and surveillance to which they are subject.
>
> (Smith 2003: 88)

Audit and inspection

The impact of audit, as a process on criminal justice, has not been greater than the successive Audit Commission reports entitled *Misspent Youth* (1996, 1998, 1999, 2004). *Misspent Youth*, published in 1996, identified a number of problems with the system for dealing with young offenders:

- prosecution through the courts was slow;
- not enough was done to address offending behaviour;
- the agencies involved often worked in an unco-ordinated way;
- little was done to prevent young people from offending in the first place.

(Summary, Audit Commission 2004: 1)

These reports carry a great deal of weight and despite being conducted by those not familiar with the youth justice system itself and its panache for presenting reports which purport to be good evidence-based research, there is growing concern that their reliability is questionable. To take one example, discussed by Smith (2003), where the arguments presented against repeat cautioning guided the government away from this policy to its Final Warnings system. Citing recent research he argues, 'Despite the fact that the evidence in support of this conclusion is limited and untested it has become an accepted truth' (Smith 2003: 47). An analysis of the first two Audit Commission Reports perhaps gets at some of the often unstated concerns about the nature and function of these reports. Jones observes:

> They are regularly cited but are rarely criticized or evaluated. Their findings are often taken as the final word on the topic. It is as if the critical faculties of youth justice academics and practitioners are suspended when confronted with financial costings, statistics, or 'evidence' when it is gathered by accountants, auditors or economists.
>
> (Jones 2001: 362)

Jones goes on to dissect the assertions made in these texts to illustrate how often flimsy or sometimes non-existent evidence is cited to back up arguments for change. The influence of these reports on youth justice cannot be underestimated. What they appear to form is often a legitimation for the direction in which government want to head. Evidence-based practice here is not as robust as presented yet, as Jones observes, is not always the subject of critique. With audit and inspection so prevalent and such a high visibility presence in local areas there is a concern, raised by Jones, that practitioners will begin to give auditors and inspectors what they want to tick the boxes and get continued funding, and not what may be needed.

Penal populism and risk management

The climate within which risk assessment and management flourishes is still a highly punitive one for young people which can be uncomfortable for enabling a needs-based focus to flourish. The objectifying of risk via risk assessment procedures has developed, somewhat ironically, on parallel lines to the adult correctional services. ASSET is the tool for risk assessment used in this field with no clear reference at all to the OAsys tool in adult corrections. The concern of many commentators is the way that this managed approach to intervention has accelerated punitive outcomes. Brown in this extended quote expresses this frustration on the impact of penal populism on the youth justice system:

> The so-called 'actuarial new penology' retains most of the aspects of the punitive 'old' penology within a framework of governance that is increasingly managerialized and interventionist in its 'centralized decentralization'. Inherently net-widening in both criminalizing incivilities and allocating punitive powers to non-justice based agencies and individuals, and is increasingly distanced from any notion of rights or social justice for young people in its aggressive promotion of a somewhat barbaric populism.
>
> (Brown 2005: 99)

What Brown so aptly observes is that in a context of penal populism, actuarial risk management becomes the means of framing youth crime itself as well as determining strategies of intervention. In this approach reform and rehabilitation as goals of intervention are less prominent a concern than monitoring progress and sharing information about risk which becomes the prime goal. We see this approach developing in the attitude towards anti-social behaviour where increasing the numbers on orders as a demonstration of success is more vital than securing support facilities to tackle any root cause of the nuisance behaviour itself. By giving a primacy to risk as a guide to action, the extent of offending itself becomes less central. In an interesting piece of dejà vu the very preventative practices seen in the 1970s as contributing to a rise in the use of custody for young people are now seen as the prime goal of the system and this can justify early interventions without any real evidence of a delinquent career developing (Hudson 2003). The proliferation of programmes, such as YIP and Splash programmes and indeed even such as Sure Start, target 'at risk' children and young people and risk accelerating a criminal career.

The boundaries of criminal activity become blurred in this climate. Having fuelled a concern about the state of young people today through supporting media hysteria about 'hoodies', etc., this can seemingly justify interventions through a risk reduction approach rather than on the evidence of any actual offending behaviour. The language is neutralized and the processes described in managerial terms but the outcomes are highly politicized and result in increases in the use of custody, a situation which directly led to the early resignation of the Chair of the Youth Justice Board, Rod Morgan, in January 2007. As Geoff Monaghan, Chair of National Association of Youth Justice stated in a press release on this matter:

> far too many children are coming into the formal criminal justice system who could be dealt with much more effectively elsewhere. It can only be a matter of shame that the result of this is that we continue to lock up more children than almost any other country in Europe.
>
> (www.nayj.org.uk/website/node/370)

Hudson (Hudson 2003) has identified this as a shift of emphasis from risk management to what she terms *risk control* and this is one of the real consequences of this connection between penal populism and risk management. It is not inherently the case that a concern to manage the risks that some young people pose should produce such punitive and negative consequences.

Pluralization

The particular approach of the YOTs immediately altered the relationship between pre-existing expertise and its application under the new arrangements. There were concerns at the outset that professionals from an array of agencies might undertake tasks normally the province of the statutory social services. The fact that in 1997 there was no developed system for registration of social work in youth justice meant that there was already a mix of qualified and unqualified staff undertaking similar jobs. The approach developed by the YJB was to couple together its approach to quality standards, as discussed above under performance management, with its approach to training. This continues the moves towards de-professionalization redolent of early new public management.

> De-professionalisation holds many advantages for criminal justice system managers with an iconoclastic and homogenising bent. Non-professionals have little or no knowledge of alternative ways of doing things, as a result the potential for disagreement with, or deviation from, prescribed method or procedures is minimised. This means, for example, that the integrity of the Home Office accredited 'offending programmes', discussed below, is far less likely to be subverted by the exercise of 'professional discretion'. Such training as these new recruits receive is essentially practical and any ethical issues which arise can be resolved by reference to the relevant 'values statements' or codes of practice. Over time, this recruitment strategy spawns a new division of labour in which non-professionals 'deliver' the 'programmes' and the dwindling number of professional workers become, essentially administrative, 'case managers'. This produces a cheaper, more flexible and far more manageable workforce.
>
> (Pitts 2001a)

Although a qualifications framework was developed by the YJB the central focus and most of the initial funding available went to an award known as the Professional Certificate in Effective Practice (Youth Justice) (PCEP). This award is really a short course set at Year 2 of an undergraduate degree but lasting for only a third of the year. The PCEP was championed as the central requirement for all those working in the youth justice system with a YJB target of 80 per cent completing this award by 2006. Linked only tangentially to Occupational Standards and set outside the developing framework for Occupational Standards being developed by the new National Skills Sector Council – Skills for Justice – this award occupied a rather grand position at the centre of a youth justice commitment to quality standards. There are a number of concerns about this programme despite the fact that it involved a good quality but limited training programme:

- it contained no assessment of practice;
- it stretched to the limit those coming to it without any formal qualifications; and paradoxically
- was often too perfunctory for those with relevant professional training.

It served one clear purpose and that was to create a 'licence to practice' across the system whatever the occupational role of the individual prior to coming to the YOT for employment.

Explicitly built around the 15 KEEPS (Key Elements of Effective Practice) booklets and despite being on the whole well administered and delivered by a small clutch of higher education institutions it creates something of a mirage that youth justice workers can now assume they have enough training to practice. This dumming down of training is a feature which allows and encourages a plural, compliant and cheap workforce to develop.

Joined-up justice

Why the YOTs approach to joining up has not been followed by other criminal justice provision is interesting and puzzling. The dynamics involved in putting individuals from different agencies together to work in a coordinated fashion did cause teething problems which have been well documented (Bailey and Williams 2000; Burnett and Appleton 2004). It required good management and a supportive culture which was not easy at a time when their home agency may also be undergoing changes. As the YOTs developed working relations so the YJB could set the change agenda.

Of course, one of the key tensions of working in the same office setting was ensuring that the focus of one particular agency was shared across the whole team. This could lead to tensions between various members sometime representing and mimicking disputes at an organizational level. This was most acute where the big systems – criminal justice, health and social care clashed. Pitts noted this as early as 2001, 'It seems that in its effort to construct a corporate youth justice system, the YJB has systematically confused the building of an effective multi-agency team with the eradication of professional difference and the denial of structural conflict' (Pitts 2001b: 7).

In one piece of research (Minkes *et al.* 2005), evaluators noted that major disputes arose between projects commissioned to deliver drug services. This reflected a difference in value base between voluntary sector providers and the YOT and/or between systems to support drug treatment from a health rather than a criminal justice perspective. Joining up in this context merely shifted the pre-existing disjuncture over philosophy and practice often felt to occur in the drug treatment field. In some projects commissioned by the YOTs, workers engaged chose to work in the same setting as the YOT worker and others in different offices. The former can often be seen as providing a shared experience of the issues which contributes to shared understanding and mutual support. Minkes *et al.* (2005: 263) indicates 'they were defined by cultural differences between YOTs and drug projects, which could result in difficulties over confidentiality and information sharing, referral criteria and practice, and responses to non-attendance'.

Drug treatment is a central part of the work with young people today. Yet the modernisation approaches have stifled initiative and produced ever lengthening bureaucracies and conflicting objectives which curbs the supposed heart of the project to reduce dependency on drugs and help restore a future for young people. A damning report by Nick Davies in the *Guardian* drawing on the work of one DAT co-ordinator indicates the worse side of what joined-up action on drugs can actually mean:

> the bureaucracy – the 44 different funding streams, each one with its own detailed guidance and micro targets from the centre, each one with its own demand for a detailed business plan and quarterly reports back to the centre; the endless service agreements he had to sign with every local provider with their own micro targets and a demand for quarterly reports back to him so that he could collate them and pass them back to the centre; the new annual drugs availability report to the centre; the annual treatment plan to the centre over 68 pages and nine planning grids with 82 objectives . . .
>
> (Davies 2003)

Responsibilization

In the context of services for young people, governments of both political hues have pursued a policy of what Brown describes as '*punitive responsibilization*' (Brown 2005: 97). The particular objects of this responsibilisation process are firstly young people themselves and then parents. The latter have particularly been targeted for reform and increasingly punitive court orders and compulsory parental training has been introduced to deal with their supposed neglect of duty. For young people the adoption of 'naming and shaming' as a tool of control is another example of this punitive approach to making individuals responsible for their behaviour. Brown goes on to identify the role of the media in this process defining their role as 'contemporary stocks' a vivid but accurate portrayal of how it must feel to be a young person in our society today.

Fitting uncomfortably and somewhat paradoxically with this trend is the apparent commitment signalled by Straw in 1997 and gathering pace a little since towards restorative justice as one arm of the strategy for dealing with young people. The court-directed Referral Order is the flagship of this approach and suffers from being set in such a judicial setting. Nevertheless, there seems to be a genuine commitment to roll out restorative justice approaches to the work of young people. A process which can responsibilize the young people themselves and their communities in taking responsibility for the harms caused. How far this element acts in spite of the system rather than because of it is certainly questionable.

Permanence of paradox

> the essentially incompatible time frames with which youth justice professionals are having to contend (as a result of the over-politicization of the field on the one hand, and the impact of managerialism on the other).
>
> (Pitts 2003: 15)

Pitts identifies political time, funding time, project time, multi-agency time, penal time, programme time, developmental time, research and evaluation time, are all out of kilter in what is required to develop a positive youth justice system for the twenty-first century. The insistent political demands in a penal populist climate, buttressed by well honed managerialist processes risk yet another failure of the system, historically a cyclical event for this area of criminal justice policy as we saw in the contextual outline at the start of this chapter. Paradoxes abound in the way in which modernisation has been played out over the past decade.

Faster delivery vs. better delivery

Reducing delay has been at the forefront of New Labour's criminal justice policies since 1997 particularly focused on youth justice. To reduce the delays in court proceedings was one government target they failed to meet in time for their first re-election but continually poured money into its achievement. However, while there is some merit in achieving a faster throughput of those arrested for offences there is no particular relationship to rates of reoffending. Administrative delay is wasteful of resources and it had been allowed to grow in the court system unchecked. But its achievement does not impact upon whether the outcomes for offenders themselves are any different as a result of a quicker throughput.

Welfare vs. punishment

The pursuance of punishment in the absence of rehabilitation and reintegration leaves the young person excluded from meaningful participation in the communities they come from. The uneven way in which punishment focuses on certain groups also means that human rights can be violated in the treatment of such groups as they move through the system. The imposition of ever stricter enforcement requirements on curfews or electronic surveillance must not be done at the expense of support and welfare measures.

The more young people become alienated from the system the more likely are the outcomes to be longer periods of exclusion from meaningful participation in society. A focus on rights, welfare and rehabilitation not undermined by National Standards which inhibits and undermines such work needs to be pursued if we are not, yet again, to see escalating numbers of young people unnecessarily and unproductively incarcerated.

Local vs. central control

YOTs are formed at the point of delivery and sit within local authority areas. They can make judgements about what is required to reduce crime and offending behaviour and can work with communities to develop a positive response and solutions to youth crime. This is at the heart of a localized strategy for youth justice and exemplified in the YOT structure which through its multi-agency construction should have access to the related welfare and health agencies to support plans and developments. The paradox is that the requirement to prepare an Annual Youth Justice Plan showing how the targets set by the centre are to be met and through its quality assurance processes and the Key Elements of Effective Practice the opportunity for meaningful local practices is reduced if not eliminated.

Conclusion

Managing youth crime in a volatile and punitive climate is not easy. The punitive atmosphere created in England and Wales in the past two decades has often begun, indeed been actively constructed, around an identification of youth as the problem. This shows no sign of abating as the current sound bite on the 'Respect Agenda' builds on these basic assumptions. It was unsurprising that Jack Straw majored on youth justice when he became Home Secretary in 1997. He created some innovative structures seeking a multi-agency localized response to youth crime. In the context of a rampant modernising agenda we have seen that some of those aspirations have been shaped and distorted by political events and central government imperative. We have also observed, in this chapter, the importance of seeing the various dimensions of modernisation in their political context as changes which have occurred are not the only routes which could have been taken. A greater commitment to restorative justice, a recognition of the local nature of juvenile offending and the need for a more individualized needs-led response, a successful campaign to cut the use of juvenile custody and reform of its institutions would have taken youth justice into a different direction. For now it remains part of the problem and exclusions, demonization and alienation are the current likely outcomes for young people caught up in the modernising of this sector.

Further reading

Brown, S. (2005) *Understanding Youth and Crime: Listening to Youth*. Maidenhead: Open University Press.

Burnett, R. and Appleton, C. (2004) *Joined-Up Youth Justice: Tackling Crime in Partnership*. Lyme Regis: Russell House Publishing.

Smith, R. (2003) *Youth Justice: Ideas, Policy and Practice*. Cullompton: Willan.

chapter five

Modernisation and the correctional services

Introduction

This chapter will be concerned with tracing the way in which the correctional services, in this case defined primarily as the Prison and Probation Services, have been affected by the modernisation agenda over the past decade. The different response of the two agencies will be traced to unlock the way in which organizational and occupational cultures impact upon the way in which change is both perceived and delivered and the ways in which the response to that change has produced a real crisis of mission, particularly for the Probation Service. The tension between dimensions of the modernisation agenda and the resulting examples of paradoxical disjunctures will be analysed and evaluated. The impact on performance will be interrogated. This chapter will conclude by looking at how the modernisation agenda around joined-up justice has shaped the moves to integrate the correctional services under the, as yet, nascent, National Offender Management Service (NOMS). The growth of a mixed economy of provision including the impact of privatization will be incorporated into the analysis.

Contextual outline

Historically the development of the Prison and Probation Services has proceeded on parallel lines. Indeed until the Morison Committee of 1962 the Probation Service had no active relationship with prisons at all, the after care work of prisoners was held by the Discharged Prisoner's Aid Society. The growth of welfare work in prisons post-1962, after care services in the 1960s and in particular statutory license services, such as parole in 1968, increased the points at which probation brushed alongside the prisons but both retained separate identities, cultures and histories. As Nellis identifies, 'part of what it has meant to be the Probation Service, to be a probation officer, is to be sceptical of imprisonment, to stand for something different for very many – albeit not all – offenders' (Nellis 1999: 312).

In the 1980s Napo (National Association of Probation Officers) had campaigned against probation officers working inside prisons at all regarding the stigma of such close identification with such a dehumanizing institution as anathema to its core aims and goals. This separate cultural identity has impacted upon the distinctive responses to change in the organization of criminal justice and in the modernising process itself. It should not be surprising to find that each agency has made sense of the intended reforms with a distinctive set of actions and reactions. Indeed proposals since 1990 for joining the two services together have received somewhat polarized reactions from prison and probation personnel.

Joining Forces to Protect the Public, published by the Home Office in 1998, set out a blueprint for a centralized probation service, to be developed as a Next Steps agency, a status achieved by the Prison Service in 1992, and working in tandem with the Prison Service. For the Probation Service the attendant diminution of professional autonomy and greater central control were seen as explicit consequences of this move. In this sense probation comes closer in such a reorganization to the centralized operation of the Prison Service. Indeed, according to the report, the Prison Service was to become more of a reference point for the work of the service than the locality although the rhetoric of local accountability was retained at this time. Coterminosity with the ten Prison Service regions is mentioned in this report, a theme which has gathered pace since then. Merger of the two organizations was eschewed at this time as a bridge too far but the term 'corrections' which began to be used reflected a growing international trend for the two arms of corrections – prisons and probation – to be seen as complementary, if not joined-up, services.

The gradual working in tandem of the two services was certainly a growing phenomenon towards the end of the century. The optimism of 'What Works' impacted within prison as well as in community provision. Sentence planning for resettlement which was seen as a shared enterprise and partnerships with the voluntary and community sector, grew in both services. This positive approach to custody encouraged a governmental belief that the missions of the two services were ones that could be shared in a joined-up justice system. Such a vision tended to sidestep the uncomfortable truth that prisons were often experienced by its residents as destructive and dehumanizing, in spite of its best efforts (Stern 2006), and has never been able to rid itself of its punitive ethos, not unsurprising given the continued stories of drug and alcohol abuse, bullying, suicide and mental illness which dominates prison life (Ramsbotham 2003). Somewhat ironically the negative aspects associated with prison, reframed as part of the consequence of the demands of public protection, were transferred by association to the Probation Service now seen as the agency to deliver 'punishment in the community'. The uncomfortable image of 'screws on wheels' first coined, and then successfully resisted, in response to the Younger Report of 1979, was now a more insistent feature of how probation staff were to be viewed, as risk management and public protection became their more pressing agendas. The argument gained ground that if they were to be seen as complementary arms of corrections, and if their work was to be better co-ordinated, a criticism levelled at the performance of the two services through research and inspection reports, then joining up to create a single point of reference gained a political and policy foothold.

Any attempt to join these two disparate and sometimes uncomfortable partners would cause difficulty and opposition. Policymakers eschewed the notion of merger and it was left to a business entrepreneur, backed by David Blunkett as Home Secretary of the day, to come up with the organizational template for the future. The Carter Report (2003) proposed the setting up of the National Offender Management Service but with both probation and prison retained in some form, not precisely delineated, at the same time.

Reforming the prison and probation services

The drivers of global crime – identified in Chapter 3 – were core to the way in which reform has been experienced by each of the correctional services.

The Probation Service has certainly felt vulnerable to change. A prolonged period of fear stemming initially from Thatcher's scathing and censorious attacks on public services, particularly those whose liberal credentials were worn on its sleeve, has continued under New Labour. Threatened with reshaping, replacement and reorientation and, seemingly without influential friends anymore, probation allowed itself to be persuaded to change and adapt to the insistent demands of penal populist thinking. Lacking structural power in comparison to police, courts and the Prison Service, and, in part, keenly embracing key agendas, such as risk management and What Works, probation managers saw survival as being about giving government what they wanted. The Probation Service was thus a particularly hapless victim of censorious criticism and seemingly complied with all requests to change. This should not be too surprising in that probation has always shown itself willing to adapt to political demands even in more positive climates. The compatibility of such diverse roles as parole (1968), community service (1972), Day Training Centres (1972), negative conditions in probation (1982), curfews and electronic surveillance (1991), National Standards (1992, 1995, 2001, 2005), risk assessments (1990s), public protection (1990s) and many others, shows a service whose responsiveness to reform appears ready to accept almost anything. This can be interpreted as a positive feature in its readiness to adapt but shows also its reform vulnerability. Since 2001, particularly on the advent of the National Probation Directorate, its capacity to resist changes has been not only not in evidence but seemingly not on the agenda. Censure had created the climate of fear which produced an attitude of compliance to any innovation. Indeed the then Director General of the new National Probation Service said directly to the then Home Secretary, David Blunkett, at Probation 2002, 'we will do whatever you want us to do', a statement of compliance which signalled both magnanimous co-operation with the government and total abdication of responsibility for self-direction and professional autonomy. The simultaneous retirement in 2001 of 17 chief probation officers at a stroke ripped out the professional leadership of the service while creating a managerial corps of individuals appointed for their willingness to work within the new parameters. Modernising probation was not a difficult endeavour in this context.

The Prison Service approached policy change in a rather more reform resistant way. Institutionally and historically committed to secrecy and with its work often out of the public eye and with a powerful union, the POA, which could resist and derail attempts at change, the Prison Service has a history of obstructing change. Attempts to restructure were resisted but Thatcher's wider assault on trade unions impacted upon the ability to resist and it came increasingly under central scrutiny. Crucially privatization was an early battle ground for the Prison Service which found itself, after the 1991 Act, at the forefront of that process. Although unhappy about these developments, the development of that policy produced some considerable resistance and reorientation which will be discussed in more detail next.

The breakdown of the attempt to market test three prisons in the Isle of Sheppey in 2005, shows that the Prison Service has developed its capacity for reform resistance such that current attempts at contestability seemed almost entirely focused on the Probation Service. As we shall see below, the traditional task orientation of the Prison Service makes it a comfortable bed fellow with many of the modernising trends. Its willingness to do whatever is required provided it appears on the task list means that there is less ideological resistance to change as in the Probation Service.

The next section focuses on the detailed dimensions of modernisation which accompany the recent modernising agenda.

Key dimensions of modernisation

Mixed economy of provision

Both prison and probation are traditionally and quintessentially public sector agencies. Prisons became state-driven in the late nineteenth century and probation followed through the 1907 Probation of Offenders Act. Interestingly prisons had a more ancient history as private institutions but in the modern context this history now seems less relevant. Co-operation with other agencies to further their own agenda also has a long history. Prisons have allowed voluntary agencies, notably faith-based organizations to offer a variety of pastoral care and specialist services for many decades and probation staff have utilized community agencies as sources of referral and support over the same period. More formal usage of the voluntary and community sector began in earnest during the 1990s. The so-called Peppermint Paper (Home Office 1990b) introduced a 5 per cent rule (later raised to 7 per cent) requiring probation to be in partnership with other agencies, an approach that in 2006 has been reintroduced by government intent on pursuing, with more vigour, a mixed economy of provision. The growing focus on resettlement also induced prisons, with central financial support through Custody to Work, to develop contracted services with the voluntary sector over the same period.

The context of these changes was a positive appreciation of the complexity of service delivery and the availability of skills and expertise in other sectors. The needs of the service drove this development, albeit in the case of probation, reluctantly and haltingly. The early days of so-called partnership work in the 1990s saw innovative ways of claiming how the 5 per cent had been achieved and while partnerships were often lauded as examples of a community orientation, this happened as much through the compulsory nature of the target as a genuine desire for partnership. This varied across services. This reluctance can be noted when the requirement was taken away and some services increased, or at least maintained their levels of engagement, while others reduced partnerships back to the periphery. What this process demonstrated was that a comprehensive service could not necessarily be delivered by a single agency and the more insistent demands for a mixed economy under New Labour already had evidence of the potential of this process in action.

The Prison Service, required to go beyond its traditional warehousing role for prisoners, found it useful to contract services to deliver key elements of its resettlement agenda. The appointment of VCS co-ordinators, required by a prison circular (Prison Service Order 41/90), was formal recognition of the significance of these agencies to the work of the prison. Chapter 9 pursues that history in more depth.

However, a mixed economy of provision under New Labour was not simply about extending the reach of the VCS but more fundamentally about challenging the monopoly of the public sector in the delivery of services motivated by the assumed benefits which a competitive arena would create. The commitment to grow the VCS was a central feature of all the modernising agendas and funding to support capacity building, such as Futurebuilders and Change Up, were part of this government commitment. Commissioning processes indicated a key change. No longer were probation and prison to be the commissioners of services but there was to be encouragement to bid from consortium of agencies from the three sectors. This fundamentally changes the nature of the relationships between the VCS and the public sector and also potentially offers a vehicle to enhance a key role for the private sector to develop.

Contestability

The concept of contestability, coined by New Labour, was ostensibly about creating the opportunity for competition while not implying that another agency, private or VCS would necessarily take over service delivery. A recent NOMS document defines it in its glossary as:

> Contestability is not another word for competition. It is a situation where a provider faces a credible threat of competition in the provision of some or all of the services they deliver. For NOMS it is a programme for Prison and Probation Services to demonstrate that services are provided to the highest possible standard and achieve results.
>
> (NOMS Commissioning Framework 2007: 19)

However, it is clear in political statements that the intention with regards to the Probation Service is to force it to lose its monopoly as a way of galvanising standards. The support for contestability nurtured by the then Chief Executive of NOMS, Martin Narey, was reflecting a belief that the Prison Service had benefited from this process, first introduced in 1992, with the privatization of HMP Wolds. The subsequent development of private prisons, though remaining at no more than 10 per cent of the prison estate seemed to galvanize the public prisons into looking at their own practices to such a successful degree that not only were they able to win back two contracts from the private sector, but also forced Charles

Clarke to abandon the attempt to market test three prisons in the Isle of Sheppey in 2005 and, as yet, no public sector prison has been put into private hands. The performance testing of prisons to determine capability has revealed a Prison Service well able to deliver what its political masters require, 'The public sector has been successful in all the performance improvement programmes conducted without competition' (Liebling 2006: 70).

The Sheppey fiasco, which undermined Martin Narey's support for contestability and maybe led to his resignation, seems to have weakened the political desire to further market test the prison estate, but with John Reid becoming Home Secretary a renewed attack on the Probation Service, a softer and somewhat demoralized target was renewed and contestability was to be the tool of reform. The Offender Management Bill due for passage through Parliament in 2007 will, if not derailed by opposition, set in motion the enabling legislation to pursue the reshaping of probation into trusts and the market testing of interventions. This is in spite of evidence that the Probation Service has increasingly met the government targets. The ideological support for this process remains and has kept the service insulated from any more fundamental challenge about the future direction of offender management. The Probation Boards Association in concert with Napo have been the focal point for more general resistance to the NOMS concepts and with some success.

It is important to note that the market testing of services in the criminal justice system is a principle which, while one of the key dimensions of modernisation, is operated selectively. So, for instance, the development of electronic surveillance, prison escort services, the running of voluntary sector approved premises among many other services in policing and the courts, have not been subject to contestability. The targets chosen are soft ones to make political headway not necessarily for evidence-based reasons.

Performance management

The setting of targets and key performance indicators has been a central theme of new public management since it was first introduced. We are now familiar with the use of league tables and assessments of how well a public agency is doing, measured on its achievement of selected targets. Indeed internal processes for improving performance are a necessary feature of public services and strongly correlated with the need for public accountability and cost effectiveness. The supporters of performance management, as a tool for measuring standards, regard it as a politically neutral mechanism (Armstrong 2006).

The Prison Service has a long history of organizing its work to specified tasks and its command and control organizational structure adapts easily to changes in the required direction it takes. The ease in which prison has adapted to the modernising environment in part lies in its ability to absorb the key performance indicators into its daily routines. As an organization it decided that its survival depended on delivering an improved service, at least improved as measured by the targets set. At the grass roots level it may be felt that the chase for particular indicators may be unhelpful or even counter-productive to good practice but as money follows achievement of targets senior managers will still seek to meet what is required. It took the Probation Service somewhat longer to realize this fundamental truth about performance management.

The contradictions in this approach can be seen in the way that political changes can alter, even negate, the direction which a performance measurement was taking a service. As political priorities change, sometimes within a timescale where other targets had already been set (recall, for example, the Street Crime Initiative – where targets for agencies changed mid-year because of a new centrally-driven political target around the moral panic on street crime), this can impact on developing good practices. Indeed good practice may only be marginally related to achieving good performance. Thus there appears a fundamental contradiction between What Works and key performance targets as will be developed later. Even more worrying, the Probation Service has demonstrated a good track record of progressively meeting its targets but this has not dulled the desire to introduce other providers of interventions.

Deconcentration and regionalization

The rhetoric of local devolution of powers sat uneasily with centralizing tendencies in setting targets and policies. This is well illustrated in the shifting sands associated with the organizational restructuring of both the Prison and the Probation Services. The regional restructuring of the Prison Service reflected a growing regionalization of the locus of delivery. We have seen attempts to create this level of government in the regions across most of the services. The Prison Service approach still maintained policy at a national level and the requirements of circulars ensured that all parts of the sector operated in similar ways. However the traditional independence of individual prisons and indeed individual governors has never entirely been overcome. It is therefore unsurprising to find that policy on the ground may feel very different in different prisons where local cultures and practices shape the national agenda. The roll out of VCS co-ordinators initiated by the Prison Circular 41/90 has guaranteed such a role is present in each institution. However in one region, different individuals from different agencies occupied these posts and each approached the task with individuality within that national policy (Senior *et al.* 2005: 35).

For the Probation Service, a tradition of local independence and indeed local accountability was dramatically challenged by the formation of the National Probation Service which came into being in April 2001. The centralizing tendencies of government policy had seen progressively interventionist approaches since the somewhat weak first attempt to exert central control through the Statement of National Objectives and Priorities of

1984. Cash limits on local expenditure marked one increase in central control and then National Standards in 1992 another. At first these measures were introduced in a permissive fashion, encouraging services to adopt these directives but, by increasing degrees of persuasion, which became more and more prescriptive, until discretion and autonomy as a concept of professional practice has almost been completely written out. National Standards bring together targets and practice in a managed environment. Of all the features of probation, modernisation, the control of professional autonomy has changed the shape of practice. The demands of the centre combined with centralized training regimes, both for the training of new officers and underpinning Offending Behaviour programmes, has tightened professional discretion to a point that only longer serving officers can even remember its existence. Local areas have been retained but their independence much reduced. Some remnants of local initiatives can be seen in probation's participation in CDRPs or through the probation role in youth offending teams. Interestingly prisons have never become members of these partnership bodies. Criminal justice boards which operate on an area level are another example of more local influence over some joined-up aspects of service delivery.

With the advent of NOMS, further regionalization has been signalled. The intention to set up regional offender managers with a commissioning remit for both prisons and probation will create another tier of government. However, talks of merger of some Probation Service areas appears to have disappeared, maybe partly as a result of the failure to insist on such regional mergers for the Police Service. It remains to be seen how the balance between local delivery and central control will be mediated through this new regional process. What is clear is that local accountability via local authorities remains at the margins for correctional services delivery, and it is government defined localism – criminal justice boards – which are the locus of control.

Audit and inspection

Although the Probation Inspectorate has a long history dating back to 1936 its role and focus has changed dramatically in recent years and in particular since the Criminal Justice Act 1991, when the Inspectorate was given a statutory basis for the first time, placing it on a comparable footing to other central government inspectorates, such as the Prisons Inspectorate. When it had responsibility for inspecting training it developed a regional structure but now operates from just two office bases. The Prison Inspectorate was established in 1980 as a result of the recommendations of the May Committee of Enquiry into the United Kingdom Prison Services.

In the past ten years as part of government's interest in joined-up justice there has been calls for a single inspectorate. This has been resisted including in a key debate in the Lords, where the principles of seamlessness were not questioned but the timing was:

> No one would argue that a seamless system requires a single inspectorate looking at various aspects of the criminal justice system. We do not have a seamless criminal justice system, yet we are moving in that direction. Each of the agencies has a specific role. It requires specific expertise to ensure that the system operates with fairness.
> (Lords 2000: 1202)

Current plans of the Home Secretary, John Reid, are for a single criminal justice regulator, but this has been heavily criticized on human rights grounds. This has particularly exercised the Prisons Inspectorate who feel that they offer a buffer against inhuman treatment in prisons. The current Chief Inspector of Prisons, Anne Owers, has recently said, 'the sharp focus and direct voice of prisons' inspection will be lost or muffled' (quoted in Travis 2006). One of the key concerns is that the Inspectorate will be much more concerned with efficiency and effectiveness of the system and not with the identification of abuse, thus removing a key role as a safeguard of human rights. Inspectorates of course are limited to inspecting what targets have been set by government but its relative independence and focus on either probation, prisons, courts or police, allows it to conclude in ways which air difficult questions but which must be seen as a mark of a civilized and open society.

Audit is another means in which both probation and prison have been assessed. Starting in 1989 with the Probation Reports (Audit Commission 1989) there have been a series of reports which focus on efficiency and effectiveness. This brief is part of the way in which attitudes towards the sectors are shaped for government purposes. Measuring success is reduced to those elements of efficiency and effectiveness which the audit reports put under scrutiny. There is a clear risk that the wider context within which practice is developing both for prison and probation is understated in such reports.

Penal populism and risk management

One of the key global drivers of crime is the focus on a punitive populist approach to law and order alongside an actuarial approach to justice. Ironically in terms of business, prison can benefit from this approach, as prison numbers soar so does the demand for prisons. However, at the same time the risk associated with unregulated prison growth – overcrowding, reduction in human rights, longer sentencing leading to problems of regime, suicide, drug abuse, bullying, etc. – makes this coercive tilt problematic. Decisions about release have also been crucially affected by an actuarial approach imbued with a penal populist veneer. Eligibility for early release under home detention curfews or various forms of conditional release including parole and life licences, have become circumscribed by both the forces of penal populism and risk management.

First, a more punitive climate for those sentenced leads to the imposition of longer sentences, most noticed recently in the growth of tariffs for lifers, which now means that on average inmates are spending considerably longer inside before being considered for release. When decisions about release are considered the impact of rehabilitative thinking on that process is much reduced. A prior consideration is public protection and the cautious use of risk assessments to structure release decisions.

Risk management has become a central feature of probation practice (Kemshall 2003). High 'zero risk' expectations subject to increasingly close media scrutiny accompany this aspect of modern practice. While risk has always been a feature of probation work its modern actuarial accounting purports to create a scientific process of assessment which, though largely based on whole groups of offenders, can help predict both risk of re-offending and the more complex and potentially sensitive risk of harm to self or others. In many ways the careful assessments associated with high-risk offenders, such as represented in the improved MAPPA arrangements, represent real and worthwhile progress towards public protection, agency co-ordination and targeted interventions.

However whether that satisfies the public appetite for risk surveillance of whole populations, particularly sex offenders, is less easy to assess. Sex offenders have been put under increasing scrutiny with registers and panels, and the professional perspective is very positive. However, there is a fundamental truth not willingly acknowledged by government policy-makers. Expectations concerning risk protection are in essence unrealizable. It is certainly possible to increase public protection and to institute positive programmes of intervention but without resorting to such levels of technological and intrusive surveillance which may not be compatible with a civilized society, all such approaches will not necessarily prevent re-offending. Indeed it cannot by its nature prevent new offenders offending as they fall outside the radar, although there are, occasionally, calls for so-called 'pre-delinquents' to be identified and tagged as a precaution against future unspecified offending. Indeed anti-social behaviour orders convert nuisance youngsters into criminals simply through a breach process.

Probation has had to endure such unrealistic expectations in reactions to recent incidents, most notably the Monckton Enquiry in 2006. Though there were mistakes made and documented through the Inspection Report (HM Inspectorate of Probation 2006b) at the heart of such an enquiry is a contradiction in practice. The report was ultimately concerned with whether the correct decisions and procedures had been invoked. This can be counterproductive in that attention to agency protocols is not the same conceptually as attention to dealing with issues which required professional judgement. Also the desistance literature (Maruna 2001; Farrall 2002) points out how individual actual change is. So any risk protection procedure will induce false positives and false negatives (Bottoms 1977) no matter how well calibrated.

The criminal justice climate remains highly punitive and thus the context within which risk assessment and management has developed is mediated through this particular late modern obsession with crime and disorder. It will be important to identify correctional services in jurisdictions where penal populism is less evident and to see how far they can work in a climate with more inclusive offender strategies.

Pluralization

The Probation Service was in the 1970s almost entirely probation officers except for a smattering of administrative grades. The professional development of the service in the 1970s and 1980s rested largely with university educated professionally trained staff with some support staff derisorily known as ancillaries, and thriving volunteer schemes. Massive growth in other grades within probation has been a key feature of the pluralization of the service delivery. This has led to a blurring of boundaries between different grades and an increase in responsibility and authority for lower grades effectively leading to a deprofessionalization of the service. Indeed, Michael Howard would have abandoned the graduate training of probation officers if his plans for an NVQ qualification, without supported learning, had not been resisted in the mid-1990s. New Labour introduced a new award without its social work base but made it fit for purpose for the changing service. However, ten years into this training uncertainty has once again reared its head as the future for offender management training has not been unequivocally set at higher education levels.

There are a number of reasons for this. First, there has been an increase in what can be termed 'bespoke training'. This has proliferated with the growth of accredited programmes which run tightly prescribed programmes of intervention. They require the leaders to operate in a particular fashion to ensure programme integrity. Training does not encourage questioning as a number of probation officer trainees found out during their courses, where the contrast between the approach and that encouraged on the DipPS meant they were failing because they questioned the methods! Clearly reflective practitioners are not encouraged in this model and it is easier to 'train' those who do not have that broader critical thinking approach. Hence accredited programme delivery and thus training has been targeted at those with little or no generic training.

Second, it is argued that a generic probation officer training is inappropriate as it is too expensive, takes too long and is too broad in content. The question asked has been, as prison officers can be trained in six weeks why does it take so long to train probation officers? Of course, this comparison misunderstands the complexity of a job which is required to meet exacting standards of professional practice with difficult, often recalcitrant and reluctant people. The current DipPS has been widely seen as a 'Rolls Royce', high quality, 'fit for purpose' training whose basic tenets can be adapted for offender management training.

Third, what is at the heart of this is the pluralization process itself?

The more fractured and fragmented modules of training become, where reflective practice is not encouraged, the more the training can be a means of control of its workers in terms of how they operate and how they stick to the national standards. This is both dangerous and disingenuous. As the Monckton Enquiry (HM Inspectorate of Probation 2006b) revealed it was a lack of judgement about what was happening which precipitated tragic outcomes and following the rules may not have prevented this result. Greater differentiation of staff roles is often a cheap option as well as a control option. It can be postulated that prison officers' training is a long-term example of a reductionist approach to training, making it easier to run a command and control structure in individual prisons. This can produce unforeseen outcomes in prison and will likely produce negative outcomes in the community.

Specialization is important. Training staff to do particular jobs, for example, targetting NHS and prison medical needs; drugs counselling through CARATS; and ETE through the VCS demand forms of bespoke training. But this could be done in ways which encourage a 'building block' approach to training which can, cumulatively, lead to degree level outcomes, a high quality professional training environment and ultimately to the generation of a skills set which will produce high quality offender managers in the future. This is not what the modernisation agenda projects for staff in the correctional services. Workers being trained in particular programmes/procedures, which are delivered in a paraprofessional manner, is a potential recipe for mistakes to happen in the future.

Joined-up justice

The refrain of 'joined-up justice' has echoed insistently around the changes in the correctional services since 2003. The invention of this new NOMS approach, rather than a merger of prison and probation, has been predicated on the need to reduce the fragmentation of practice exemplified or supposedly exemplified in the past two decades. The argument put by Carter (2003) was simply thus:

> Building on the significant improvements in delivery over the last seven years, a new approach is needed to focus on the management of offenders.
>
> - Prison and probation need to be focused on the management of offenders throughout the whole of their sentence, driven by information on what works to reduce reoffending.
> - Effectiveness and value for money can be further improved through greater use of competition from private and voluntary providers.
>
> This means . . .
>
> - The establishment of a National Offender Management Service – restructuring the Prison and Probation Services – with a single Chief Executive accountable to Ministers for punishing offenders and reducing reoffending.

- Within the new service there should be one person – the National Offender Manager – who is responsible for reducing reoffending – supported by Regional Offender Managers. They would supervise offenders and commission custody places, fine collection and interventions – whether in the public, private or voluntary sector.

(Carter 2003)

This simply encapsulates Carter's and immediately the government's vision (simultaneous release of Carter and government response) of the future. Its contextual analysis was generally felt to be apposite – there were problems in the way the two services functioned both individually and in relation to each other. This had, however, already changed over the preceding period such that the issues were being effectively tackled as hinted at in the opening line of the quote above. However there has been little justification for joining up in the manner prescribed. The key question is, why does NOMS mean? In fact there is a real danger you can end up with different forms of fragmentation rather than greater integration. Prisons and probation remain, offender management and intervention is separated and, with contestability, interventions could be any combination of public, private and voluntary sector providers. Thus NOMS is not a required feature for joining up. In other jurisdictions, for instance in Sweden, joining up has meant the merger of Prison and Probation Services: a different solution with just as much possibility and potential weaknesses as the NOMS solution for joining up.

The NOMS solution has produced an identity crisis for probation which has split its organization as some of its leading personnel have rushed to become NOMS personnel while others, notably and ably led by the employers organization, Probation Boards Association and the union, Napo have rushed to the defence of traditional organizational structures. No one seems to disagree with the need for seamless provision in delivery but there is much disagreement about the nature of the joining up proposed. This will be further developed below.

There is a real risk that the new structures of NOMS will simply increase fragmentation and not achieve the goals it sets itself. This is of course an empirical question the answer to which will emerge in the next five years. However, fundamental to joining up any services is the existence and support for a shared sense of vision and purpose, a feature which, for instance, joint training between prison and probation is more likely to achieve than simply changing the organizational boundaries.

Responsibilization

Responsibilized communities are very evident in government campaigns against crime focusing on what individuals, parents and communities can do to support crime reduction activities. If you are not seen as part of the solution you will be seen as part of the problem. However, many of these activities are not part of mainstream correctional activity. Probation has ceased to have any resemblance to a community-based organization and prisons are often seen as the ultimate exclusionary symbol. What government needs to focus more on, if the impact of its policies are to have an effect across all groups, is creating a more inclusionary approach by responsibilizing offenders.

Offender perceptions of services are now being collated in evaluation, though their limits are discussed in a recent reflection on this trend (Knight *et al.* 2007). What has been slower to develop is the direct engagement of offenders in both researching outcomes (O'Keeffe 2004) and in offering peer support and mentoring to their peers (Senior *et al.* 2007b). The treatment of ex-offenders as individuals who can offer meaningful support to their peers struggles to get a foothold because of cautious professional attitudes and, sometimes, a negative public. However, we know that restorative justice processes are successful because they seek to bridge the gap between offenders and the wider community and where experiments have taken place the results are very positive.

A little of this can be seen in prisons where there is a current debate about prisoners as citizens (Faulkner 2002). Listening schemes, schemes such as the Inside Out Trust and use of St Giles peer advisors are all examples of the involvement of inmates in helping others. The setting up of prisoner councils is also designed to give a voice to prisoners in the administration of regimes, but perhaps there is still caution in how fundamental a change this is (Solomon and Edgar 2004).

However, the political climate is not always conducive to this aspect of responsibilization. Government has spent the past two decades finding language which ensures a negative and exclusionary 'us and them' feel which is perpetuated in the name of orders and organizations: *viz* community punishment orders; curfew orders; offender managers; anti-social behaviour orders; the National *Offender* Management Service – and these are just official terms. Thugs, hoodies, rat boys, scum, etc., are the media inspired contributions. Condemning more and understanding less does not augur well for inclusive forms of responsibilization.

The permanence of paradox

The correctional services – prison and probation – have clearly different organizational arrangements and their history shows a somewhat different response to reform and change and a different capability at resisting change. It is not surprising, therefore to have charted above the very distinct ways in which the management of change under the modernisation agenda has been both received and acted upon by these two diverse agencies. The drivers of global crime act as an overarching context within which such micro-management of change occurs. A more punitive climate affects prison and probation very differently – producing more customers for prisons and maybe a greater public acceptance of prison as the containers of such criminals. Prisons serve as a helpful repository, symbolically and in practice, for society's punitive impulses and the symbols of prison – exclusion, segregation, punishment and surveillance – also impact on the nature of the community sentences delivered by probation. No agency in criminal justice has had to change and adapt more to this punitive climate than probation. Its capacity for resistance is weak and its tactics such as it was articulated was, in a censorious and coercive atmosphere, to be compliant towards any changes imposed. This has weakened its professional standing and made it more vulnerable to change. Prison has had to face threats to itself as a public service notably with the advent of private prisons, but has been able to respond quickly to manage that threat and indeed currently to suspend further moves in that direction.

Within the dimensions of modernisation, however, we have seen some key contradictions that fundamentally weaken the modernising process.

What works and performance management

Logically you would expect a commitment to an evidence-based approach to directly influence performance indicators. However, some commentators have noted an 'evidence-free' approach to such indicators, which can also serve directly to undermine the intervention programmes themselves. First, the setting of targets involved, for example, in reducing delay, prompt breaching processes or achievement of particular outputs, such as accommodation on release, all serve to get in the way of good practice in programme interventions. To take one of the examples given above it is worth tracing the process to illustrate the paradoxical outcomes.

The Prison Service had a target to ensure everyone is accommodated upon release. The mark of this target is that they have an address to go to. Prisoners knowing that failure to provide an address would inhibit their chances of early release have found many ways of ensuring they have an address – be it a mate's floor, their family (for one night only) or a night shelter. However, when working on a research project (Senior *et al.* 2005) I discussed this with the Resettlement Governor of a prison in the northeast. She indicated that this target inhibited real efforts at securing meaningful accommodation. Once an address had been secured it did not matter if this broke down within days of release, the target had been met. She commented that this was revealed when prisoners returned to jail on breach of orders. A more meaningful target, such as securing accommodation for three months post-release, would have initiated different levels of investment in achieving it. This is simply illustrative of the conflict between What Works and performance indicators and this is also even more poignantly illustrated in relation to the failure of offending behaviour programmes. It is now becoming clear that this failure is, in part, due to the high breach rates and therefore non-completion of programmes. One key tenet of such programmes is completion and a performance target of breaching absence undermines the ability of programme managers to complete their investment and thus reduces programme integrity.

Locality vs. central direction

Modernisation is sold in political circles through its hollowing out of the state and the transfer and devolution of control to the local areas. Certainly the rhetoric of this is evident in work in the corrections field. However, we have seen that this is not carried through in practice. The centre has maintained a hold over local practice particularly the Probation Service. Indeed the explicit agenda of the new National Probation Service in 2001 was to ensure standardization of practice and the ever increasing numbers of probation circulars further emphasized this central oversight. The accredited programmes approach further sought to apply a stranglehold on individualized practice. It is doubtful that this strategy actually stopped practice judgement being expressed by local areas. Indeed the desistance literature supports such individualization of practice. But it creates a climate in which variations from the central directive are regarded as delinquent rather than positive local variations. The introduction of a regional tier of government and following this the regional offender managers further adds a layer of confusion to the locus of control.

Prisons have retained a stronger hold over their business within a more compliant response to central directives. Governors concentrate on creating their own atmosphere within prisons, resulting in many nuances of practice on the ground. Given that they are closed to the public eye such differences only emerge in inspection or moments of crisis.

Risk management and penal populism

We have seen that in some senses risk and penal populism appear to work in tandem. An approach to control of offending which makes public protection paramount needs a vehicle for deciding the degrees of protection required from particular offenders or classes of offending. Thus a risk management system is essential. However, what or who is defined as a problem deserving of higher levels of surveillance and incapacitation is in part a political decision. Given that over a ten year period crime rates have fallen it could be argued that risk has reduced. Yet the tone of debate both in the popular press and in government circles is one of increasing concern about the risks to individuals and this is fed by occasional high profile cases, which genuinely do challenge our protective capacities, for example, the Soham murders. Another feature of this process is the primacy of the private sector in delivering protective services – electronic surveillance, prison escorting, satellite tracking, lie detectors, etc. – their desire to develop their business and in a market in which contestability seems somewhat absent, can lead to an unregulated desire to extend control. It has been argued elsewhere that unless there is a balance between the aims of protection, rehabilitation and restoration (Raikes 2002) then the system ceases to be fit for purpose.

NOMS and joining up

A final paradox surrounds the very solution proposed to achieve joined-up justice. It has become axiomatic that NOMS is the way in which the Prison and Probation Services can be effectively managed to ensure end to end offender management. An increasing amount of criticism has questioned the validity of this claim and the dangers inherent in a structure which could fragment and fracture integration as much as it can create a unified working environment. The Prison Service continues to operate in its own sphere resisting incorporation into the NOMS empire and while the latter has now swallowed up the National Probation Directorate, there remains resistance and demoralization at local levels of the probation service. If the Offender Management Bill were to fall in 2007 or be substantially amended now, an increasingly likely outcome, then there would be other more viable ways of achieving this joining up agenda. The advent of the Ministry of Justice in May 2007 and the different tone of political direction initiated by Lord Falconer, immediately creates a climate for change which is distanced from the punitive aspirations of John Reid and the Home Office.

Conclusion

Modernisation has impacted directly on both Prison and Probation Services. The dissonance has been felt most directly by the Probation Service and continues to reverberate around its very future. The Prison Service has managed to soak up the changes, partly as a result of its command and control structure which is conducive to a managerialist approach to change and partly through its strength to resist those features it finds less palatable. Any government which puts primacy on law and order needs a compliant and committed Prison Service to house all those they wish to exclude from participation by dint of their proscribed behaviours. Prisons are ever willing to undertake this function, after all it contributes to its own survival and growth.

The Probation Service has been seen to make a more uncomfortable bedfellow to the modernising imperative. Stripped of the global context of crime and disorder, some of the key dimensions outlined would be unobjectionable in themselves. However it has been strongly argued in this chapter that it is very much the context which has dictated the way in which the Probation Service has had to respond. There is no doubt that it has missed key opportunities to influence the precise direction in which modernisation has taken it. Its compliant approach to changes, albeit as a response to the censorious climate, has been taken as a sign of weakness and its needs have been accordingly ignored. The year 2007 is in the century of probation and while the tasks it has traditionally undertaken remain key to a social justice and a human rights approach to the administration of criminal justice, it has lost its monopoly on delivery. As we shall see in the Chapter 9, the VCS has taken some opportunity to come centre stage, an opportunity probation failed to take in 1991 and now may forever be unable to recapture.

Further reading

Hough, M., Allen, R. and Padel, U. (2006) *Reshaping Probation and Prisons: The New Offender Management Framework*. Bristol: Policy Press.

Hudson, B. (2003) *Justice in the Risk Society: Challenging and Re-affirming Justice in Late Modernity*. London: Sage.

Kemshall, H. (2003) *Understanding Risk in Criminal Justice*. Maidenhead: Open University Press.

Mair, G. (2004) *What Matters in Probation*. Cullompton: Willan.

Nash, M. and Ryan, M. (2003) Modernising and joining up government: the case of the prison and probation services, *Contemporary Politics* (June), 9(2).

chapter six

Modernisation and community safety

This chapter examines the ways in which modernisation has impacted upon the organization and delivery of crime reduction services in the wider community. Crime reduction was at the forefront of modernisation when New Labour came to power. The role of the Crime and Disorder Reduction Partnerships (CDRPs), the local criminal justice boards and their predecessors will be placed into context with particular focus on sections 5–7, 17 and 116 of the Crime and Disorder Act (CDA) (1998). It is argued that an important rationale underlying this legislation is that the solutions to localized crime problems are best achieved locally. More than that, it shows that partnerships are a relatively new mode of governance (see Chapter 1). The role of local strategic partnerships in delivering the government's community safety agenda will be explored.

The chapter is split into three main parts. The first, and the shortest, introduces the concepts of community safety and partnership in order to familiarize the reader with its contested meanings. The second part revisits the legacy of five successive Conservative governments (1979–97) and New Labour's efforts to address some of the most persistent problems facing community safety professionals, which are related to a socially excluded underclass. Under New Labour the joined-up work of CDRPs and the Social Exclusion Unit (SEU) have been there to tackle this. The relevance of the drivers of global crime for understanding these concepts is also sketched where appropriate. In the third and main part, the key dimensions of modernisation are scrutinized with reference to specific examples taken from the criminological literature. In accordance with what was said at the outset of this book, some of these factors are more relevant than others and in discussing the modernisation of community safety it is argued that joined-up justice, responsibiliziation, penal populism and risk management are the most pertinent, although some comments will be made about each of the dimensions. Towards the end of the chapter it is argued that under New Labour's modernisation strategy the prevailing political tactics have been commitment with a transformative orientation towards reform; although in the early days there was conceivably some compliance realized through primary legislation and a degree of resistance to some aspects.

Contextual outline

The context behind the concerns of this chapter is complex and the terms in currency in relevant debates are contested. Community safety, and its modernisation, is the main focus, but this necessarily involves us in the consideration of crime prevention and crime reduction. As many commentators are keen to point out these are all different phenomena but their usage is sometimes intertwined and frequently the distinctions are not hard and fast (Hope 2002; Pease 2002). Although the contested meanings of these concepts is of importance, it is their application in the context of partnerships that will preoccupy us most. The notion of partnership is also subject to debate and there are both normative and practical perspectives (Gilling 2005).

Although an awareness of the history of partnerships in crime and public policy is indispensable, for the purposes of this chapter, most time and space is dedicated to New Labour's CDA (1998) and its intersections with modernisation. In contrast to the other agencies examined in this book, modernisation has not been made an explicit feature of debates about the meanings of community and community safety (Hughes *et al.* 2002; Matthews and Pitts 2002; Squires 2006; Hughes 2007) or more administrative and technical concerns relating to the phenomenon (Tilley 2005; Farrall and Pease 2006)[1]. We redress this next.

Thinking about community safety

Crime prevention, community safety and crime reduction are sometimes used synonymously, though each has its own peculiar conceptual history. For example, the ideas underpinning community safety have been around for a long time, even though the terminology is relatively new. The Morgan Report (1991) put the idea on the agenda of policymakers. Since then the meaning of the term has been contested (Pease 2002; Hughes 2007) but for the purposes of this discussion a relatively old Home Office definition is useful. Community safety is:

> an aspect of 'quality of life' in which people, individually and collectively, are protected as far as possible from hazards or threats that result from the criminal or anti-social behaviour of others, and are equipped or helped to cope with those that they do experience. It would enable them to pursue and obtain the fullest benefits from, their social and economic lives without fear or hindrance from crime and disorder.
>
> (Home Office 1998: 7)

Community safety refers not just to crime and unlawful activities but also to 'chronic' social conditions brought about by anti-social behaviour, such as low level disorder and incivilities, which cause people to fear for their own safety. This feeling may be real or perceived. Community safety thus has a wider meaning which is of relevance to social policy. Community safety includes a range of protective functions provided nationally and locally, some of which are concerned with more than crime and disorder. For example, drug abuse and drug dealing, racial harassment and hate crime, tackling social exclusion, consumer protection, household safety, road safety, fire prevention, and health and public health (Phillips *et al.* 2002). Crucially, it is recognized that these problems are interrelated, concentrated in the same geographical areas and require a 'joined-up' set of responses and solutions. However, it should be noted that the main focus is on crime and disorder, which indicates that in some instances social policy may be being displaced through crime policy (Stenson 1998). For that reason, crime prevention and crime reduction are ascendant. A burgeoning industry has developed to prevent and reduce crime and both aims are very closely related to community safety. CDRPs and their crime reduction strategies are multi-dimensional, involving situational and social measures (Clarke 1980; Pease 1997; Crawford 1998). Situational measures are concerned with issues of design, security and defensible space. The view is that crime can be designed out of estates through the use of locks and bolts and improved street lighting (Pease 2002). Social measures are concerned with community development and the management of properties as well as people. Both elements are relevant but since 1998 there has been a tendency to prioritize crime reduction, although in the most recent national community safety plan the fire service and PCTs from the domain of health policy may suggest a situation that is slightly more complex (Home Office 2005). Perhaps, instead of crime policy subordinating social policy in all instances there are hybridized policies amalgamating concerns about crime and the social, where in some instances social priorities may be pre-eminent. This observation requires detailed empirical evidence that is not yet available, however.

Although community safety, crime prevention and crime reduction clearly have their own unique meanings they are all too frequently treated as if they are the same thing, which certainly creates obfuscation in the policymaking process. However, to avoid unnecessary complication this chapter will use them interchangeably rather in the same way that central government does.

Thinking about partnership

Partnership working is sometimes described as multi-agency or inter-agency working, each of which are methodologically and practically different entities (Crawford 1997, 1998). It is also an example of the new modes of governance described by Rhodes (2000b; see Part One). Heuristically it is perhaps helpful to think about the multi-agency partnerships in terms of agencies sitting together in a room, possibly discussing the same issues, but quite conceivably mutually talking past each other. What is said in meetings of this kind will be *minuted* and certain points will be *actioned*, but following the meeting there will be no genuine synergy resulting in partnerships, which have any material effect. In the case of inter-agency partnerships, it is more likely that the ideas and practices of agencies are linked, resulting in genuinely integrated policy formulation, implementation and evaluation.

More importantly, the notion of partnership quite clearly pre-dates the modernisation agenda and although they emerged during the period in which the principles of the NPM were shaped, partnership as an idea and activity is independent from these political rationalities. Partnership implies integration, co-operation and co-ordination, or in the discourse of New Labour, 'joined-up' thinking, policy and practice. This is intended to occur in terms of the operation of organizational structures and it is also expected to be embedded in the hearts and minds of the social actors participating in partnerships. However, the extent to which these aspirations are realized is influenced to a great degree by the context in which partnerships are situated, including local, national and increasingly global settings. In this chapter, the statutory partnerships established as a result of the CDA (1998) need to be related to earlier informal partnerships. From the mid-1980s onwards successive Conservative governments attempted to energize partnerships to tackle crime and disorder, evidenced by the recommendations made in the Scarman (1981) report, although the same governments rejected the Morgan report (1991) and its recommendation for primary legislation to make their creation mandatory. In the aftermath of the latter, many agencies throughout the public sector endorsed Morgan's thinking, which was to become the conventional wisdom among policy elites and senior managers across the public sector in general and criminal justice sector in particular (Crowther 2000b). This was especially the case with regard to the police (McLaughlin 1994), an observation that continues to have resonance to this day. Partnership is not exclusive to criminal justice and professionals in health and education, for example, are experienced in this type of working (Glendinning 2002). In short, each of the agencies eventually involved in community safety and crime reduction, bring with them their own histories of joined-up thinking and practice. This in turn has a bearing on the degree of co-ordination, integration and joined-up-ness that is actually achieved in intellectual and practical terms.

What are the main drivers behind the growth of partnership? To answer this it is necessary to briefly revisit the policies of the Conservatives for two reasons. First, they set the agenda for New Labour. Second, the Tories were well positioned in 2007 to re-enter office and hence were given an opportunity to exercise their political agency to determine the future directions of modernisation (see the Conclusion).

New Labour and the neo-liberal legacy

Crowther (2004) has written elsewhere that between 1979 and 1997 the issue of poverty did not attract much attention from four successive Conservative governments, despite intensive activity on the part of the anti-poverty lobby. A closer analysis of debates about poverty soon reveals that there are two distinct perspectives. On the one hand, there are behavioural accounts, which explain the poverty and criminality of individuals in terms of their perceived moral and psychological flaws. On the other hand, structural versions suggest that the material and social circumstances which surround individuals may explain, albeit not excuse, these phenomena. During the early to mid-1990s the idea of an underclass was in circulation in political and media discourse to describe a section of the poor that had become detached from mainstream society in terms of its behaviour rather than its structural location. The central argument is that the provision of welfare and the legacy of the permissive 1960s created an idle, immoral, state dependent and ultimately criminogenic underclass. This was also associated with a rise in lone parent households, crime and disorder. Neo-liberal commentators, such as Charles Murray (2000), refused to accept that the actions of the underclass were in any way an effect of government policies, claiming instead that they were caused by individualized personal deficiencies. There was no shortage of counter-arguments from academics who suggested that some measure of structural change was necessary, particularly the redistribution of income from the rich to the poor, but they lacked a sympathetic audience among politicians, the media and the electorate. The election of New Labour on 1 May 1997 led to several changes (Lister 2004).

Tony Blair (Prime Minister, 1997–2007), shortly after being elected into power, made an important speech on the Aylesbury Estate, Southwark on 2 June 1997 which changed, at least at a rhetorical level, what the Conservatives had said and done before in social policy and criminal justice policy. In his address, the PM pledged that the government would confront the problem of an underclass 'cut off' and excluded from mainstream society. He referred to unstable families, welfare dependency, crime, drugs and alienation. Blair added 'millions have simply dropped out of society, forming alternative systems of living and language . . . that is the threat if we do not stop the break-up of society' (Blair 1997, cited in Cook 2006). As noted in the introduction, the Social Exclusion Unit was set up by the end of that year. This unit focused on social problems from a joined-up perspective and set up 18 Policy Action Teams. The SEU published reports concerning homelessness; neighbourhood renewal; school exclusion and truancy; teenage motherhood; and 16–18-year-olds that are not in training or employment.

The concept of social exclusion has a long history in European social policy but it did not enter into political discourse until the mid-1990s. According to Levitas (2005), there are three discourses on social exclusion:

> a redistributionist discourse (RED) developed in British critical social policy, whose prime concern is poverty; a moral underclass discourse (MUD) which centres on the moral and behavioural delinquency of the excluded themselves; and a social integrationist discourse (SID) whose central focus is on paid work.

In short, it refers to multiple social problems and their many causes. In modern Britain, discourses on social exclusion tend to overlap with discourses on poverty, particularly Townsend's (1990) notion of 'relative poverty', but rather than focusing solely on the distributional (RED) aspects of poverty and deprivation its relational aspects attract more attention. In contrast to their Conservative antecedents New Labour stated quite unequivocally that, 'It would also be a mistake to tackle crime as if it is only a matter arising from the criminality of individuals or families'. In other words, the causes of social problems are multi-faceted and are not found solely at a behavioural (MUD) level, but also at a structural level. However, some aspects of the behavioural version are still in place. As part of the modernisation strategy the government stated that it did not share the Old (as opposed to the New) Labour commitment to equality and the redistribution of income underpinned by social rights for individual citizens (Dean 2006). The new mission statement was based on the premise that citizens needed to be responsibilized, amounting to equality of opportunity linked with personal responsibility for one's behaviour and social obligations. For example, in terms of internal affairs, 'the principal aim of the Home Office is to build a safe, just and tolerant society in which the rights and responsibilities of individuals, families and communities are properly balanced and the protection and security of the public are maintained'. This indicates that New Labour departed from its traditional emphasis on the rights of citizens as a prerequisite for the creation of the good society. Instead of rights, individuals are to be given opportunities, mainly work, and it is their duty and responsibility to take these up (Driver and Martell 2006). Thus government policies concentrated their attention on social exclusion, rather than poverty *per se*, and social inclusion would only be achieved by changing the way citizens behave, the redistribution of opportunities in schools and the labour market (SID), instead of giving people extra income (Levitas 2005).

The original remit of the SEU was to encourage co-operation and joined-up working between government departments, local authorities, voluntary agencies, and private financiers from the business sector and the wider community to develop anti-poverty policies. Its efforts were concentrated on:

> groups who are in poverty, lacking the means to participate in the economic, social, cultural and political life in Britain: . . . 5 million people in workless homes; the three million on the nation's 1300 worst council estates; the 150,000 homeless families and the 100,000 children not attending school.
>
> (Home Office cited in Crowther 2000b)

The above are also placed in the context of the government's anti-crime and disorder strategies.

During the period in which the Conservatives were in government there was evidence of a growing underclass and social exclusion. New Labour was elected to government in 1997 and as part of its commitment to modernisation made a commitment to address the multiple problems linked with social exclusion. Government agencies were enlisted to participate in this political project and at a macro level there would appear to be a general commitment to New Labour's agenda in crime and public policy. This framework is described in the following section.

Before that the drivers of global crime underlying community safety and crime reduction are briefly rehearsed.

The *penal punitiveness* set in motion as a result of Michael Howard's 'prison works' speech in 1993 was continued with a vengeance by New Labour. This issue, covered in Chapter 5, also has an impact on community safety. At the time of writing in 2007, the prison population is near capacity and there do not appear to be any immediate solutions to the impending crisis facing John Reid, the New Labour Home Secretary until the spring of 2007. Reid also encountered a public that was purportedly fearful of dangerous offenders presenting serious *risks* that have either not been *assessed* or *managed* properly. Few may be actually victimized by or witness these offenders, but the existence of predatory and violent offenders does quite rightly make the citizenry fearful. Anxieties about the need to protect communities – including the vulnerable as well as the respectable majority – reflect not only government priorities but also the deep seated concerns of both 'middle England' as well as socially excluded communities (Respect Task Force 2006; Hughes 2007). New Labour's punitive orientation is also demonstrated in their attitudes towards anti-social behaviour and young people where non-criminal behaviours are increasingly being criminalized (Squires and Stephen 2005; France 2007; see also Chapter 4 on youth justice in this text).

Beyond these developments, perhaps the basic point is that community safety is fragile, exposed by the contradictions of crime reduction policy more widely. The roles and responsibilities of all criminal justice agencies – and to some extent voluntary and private sector agencies – have all been augmented by the diversification of tasks they are required to undertake. The conditions of authoritarian austerity under which community safety is to be attained also presents some difficulties. For instance, community safety is also being modernised by the application of NPM principles but they become hybridized as different criminal justice agencies interact. More than that, the involvement of other government departments in community safety who have also been exposed to NPM produces a range of effects. Overall, different agencies are, in the last analysis, driven by the variant of NPM that is specific to their agency, even if this clashes with other agencies.

There are more specific developments belonging specifically to modernisation, however.

The modernisation of community safety: key dimensions

Arguably the most germane dimensions of modernisation in community safety is the notion of joined-up justice or, to be more accurate in this case, joined-up policy and practice. The bulk of this section is taken up with this topic although each dimension is of some significance.

Joined-up justice

For many years academics, politicians and practitioners in the field of criminal justice have argued that individual agencies cannot effectively reduce crime and disorder if they do not work together. Moreover, there is the view that criminal behaviour can only be addressed by looking beyond the criminal justice system towards wider society, including a host of statutory as well as voluntary and private agencies. The latter is an indication of the government's commitment to commercializing crime reduction policy (Johnston 2000; Crawford *et al.* 2005). The causes of and solutions to crime are dependent on recognition of the complex linkages between institutions and processes at macro and micro levels. In England and

Wales, for example, there has developed so-called 'joined-up' thinking and policies to reduce crime and disorder and create safer communities. In this part the structure of these ideas and practices are described, followed by an assessment of their impact and effectiveness. More specifically, this section shows how crime reduction and community safety strategies are 'joined-up', or connected, with policies intended to promote social inclusion. The idea of 'joined-up' government is based on the assumption that the causes of, and solutions to, social exclusion are multi-dimensional and cut across government departments. A wide range of agencies and organizations are therefore involved in any response to social exclusion. It is an holistic approach to policymaking that seeks to overcome departmental compartmentalization within government and its departments. The aim is to create an institutional framework and set of mechanisms which facilitates the development of cross-departmental networks to respond to interrelated problems. For example, in the early 2000s the working of the following departments were 'joined-up':

- Home Office
- Department for Education and Skills
- Department of Health
- Department for Work and Pensions
- Department of the Environment, Food and Rural Affairs
- Department for Transport
- Department for Trade and Industry.

Each of the agencies working within the criminal justice system are now required to work with other agencies belonging to the welfare state to address reducing crime, creating safe communities and creating a more inclusive society.

It is not the aim of this subsection to summarize all aspects of the CDA but to focus on its main provisions regarding crime reduction, leading in due course to an appraisal of the ways in which it has been modernised. As noted above, the relevant sections are 5–7, 17 and 116.

The CDA includes a statutory framework for police, local authorities and other interested agencies in order to establish anti-crime and disorder partnerships, setting out the main priorities, objectives and targets of Community Safety Plans. Separate from this, the National Criminal Justice Board was set up in 2003 to oversee activities at a local level where there were 42[2] Local Criminal Justice Boards charged with the responsibility for running criminal justice policy in their respective geographical area. The framework informing these activities is derived from a basic problem solving structure that is designed to create effective crime prevention and community safety strategies (Hough 2004).

National guidelines laid down by the government are modified at a local level to meet the needs of specific localities. In the first instance, local police commanders (known as 'directors of intelligence') and the chief executives of local authorities (councils and districts) conduct crime and disorder audits within given geographical territories. The rationale of these audits is to produce information about the scale of, the impact on and cost of each crime and disorder related problem for communities. This information will enable the participating agencies and groups to discover which problems they share in common and the ways resources may best be deployed to resolve them. The participants are police and local authority departments, such as housing, education, youth, planning, environmental health and highways. The other parties include community safety partnerships; health authorities; probation committees; victim support; local community groups; racial equality groups; cultural associations; chambers of commerce/business groups; and regional transport networks.

There are no typical partnerships and there is considerable variation from area to area. Each partnership has different core and peripheral members and the participating agencies perform different functions in order of their importance.

At the time of the CDA the Home Office (1998) identified three key groups in an illustration of what a local Crime and Disorder Reduction Partnership may look like: the partnership group, publicly accountable bodies and working groups.

1 *Partnership group*
   - Assistant Chief Constable (Police)
   - Chief Probation Officer
   - Chief Executive Local Authority
   - Primary Care Trust
   - Director of Social Services
   - Director of Education
   - Voluntary Sector
   - Transport
   - Fire Service
   - Magistrates
2 *Publicly accountable bodies*
   - Police Authorities
   - Health Authorities
   - Elected members of Local Authorities
   - Probation Committee
3 *Working groups*
   - Street robberies working group
   - Car crime working group
   - Domestic burglary working group
   - Anti-social behaviour working group
   - Racial harassment working group

It is notable that the Prison Service is omitted from this ideal-typical list as is the VCS. The latter has been incorporated in some initiatives but the former has not really been there suggesting that partnerships are orientated towards crime reduction, and that this function is defined in such a way that it excludes convicted offenders from their remit.

Each partnership was required to formulate crime reduction strategies with clear aims and objectives. In a sense the CDA has formalized many of the pre-existing informal networks of governance, philosophies and mechanisms associated with partnership and inter-agency work and community safety partnerships (Gilling 1997; Crawford 1998; Stenson and Edwards 2003). The aim was to get the police, local authorities and local people to join forces to work together to rebuild communities by addressing complex social problems in communities. Crucially, the legislation provided a mandatory framework for tackling social problems, but ultimately change would be brought about by the commitment of the individuals and communities involved.

A diverse array of tactics was used, which involved working with those groups deemed to be at most risk of offending, in particular families, children and schools, in order to prevent young people from becoming offenders. These duties cut across the different government departments and focused on social exclusion; school performance; drug-related crime; economic regeneration; and the promotion of family life (Cook 2006; Dean 2006). This is in accord with the view that the causes of crime include poverty; poor housing; poor parenting; associating with delinquent peers; poor school performance; and persistent truanting. These strategies fit into the context of the government's wider strategy, which form part of the statutory partnerships (both at local and national levels) designed to take comprehensive action against crime and its causes. The investment of resources would be based on evidence of *what actually works* rather than unfounded assumptions about what is effective, and the performance of each initiative would be evaluated.

It has been shown that the CDA (1998) created a framework for dealing with crime and disorder that involved a range of agencies beyond the criminal justice system. The section below examines more closely the mechanisms involved in New Labour's joined-up policy framework. The principal mechanism used to deliver joined-up approaches to crime reduction and social exclusion are Crime and Disorder Reduction Partnerships (CDRPs) but there are other factors, such as the Crime Reduction Programme (CRP), which ran between 1999 and 2002 (Home Office 1999; Maguire 2004)[3].

The CRP was concerned with five broad themes, with varying degrees of relevance to wider social policies:

- Working with families, children and schools to prevent young people from becoming offenders in the future (risk assessment and management).
- Tackling crime in communities, particularly high volume crime, such as domestic burglary (linked to performance management).

- Developing products and systems which are more resistant to crime.
- More effective sentencing practices (crime reduction).
- Working with offenders to ensure that they do not reoffend (rehabilitation).

(Home Office 2000a: 59)

These initiatives were required to tackle crime and its causes, including its structural or social and individual or behavioural causes. However, each programme had to be 'cost effective', provide 'value for money' and be evaluated according to their effectiveness, efficiency and economy (Hough 2004). Early initiatives included burglary reduction, targeted policing, tackling school exclusions, the installation of CCTV systems in high-crime areas, improving the information available to sentencers and tackling domestic violence (Home Office 2000a: 59).

The CDRPs and the CRP were co-ordinated by the Crime Reduction Task Force, which included representatives from police forces and local and central government. The Task Force supported, advised and guided the local CDPs/CDRPs and Regional Crime Reduction Directors by given them a national focus. For example, guidance was given in relation to target setting, the best ways of involving different agencies and the development of good practice. Also at a regional level there were Regional Development Agencies (RDAs) that co-ordinated multi-agency initiatives, joining up central government, local authorities and local people to regenerate communities. The question is, what effects did RDAs have on the local delivery of area regeneration packages. In principle, health trusts, the Employment Service, the Benefits Agency, the police, businesses and local people could all have become involved in regeneration projects. The aim was to design strategies, which link the objectives of different departments.

In sum, joined-up approaches are based on several assumptions. The idea that crime cannot be tackled effectively by the criminal justice system alone can be traced back to the Morgan Report (1991). Accordingly, New Labour placed joined-up and cross-departmental approaches to tackling crime at the centre of its policy framework. The Crime and Disorder Act (1998) has had a tremendous influence on crime and public policy.

Key issues in the modernisation of community safety

Following on from the previous example, joined-up justice underpins the notion of partnership. Chapter 3 hinted that partnerships are sometimes beset by disagreements between the different agencies involved, possibly relating to different professional cultures. Numerous reviews of community safety partnerships have documented the sometimes uncomfortable relationship between local authorities and the police, for example (Hicks 2002; Gilling 2005; Phillips *et al.* 2002).

Modernisation in this area needs to focus on the fact that there are sometimes necessary tensions between strategic aims and objectives, and their priorities, and operational attempts to develop local solutions to local problems. The lines of communication within partnerships to this day require reform to ensure information is effectively cascaded and filtered through to the relevant actors. It is also known that the different subgroups responding to a host of problems need to use meetings not only to identify problems and potential solutions, but also to circulate an action plan to all the parties concerned. Finally, if joined-up justice is to be realized it is necessary to build in systems, which facilitate the measurement of the effectiveness of the processes through which partnership products are delivered.

A concrete example of joined-up justice is the Multi-Agency Public Protection Arrangements (MAPPA), set up in each police/probation area in England and Wales, as a requirement of sections 67 and 68 of the Criminal Justice and Courts Services Act (CJCSA 2000). MAPPAs bring together the Police and Probation Services to work together as Responsible Authorities for assessing and managing the risks posed by sexual and violent offenders. This formalized and placed on a statutory footing pre-existing arrangements, which tended to be informal. In 2003 HM Prison Service was made a third Responsible Authority by the Criminal Justice Act (2003). Furthermore, other agencies were brought into these arrangements, including Social Services and health organizations, which were expected to co-operate with the Police and Probation Services (Fox and Jenkins 2005).

Each MAPPA is managed by a co-ordinator at the centre that works within a multi-agency Public Protection Unit (PPU). This co-ordinator reports to a Senior Management Board made of up representatives from each of the constituents. Sex offenders account for the bulk of cases that are managed by MAPPAs (Kemshall *et al.* 2005).

The success of the MAPPA is dependent on mutual support and increased co-ordination across and between agencies where partnerships are created to ease the exchange of information between agencies. The sharing of information is crucial with regard to sex offenders so partners can produce accurate community-based risk assessments about sexual and violent offenders. The pooling of information and available resources is the foundation of effective interventions to manage risk (Nelson and Griffiths 2001; Maguire and Kemshall 2004).

However, as governments have made clear their commitment towards these joined-up approaches to dealing with sex offenders, the media has stepped up its interest in exposing the ineffectiveness of professionals when things have gone wrong. For example, there is the case of the release on license of the dangerous sex offender Anthony Rice in 2004 who went on to reoffend with tragic consequences. Mistakes were made but the media was not hesitant in simplifying complex decision-making processes (Department of Constitutional Affairs 2006).

Mixed economy

Activities such as competition and market testing are both key elements of modernisation and govern the mixed economy of service provision in various parts of the sector, including the Police, Probation and Prison Services. Other agencies outside of the criminal justice sector, such as health, have been profoundly affected by this trend too. Crime Reduction Partnerships clearly involve agencies who in their respective domains are influenced by a mixed economy of service provision but the impact of this logic or political rationality on community safety is less clear cut. Community safety and crime reduction policies are formulated and delivered by players from the statutory, voluntary and private sectors and while the initiatives are in a sense mixed the underlying aims and objectives are not as a matter of course explicitly about competition. However, competition may occur where different agencies are applying for short-term funding to finance partnerships and specific initiatives (for example, European Social Fund funding).

Senior *et al.* (2002) show that short-term funding by councils for human resources may also be an issue, which in turn can jeopardize the effectiveness of partnerships. Partnerships may also be committed to applying for funding to assist initiatives/groups to address crime and disorder problems, but this can prove to be a problem. For example, the aforementioned piece of research revealed that funding for one partnership was obtained from different sources and much of it was short term. More than that, even when funding was secured, it was available for different time frames. It was not an infrequent occurrence for partnerships to devote a lot of time to bidding, which is time consuming and diverts attention from the real issues. These factors led to insecurity among some staff who feel unsettled about the future. This has an effect on the morale and working practices of the partnership members and arguably the overall effectiveness of the partnerships. Heavy workloads sometimes place an impossible burden on practitioners as demand for services frequently outstrips supply.

A potential pitfall of having to compete for funding is that competing for funding when resources are scarce and spread thinly militates again notions of partnership, an issue discussed further in Chapter 9, on the VCS.

Contestability

Chapter 3 discussed the relevance of this discourse in the context of the correctional agencies and it has no obvious direct bearing on the day-to-day workings of crime reduction partnerships. However, a similar observation to the one made in the previous section applies: when agencies are involved in competition elsewhere it can prove distracting and divert their attentions and energies away from other commitments, such as full and active participation in community safety partnerships. Perhaps a more significant point is that this principle is most germane to the correctional agencies that are working with offenders. CDRPs are preoccupied with reducing crime (e.g., target hardening, ASB strategies) and the involvement of offenders in terms of resettlement and social enterprise peer groups is negligible. This reflects the prioritization of crime reduction at the expense of responding to the criminogenic needs of offenders. The dominance of the police agenda and the general compliance to this negates any need for contestability to upset the status quo.

Performance management

In the spirit of 'best value' discussed in previous chapters, the mission of many partnerships is to achieve continuous improvement in performance and to ensure that the wider community is aware of community safety priorities and that the agencies are accountable in terms of their actions. The Home Office (2005) has introduced internal performance management arrangements so Home Office Regional Directors, based at regional government offices, monitor the performance of local partnerships. The aim is to formulate performance management systems that are robust and of use for the effective monitoring of local delivery. Moreover, the accountability of partnerships can be realized as they demonstrate reductions in key areas of activity, such as crime, anti-social behaviour and the misuse of drugs (Solanki *et al.* 2006). The Home Office (2005) argued that performance can be enhanced by requiring partnerships to make a clear distinction between strategic and operational functions with performance management belonging to the former.

Performance management is also ensured with reference to evidence-based policy. Policymakers base this on understanding a specific problem, its causes and the likely impact of any policy interventions. More than that, this approach to policymaking is dependent on evaluations of interventions to find out which policies are effective, or 'what works' and under what circumstances (Tilley 2005). The findings of these evaluations are then fed back into the policymaking process as examples of good and best practice. It is important that the evaluations are appropriate assessments of specific interventions.

According to Paul Wiles (1999), Director of Research at the Home Office Research and Statistics Directorate, evidence-based or evidence-led policy altered the relationship between the government, policymaking, research, evaluation and the development of programmes. This is an unusual innovation because immediately before 1997 it was unusual for government to refer to evidence obtained from scientific evaluations of existing policy and practice. Instead, they often acted 'on the hoof' by prioritizing short-term political goals, such as maintaining a lead in the opinion polls, instead of sound policy based on research evidence (e.g., Michael Howard's 'Prison Works' campaign launched at the 1993 Conservative Party conference or the 1997 election campaigns of both the Conservatives and New Labour who tried to out tough each other on the issue of Zero Tolerance Policing (ZTP)) (Hopkins-Burke 2004; Cook 2006).

The main aim of the evidence-based approach is to strengthen the relationship between policy interventions and evaluations of such strategies and initiatives. In particular, evidence is not just used to introduce a programme but is also gathered and evaluated as part of its development. Thus policy formulation, implementation and the ideas and knowledge derived from research or evaluations are inseparable.

The constraints imposed by NPM dictate that evidence is used to decide where resources will be invested in order to have an effective long-term impact on crime. Thus the CRP is intended to use available resources prudently, initially to slow down but eventually to curb the long-term growth rate in crime.

Deconcentration and regionalization

Modernisation clearly has a spatial component in the field of community safety, not least because it redefined the relationship between central and local forms of governance. Central government has given more responsibility to local agencies involved in partnerships and they have been given the role of identifying local solutions to local problems. However, the centrally determined targets imposed on each of the participating agencies influence partnership working. In the last analysis, with finite resources and the ethos of 'what gets measured gets done' the organizational goals of the police and local authorities, for example, are likely to come before the specific priorities of partnerships. The introduction of Local Criminal Justice Boards under the auspices of the National Criminal Justice Board, introduced another layer of governance above the local partnerships. Finally, the resistance of the Police Service in the mid-2000s to the proposed regionalization of the 43 constabularies of England and Wales into a smaller number of amalgamated forces, suggests the government is committed to reconfiguring the spatial organization of criminal justice. The failure of New Labour to implement this new structure is therefore significant and a recent community safety plan (Home Office 2005) seems to be more or less committed to current spatial arrangements.

Audit and inspection

The key players working in crime and disorder reduction partnerships are all exposed to audit and inspection: in criminal justice, for example, there are inspectorates for the Police, Prison and Probation Services. As pointed out earlier in the chapter, audits have been central to the working of partnerships albeit in a different sense. Since 1998 there have been triennial audits of crime and disorder problems in local communities but these have been adjudged to be a labour intensive distraction diverting partnerships from crime reduction work. The auditing principle is still important but partnerships are proving more effective in identifying community concerns. In particular, the community intelligence that is increasingly being gathered is being adapted to fit with the National Intelligence Model (NIM) framework. As noted in Chapter 8, focusing on policing, NIM was developed by NCIS to gather intelligence and information about policing activities (Maguire and John 2006). The thinking behind this approach has been applied in the context of anti-crime and disorder partnerships. Intelligence gathered by the partnership agencies is used to identify priorities at different levels and to instigate actions against offending behaviour, ranging from incivilities and anti-social behaviour right through to serious and organized crime (SOCA 2006). NIM principles can be used to make sure resources are allocated strategically on the basis of hard evidence (Newburn 2003). It is arguably significant that a tool developed by the police has been imported into a partnership setting.

On the basis of the success of NIM the Home Office (2005) recommended curtailing the triennial audits substituting it with annual three year rolling community safety plans. A six-monthly strategic intelligence assessment would be used for the purposes of consulting and engaging with communities. Furthermore, the audits are to be integrated with the Sustainable Community Strategy and Local Area Agreements as well as local thematic plans such as the Local Policing Plan, Local Area Agreements, the Youth Justice Plan, and the Children and Young People Strategic Plan. These are also intended to measure the general 'health' of partnerships to assess their effectiveness and efficiency.

Another illustration of the consequences of the audit culture are the rubbing points partnerships may experience with regard to the other priorities of agencies who operate independently as well as part of joined-up arrangements. Echoing what is written in Chapter 8, on policing, Her Majesty's Inspectorate of Constabulary (1997), for example, listed the 'key policing objectives' and 'key performance indicators' for the police as responding to violent crime, burglary, working with the community and emergency response. These were again acknowledged in the next report where it was added that there were no specific priorities, and although these objectives were still important, police performance, especially value for money (VFM), would be evaluated in terms of overall crime reduction. However, special attention would be given to multi-agency strategies which tackled youth crime, took action against drugs and created partnerships which cracked down on general crime and disorder problems at a local level. As a general rule it would appear that measures of police performance dominate most, which has all kinds of implications for the status and effective power of other players in a partnership (Phillips *et al.* 2002; Gilling 2005; Hope 2005). A paradoxical consequence of this is that it will make it increasingly difficult for partnerships to keep their social inclusion goals.

Penal populism and risk management

These twin themes are at the heart of modernisation and can be evidenced in a number of areas. The example below shows how ideas about risk are used to buttress penal populism in the context of community safety interventions.

The influence of Beck's *Risk Society* (1992) on the social sciences cannot be overstated and Foucauldian criminologists have readily absorbed his key observation that risk society has replaced social class. These approaches consider relatively recent changes in crime reduction and community safety, and its practical orientation towards the criminal populations through a range of discursive and political rationalities (Stenson 2005). For example, strategies of risk assessment and risk management embedded in the logic of actuarial justice have been deployed to segregate the hazards presented by an unruly underclass (Feeley and Simon 1994; Ericson and Haggerty 1997). Other analysts referred to below, draw on the governmental literature (Dean 1999). Here the focus is on the workings of politically constituted, differentiated and hybridized networks of statutory, voluntary and private agencies (Edwards and Benyon 2000). In contrast to radical or Marxist criminologists, proponents of the governmentality approach argue that these networks do not reflect the unitary interests of elite-type groups, such as the bourgeoisie. Having said that, the community safety partnerships sometimes mobilize themselves in order to impose sovereign control over given territories and specific social groups, some of which may be socially excluded (Stenson and Edwards 2001: 74).

Feeley and Simon (1994) have focused on the concept of actuarial justice to explain innovations in crime and control in the United States. Actuarial justice is contrasted with liberal conceptions of justice belonging to modernity, which are concerned with establishing the guilt, responsibility and obligations of individual suspects and offenders as part of a more general aim to reform and reintegrate them into society. Towards the latter stages of the twentieth century the usefulness and viability of this objective was questioned. Actuarial justice is less attentive to either the rehabilitation or punishment of individuals and is preoccupied with devising 'techniques for identifying, classifying and managing groups assorted by levels of dangerousness' (Feeley and Simon 1994: 173). Justice is no longer individualized but determined by assessing and managing the risks and hazards presented by 'groups' and 'aggregates', such as 'permanent-marginal' underclass type populations.

Like other Foucauldians the issue of social class is not at the forefront of Feeley and Simon's (1994) analysis, but what it does show is that some groups of offenders, for instance sex offenders, share characteristics equated with a predisposition to specific types of behaviour. With regard to this group of offenders, risk assessment and management have been defined by the Probation Service: the former is 'an assessment carried out to establish whether the subject is likely to cause serious physical or psychological harm to others' and the latter an 'action taken to monitor a person's behaviour and attitudes, and to intervene in his/her life, in order to prevent them harming others'. The 'desired outcome' of 'risk assessment' and 'risk management' is 'public protection' and enhanced security (HM Inspectorate of Probation 1995, cited in Hebenton and Thomas 1996: 434).

The production of 'knowledge for security' and dissemination of this knowledge or 'communications about risk' are prerequisites for 'knowledge for security' (Hebenton and Thomas 1996: 428, 431). Furthermore, the creation of security is reliant on both, hence the term 'security through knowledge' (Hebenton and Thomas 1996: 439). For example, the Police Service survey and monitor populations to produce knowledge, which may be applied in the context of risk management strategies to regulate specific categories of suspects or offenders (Ericson 1994, cited in Hebenton and Thomas 1996: 432).

In principle, intelligence systems are in place to store the data used to inform and harmonize the policy responses of the different agencies involved in community safety and crime reduction (Hebenton and Thomas 1996: 435–6). In practice the attainment of security through 'risk management' is far from simple as local intelligence systems are not adequately equipped to actively assess, monitor and keep track of all offending groups. Furthermore, multi-agency networks co-existing inside partnerships (e.g., the police, education, probation) are rarely co-ordinated.

Ericson and Haggerty (1997) develop similar ideas in their characterization of the police as 'information brokers' who collaborate with other organizations, such as welfare organizations and insurance companies, to identify the crime risks imposed on society in order to control and govern crime. Although they are writing specifically about policing, the logic of their argument can be used to consider the actions of community safety partnerships. They process and reproduce knowledge for security through systems of information technology, bureaucracy and surveillance (Fussey 2004). They then refer to prudential and actuarial models to calculate and measure the risk of particular behaviours and the scale of harm or loss they cause. The application of scientific knowledge enables different expert groups to classify, target and exclude deviant populations.

However, there would appear to be fundamental problems with this type of analysis because risk is not always calculable (i.e., the prudential paradigm) and all knowledge of risk is finite and entangled with ignorance and uncertainty (Beck 1992). Criminal justice and community safety practitioners operate with different risk management strategies not only in relation to traditional and specialized police activities, such as investigative techniques, styles of detective work, but also to a wider range of activities various agencies carry out with multi-agency partnerships. Crawford (1997) suggests that actuarial principles are invoked when agencies amass crime data, which is in turn used to inform crime prevention and community safety initiatives in specific geographical territories, such as incapacitation and community-based punishments.

Such representations of risk are over coherent and too systematic. Ericson and Haggerty (1997) have conceptualized an ideal-typical model of risk assessment and management, instead of considering how different strategies are combined in many different ways, producing hybrid forms of risk management. In other words, models of risk found in policy documents are not implemented straightforwardly as they come into contact with traditional practices and procedures as well as more novel techniques and strategies existing in crime reduction policy. The pure conceptions of risk imagined by policymakers are thus hybridized in practice. This shows there are fundamental limitations to this dimension of modernisation.

Pluralization

The promotion of community safety through multi- or inter-agency partnerships requires a range of competencies on the part of the practitioners involved in its formulation and deliverance. After all they are being required to work with professionals from very different backgrounds with different cultures and with different orientations towards caring for and controlling offenders and victims. For example, there is a requirement for an understanding of the diverse needs of individuals affected by crime and disorder, particularly their ability to deal with its consequences. Practitioners must also strive to make the effects of crime and disorder tolerable without threatening privacy, liberty, quality of life and increasing social exclusion. They are expected to support victims of crime and reassure those who fear crime and to make people aware of the objective risks posed by crime and disorder related problems. These tasks are difficult enough at the best of times but the attainment of these goals and genuine partnership may be offset by the introduction of a new corps of para-professionals, such as Anti-Social Behaviour Order (ASBO) co-ordinators and the Fire Service. This amounts to the reconstitution of some of the core responsibilities of criminal justice professionals through dilution and diversification. Deprofessionalization is occurring in several areas, witnessed by the plethora of new roles for assistants to complement professionals. In effect people with no direct professional knowledge or experience of the problems they encounter are being brought in to deal with community safety and crime reduction matters. New forms of expertise and possibly new 'silos' are being created; the results of which remain to be seen. However, the para-professionals would appear to be committed to modernisation, especially as there is a chance of work in novel areas.

Responsibilization

NPM and modernisation have resulted in the widespread responsibilization of community safety and crime reduction activities. Communities were required to identify the problems affecting them through the audits but agencies were also charged with implementing solutions. This can also be seen in the way the CDA formalized the notion of partnership but central government was not, at least on the surface, over-prescriptive (Walklate 1999). The CDA contained no detailed prescriptions of what the agenda for these partnerships should be or the structures needed to deliver them, instead advocating 'maximum flexibility'. The rationale for this approach is that the people who live and work in specific areas are in the best position to identify problems and to propose how they should be addressed. The stress is on building on existing structures of co-ordinated activity, such as multi-agency partnerships, at county, district and borough levels to tackle single, specific and local problems. These should be brought together to avoid duplication and unnecessary competition for scarce resources. In some ways this is disingenuous on the part of the government because the activities of these new localized forms of governance are enabled and inhibited by central government policy. Partnership agencies are given the responsibility for policy formulation but the government still exerts an influence, not least through the performance indicators applied to different agencies when they are not performing in partnership.

Conclusions

The notion that partnership is an effective mechanism for responding to crime and enhancing community safety is not especially new although it became a centrepiece of New Labour's commitment to modernisation (National Audit Office 2004). At least on paper it is an area that is potentially reform transformative. The Crime and Disorder Act (1998) made crime reduction and community safety a statutory responsibility for public, private and voluntary community sector agencies. This legislation was underpinned by an idea that crime cannot be tackled effectively by the criminal justice system and reflected what many academics and public sector workers had been telling successive Conservative governments for some time. The message that the criminal justice system alone cannot tackle social problems is deeply embedded in New Labour's joined-up and cross-departmental approaches to tackling crime and social exclusion. In this chapter we have reviewed the implementation of the CDA and examined its impact, paying particular reference to social exclusion. While there has been a general commitment to this agenda from all agencies there are some paradoxes.

Given the timing of the community safety partnership agenda many of the agencies implicated in joined-up policy and practice had already experienced reform, being exposed initially to censure, followed by varying degrees of compliance. Modernisation and its emphasis on inter-agency partnership are precisely what many agencies had been calling for for some time and there was thus considerable commitment to the CDA. This is accentuated most among the new corps of para-professionals, the private sector and to some extent the VCS. The situation was a little messier, though, because genuine partnership has not been firmly established everywhere and there is more of an emphasis on multi-agency working at the expense of inter-agency working (Hughes 1996). More than that, the partnership framework has been used mainly by local authorities and police to drive forward their own largely crime reduction goals at the expense of more inclusive strategies focusing on offender management issues. Accordingly, other partnership members either tacitly commit or comply with partnership strategies that may not truly reflect their more distinctive missions.

Partnerships are supposed to be holistic in their approach and there is an abundance of evidence showing that this has happened, although there are contradictions. The semantic confusion identified at the beginning of the chapter, brought about by the conflation of community safety and crime reduction has resulted in paradoxical developments. In short, crime reduction goals may go against the grain of community safety goals: crime reduction strategies may perversely undermine attempts to create a more inclusive society by sidelining and excluding permanently some groups of offenders (Hope 2005). The criminalization of anti-social behaviour is just one example.

Finally, the relationship between central and local modes of governance is the source of some friction. The aspiration to create local solutions to local problems was laudable and this has arguably been partly achieved, but centrally determined objectives emanating from the Home Office have made this difficult. In community safety, the modernisers have developed a framework that is distinctive and potentially revolutionary and it has the scope to be transformative of crime and public policy. Regrettably central government can also create stasis rather than dynamism because it is not fully committed to genuinely resourced inter-agency partnerships, thus rendering them potentially vulnerable.

Notes

1 Crawford's (1997, 1998) important work covers some ground that is relevant to the concerns of this chapter (i.e., the local governance of crime control as an explanation of crime prevention in non-statutory local partnerships) but his empirical work predates the New Labour CDA (1998) agenda. For that reason it is bracketed off from this chapter. Hughes and Edwards (2005) mention modernisation in passing but it is not examined systematically nor is the concept defined with precision.

2 This is congruent with the number of police and probation areas.

3 The original plan was for the CRP to run for ten years, but it was shelved after only three years.

Further reading

Gilling, D. (2005) Partnership and crime prevention, in N. Tilley (ed.) *Handbook of Crime Prevention and Community Safety*. Cullompton: Willan.

Home Office (2005) *National Community Safety Plan 2006–2009*. London: Home Office.
Hope, T. (2005) The new local governance of community safety in England and Wales, *Canadian Journal of Criminology and Criminal Justice* (April), 369–87.
Hughes, G. and Edwards, A. (2005) Crime prevention in context, in N. Tilley (ed.) *Handbook of Crime Prevention and Community Safety*. Cullompton: Willan.
Stenson, K. and Edwards, A. (2003) Crime control and local governance: the struggle for sovereignty in advanced liberal polities, *Contemporary Politics*, 9(2): 203–17.

chapter seven

Modernisation and the court system

Introduction

It is now common parlance to talk of a court 'system' comprising elements of the sentencers, both lay and judicial, of the legal professions, of the role of the clerks and the Crown Prosecution Service as elements in this 'system' serviced by the Police, Probation, Prisons and Youth Justice Services. This chapter will be constructed around the context of how the courts system links with other aspects of the criminal justice system and particular focus will be on the magistrates' courts and its personnel where 95 per cent of the criminal business of the courts actually takes place. A key part of the modernisation agenda is delivering cross-cutting and joined-up services.

Technological developments have been at the forefront of this systematic reorientation and forms one key aspect of the modernisation agenda. Funding of certain changes has served to restrict spending more generally and financial dilemmas have had to be faced in decisions on what to deliver. The politics of change has also inhibited organic growth of modern technologies across agencies although there are signs of this changing. Issues of data protection, confidentiality, data sharing, etc., will be addressed. The courts are often at the fulcrum of such services and their role in the modernisation agenda will be explored. Independence, including judicial independence, and the concept of the separation of powers appear at risk under joining up proposals and this will be evaluated. This chapter has a limited goal. It is concerned with aspects of modernisation as pertaining to the criminal justice functions of the court system. A broader history of the development of the court system can be obtained elsewhere (Raine 2001, 2005; Creaton 2003) and is beyond the remit of this chapter.

Contextual outline

Prior to the politicization of crime control in the late 1970s by neo-liberal and New Right politicians, no one would have questioned the right to independence of the court system. The symbolic importance of the courts as arbiters of criminal disputes and as a dispenser of justice was seen to stand outside of the political maelstrom. The ancient doctrine of the separation of powers between the executive arm and the judicial was widely accepted and seemingly unimpeachable. This view seems almost quaint and anachronistic as we write today, barely two decades on. The governance of the courts is now increasingly subject to the interference and demands of the executive arm often to the ire of the judiciary but in keeping with the managed approach of criminal justice reform and change. This can sometimes be labelled, almost framed as a threat, as a 'constitutional crisis', where the smooth operation of government breaks down as a consequence of different groups within government disagreeing on just which group retains sovereignty in any given matter. Over the past decade the unease about how this is manifest has been partially, if just symbolically, resolved by removing the Lord Chancellor as both an executive and judicial head. This, as Creaton notes, 'symbolizes the imperfect separation of powers within the British constitution' (Creaton 2003: 115). As Lord Woolf commented upon his impending retirement in 2005:

> They constitute a new constitutional settlement between government and the judiciary. For the judiciary perhaps the most striking difference will be that my successor will be the first Lord Chief Justice who is not only the professional, but also in place of the Lord Chancellor, the constitutional head of the judiciary of England and Wales.

Lord Falconer, the Lord Chancellor, speaking in 2006 was still careful to uphold the traditional notion of the separation of powers:

> All too frequently the problems of the system or the consequences of legislation manifest themselves in decisions the judges have to make. Whilst it is perfectly legitimate for Ministers to address policy issues raised by individual judgments, Ministers should not criticize judges. Just as judges don't do politics, ministers don't try cases. That has always been the core of the relationship between the executive and the judiciary. That is how it should remain. It is sometimes hard to maintain. It is sometimes in danger of being pushed – often by those beyond the relationship – towards conflict. We need to resist such attempts – together.
>
> (Falconer 2006 Speech, www.dca.gov.uk/speeches)

What price such separation, as moves to split the Home Office and the creation of a Ministry of Justice, led by Lord Falconer, has been acted upon in May 2007.

The slow but steady erosion of the core concept of judicial independence has been evident in how the system is now operated. The government, impatient to impose its imprint on sentencing practices and make the courts more efficient and consumer-orientated, has gradually reshaped the way in which this issue is presented. This has produced regular clashes over recent years and John Raine commenting on this, points to a much more restricted definition of this term as an outcome of this battle of wills:

> . . . narrowing has taken place of the concept and meaning of judicial independence, from an overarching concern to ensure 'constitutional independence' to the very much more specific and practical concern with 'independence in decision-making' within the courtroom.
>
> (Raine 2005: 297)

Organizationally the work of the courts is conducted through the Department of Constitutional Affairs now under the newly created Ministry of Justice, a unified HM Courts Service, a significant change in itself bringing together the work of the magistrates with the judiciary. This is a typical structure of modern government with the executive agency having operational responsibility leaving the state to hold policy decisions. In terms of criminal justice reform this creates some constitutional separation from the Home Office which may become even more fragmented with the division of the Home Office into two segments, Justice and Security (*Guardian* 2007). This could bring a fascinating future for joined-up justice in itself. If these plans develop as envisaged, in order to bring together prison, probation, youth justice, police and the courts system, it would involve joining up at least four departmental bases. A paradoxical feature of joining up perhaps? It was certainly argued by Creaton that this separation, both organizational and, of more ancient significance, constitutional, contributes to perhaps a rather different kind of impact of the modernisation impulses of New Labour. She writes, 'The privileged relationship with the judiciary and thus within the constitutional framework has insulated the courts and legal professions from many of the pressures and imperatives impacting upon other public sector and criminal justice agencies' (Creaton 2003: 115).

However, changes have occurred and have been most marked in the way in which the lower courts have been subject to changes. The picture going back to 1980 was one of considerable variation. Fitzpatrick *et al.* note, 'The defects were fragmentation, inefficiencies and lack of professionalism and consistency. The remedy was new court management' (Fitzpatrick *et al.* 2001: 102). In a literal interpretation of the term modernisation, the magistrates' court in particular has been 'made modern'. The desire of early new public management to be efficient drove many of these changes. This includes a more consumerist orientation, efficiency changes and some limited marketization. A centralizing approach to these changes was initiated. Responsibility for the magistrates' court transferred to the Lord Chancellor's Department in 1992. The Police and Magistrates' Court Act 1994 was another key driver. Gone are local court buildings existing in every nook and cranny of the countryside. New buildings, often financed through the Private Finance Initiative (PFI), have brought the two branches of sentencers, magistrates and the judiciary, together in bigger more 'fit for purpose' complexes. This has been pursued alongside the move to a more professional corps of 'district judges' which have been imposed in most regions of the country, thus challenging another long-standing practice of the centrality of the local lay magistrate. At present the continued existence of the lay magistracy is not being threatened, but their role in being a form of 'community representative' is severely challenged. Admittedly it is worth adding that magistrates were already seen as unrepresentative of the wider community, being drawn largely from the white, middle-aged and middle-class populations.

Modernising the courtrooms has involved the development of IT systems which have rationalized practices and been part of the imposition of a business culture to the management of court jurisdictions. The aforementioned 1994 Act also encouraged mergers of magistrates' court committees and the separation of the role of justice clerk (justice arm) from the new justice chief executive (business arm) again giving force to the bureaucratization of the court system. This particular change has been replicated in changes in the Crown Prosecution Service (CPS). In each area it is headed by a Chief Crown Prosecutor, supported by an Area Business Manager, to reflect the greater separation between legal and management responsibilities. The moves towards co-terminosity of the area structures, an early New Labour move, has now brought both the courts and the CPS into 42 areas, thus replicating the Police and the Probation Service.

A review of the Crown Prosecution Service was commissioned by the government in 1997. The CPS has always been more vulnerable to reform not having a long history (formed only in 1985) and uncertain power base. The Glidewell Report was published in 1998 and included in excess of 70 recommendations. While the majority of the recommendations focused on Crown Prosecution Service internal activities, there were also particularly significant aspects affecting the working relationships of the Police and Crown Prosecution Service. In essence, it proposed a move to a single administrative unit, permanently siting police and CPS staff in one location in order to maximize efficiency and eliminate duplication. This was building on the principles of Martin Narey who had already published his report. The Narey Reforms, implemented in November 1999, have already proven the benefits of the collaborative approach, and had provided the foundation for Glidewell.

Changes have also occurred in the legal professions though this has been slower and resisted by the long-standing professional autonomy and self-regulation to which both solicitors and barristers have traditionally operated in a somewhat protectionist fashion. But changes, nevertheless, are evident although the power of government to intervene here is as difficult for it as we have seen above for the higher courts. The Court and Legal Services Act 1990 did introduce reforms which impacted upon the governance of the legal professions including the bar's monopoly on advocacy, controls over training and the establishment of the Legal Services Ombudsman (Creaton 2003: 119).

In summarizing how far modernisation has impacted upon the court system since 1979 it can be seen that, 'centralization, liberalization, modernisation and now the "joining up" of the administration of justice have seen both the courts and the legal profession transformed' (Creaton 2003: 124). This process remains a continuing project as far as government is concerned. Lord Falconer in 2007 stated:

> While the criminal justice system has improved considerably over the past few years – with more offenders being brought to justice, and a reduction in the number of ineffective trials, with further areas introducing problem solving courts and community justice – there are still some common issues hindering the efficiency and effectiveness of the courts system.
>
> Disproportionate time and money spent on minor offences; late disclosure of evidence by the prosecution; lack of defence representation; unnecessary pre-trial hearings; poor case management and administration – all problems of process. But furthermore in some areas there was seemingly a culture of acceptance around these inefficiencies.
>
> Somewhere down the line it is as if magistrates' courts became distracted by three inch thick case files for the simplest of hearings. Over complexity got in the way of delivering justice
>
> (Falconer 22 February 2007, Speech, www.dca.gov.uk/speeches/2007/sp070222.htm)

However, as we look at the detail of reform, the context remains one in which 'old court ideologies' (Fitzpatrick *et al.* 2001) defined by Fitzpatrick *et al.* as 'localism, laity and judicial independence', have exerted a sway on how those changes have developed perhaps giving a rather different end-game to the imposition of government reforms than is evident for other criminal justice agencies.

Reforming the court system

Characterizing the court system in terms of reform orientation and political tactics feels quite different to the other criminal justice agencies. Its recourse to the law itself to challenge executive changes acts as a powerful, if largely reactionary, resistant force. Of course, Parliament can always legislate for change but if this appears to be extending beyond what seems reasonable, as defined by the judicial interpretation of the law, then this can be resisted and opposed. Again it is not a clear and unambiguous situation. Different parts of the court system have different degrees of capacity to resist change. The Magistracy have been reorganized the most, as we have briefly seen above, as its structural power has weakened – its reform resistance is low and reform vulnerability is thus much higher. This appears to be the case for the CPS too, who have managed to create little referential power. The judiciary remains a difficult group for government to confront and its powerful lobby can appear reform resistant. It is also difficult to impact upon the legal professions – solicitors and barristers – partly due to their mutual protection. However, this is not the whole story, when this breaks down, as in the case of advocacy in the high courts, reform can be achieved.

In considering how the courts exercise their sentencing duties, the government has focused criticism mainly on the outcomes of sentencing and particularly disparity. This disparity shows itself not only as 'justice by geography', though that has proved resistant to change as we saw in the youth justice discussions, but also there are gendered and racialized differences. By implication the professionalism of the lay magistracy has come under increasing scrutiny but the tactic employed by government has been one of inducing compliance rather than overt censure. Indeed as we shall see in detail below, it has been the more subtle pressure of financial constraint, as much as political bullying, which has persuaded the courts to modernise. How far the court system is committed to such changes is hard to identify. As servants of the public any increasing harshness of sentencing can be defended as being in the public good and a proper response to perceived increases in lawlessness and disorder. Idiosyncrasy in sentencing particularly where leniency is the outcome, has been attacked by government but usually as an isolated example rather than a full attack on the magistracy.

The next section focuses on the detailed dimensions of modernisation which accompany the modernising agenda of New Labour and helped shaped the way in which a modernised court system has been delivered under the third New Labour government.

Key dimensions of modernisation

Mixed economy of provision

One of the key issues, consequent upon the separation of powers, is the taken-for-granted assumption of public service underpinning the nature of the judiciary and magistracy. England and Wales has always appointed, not elected, its judicial figures and has steered away from the politicization of these roles as exemplified, for instance, by the US. This is not a democratic position, subject to election and therefore would sit uneasily if it were provided in any other way than by the due processes set up to achieve it. However, many aspects of court provision surrounding the sentencing process and just the general business of the court have been increasingly delivered by either the private or the voluntary sector. The changing perception of what the courts should be offering, generated by a consumerist view of provision, has opened up possibilities for change. In meeting those demands the court system has engaged a range of organizations. The most notable example of this, partly as a government inspired response to the Victims Charter and the rebalancing of the justice system, has been the growth of provision to support victims and witnesses traditionally lacking an effective voice in court – the lack of protective and safe facilities around the court setting identified as being a particular neglect. Government, in seeking to 'rebalance the criminal justice system' in response to the needs of victims, has sought to ensure this neglect is dealt with and that provision is increasingly available. Most recently the introduction of a statutory code of practice, building significantly on the current victims charter, puts obligations on criminal justice agencies to deliver improved and consistent support, information, advice and protection for all victims.

The delivery of many of the ancillary services, which support the court in its operation, has seen much more involvement of the private sector particularly in such areas as prison escorting and in the development of IT services for the administration of the court system. In developing services for victims, this has increased the role of Victim and Witness Services in the court setting itself.

Change in the types of courts and responses to problems are ongoing. In those changes highlighted in the latest business plan, we see an increasing engagement of different agencies in the pursuit of managed justice. These include:

- In November 2005, we published a White Paper: *Supporting Magistrates' Courts to Provide Justice*, which set out a programme of work to ensure that the magistrates' courts are *connected*, *respected* and *effective*.
- A new enforcement framework from the Courts Act 2003 has been fully rolled out to magistrates' courts.
- We invested £1m to improve the comfort and security of facilities

for jurors at Crown Court centres and more than £3m in improving accommodation facilities at courts for victims and witnesses.
- The Community Justice Centre in North Liverpool was officially launched by Harriet Harman QC MP on 20th October 2005. The centre brings together criminal justice agencies and voluntary service providers in one building in the heart of the community, working with local people to tackle local problems. The Community Justice Initiative in Salford Magistrates' Court started operating in November 2005 applying problem-solving principles to both youth and adult cases.
- The Lord Chancellor and the Lord Chief Justice launched pilots of dedicated Drug Courts at the Leeds and West London Magistrates' Courts on 13 December 2005.
- 25 specialist domestic violence courts have been established and all will be in operation during April 2006.

(HMCS Business Plan 2006–7)

Contestability

Although the courts have not been subject to contestability, the impact of financial constraints has continued to be a mechanism which has sought to bring the operation of the court system under control. The original mechanism used to encourage the closing down of uneconomic local courts was through a process of cash-limiting budgets as a means of encouraging action. The push towards amalgamation was partly created to reduce cost and duplication of effort. In general, though, this concept has not impacted in any meaningful way on the process of reform.

However, it could be surmised that the introduction of contestability in the correctional sector may impact directly on the business of the courts. For example, in their sentencing function the courts may have to deal with non-public sector agencies, such as the private sector and VCS. It will be interesting to see how magistrates and judiciary perceive community punishments provided by such agencies. For example, will they trust them? Also, how will they be held accountable in the same way as the public sector? What role will the inspectorates play in ensuring the normally secretive, private sector is scrutinized sufficiently.

Performance management

The emphasis on performance has had a marked impact on certain features of court provision. Often an austere place to visit and with little bespoke facilities to care for the needs of traumatized victims and witnesses having to sit alongside the perpetrators as they waited to enter court, performance management tools brought an opportunity to bring to the fore a more consumer-driven approach to the court service. This has clearly resulted in significant change and a more responsive service has been developed particularly for victims and witnesses. Year on year rationalizations of budget can, however, have counterproductive effects accompanying a preoccupation with balancing budgets. As much as new facilities can be developed the potential loss of vital services, or useful court buildings, can be a budgetary decision which falls unevenly on services. It is harder in such a stringent financial climate to always work alongside other agencies when the financial costs may be too great.

IT systems have been introduced widely across the court system. This was noted by Fitzpatrick *et al.* as providing the means both for managerial audit and for the particular direction it might take:

> performance indicators, aims, objectives and mission statements. For example the Leeds MCC states that it is committed to 'achieving the highest standards of local justice and service through a system which, within financial constraints, is efficient, expeditious and commands public confidence'.
>
> (Fitzpatrick *et al.* 2001: 108)

This process of centralizing the target setting mechanisms have been advanced and reached their current situation in which the unified HM Courts Service Business Plan sets out the organization's targets. A national plan is published annually, together with individual plans for each area. This quotation below will illustrate the way in which planning now is centrally orchestrated and the kinds of targets which are given paramountcy: HMCS has a strategic goal:

> All citizens according to their differing needs are entitled to *access to justice*, whether as victims of crime, defendants accused of crimes, consumers in debt, children in need of care, or business people in commercial disputes. Our aim is to ensure that access is provided *as quickly as possible* and *at the lowest cost consistent* with open justice and that *citizens have greater confidence in, and respect for, the system of justice*.
>
> (HM Court Services Business Plan 2006–07, original emphasis)

As it goes on to say, 'access, cost, reducing delay and confidence and respect are emphasized as key elements, which will make a difference for all citizens'. This illustrates how far even the court system has had to travel to meet modernisation protocols. But the focus here remains perhaps disturbingly on the quantifiable measures of the court process and not on its central mission. So, as Raine comments, the tendency to:

> focus on quantity measures such as case throughput rates, waiting times and length of sentences, rather than on the quality aspects or effectiveness measures, for example, how well cases were conducted and with what impact on subsequent behaviour.
>
> (Raine 2001: 114)

Thus, the commitment to evidence-based practice, a supposed tenet of modernisation when it does not interfere with other dimensions, seems practiced largely in the court over issues the government focuses on which can court political advantage. Again as Raine (2001: 114) goes on:

> despite all the rhetorical commitment under New Labour modernisation to develop evidence-based practice and doing 'what works,' in practice doing justice more cost-effectively may well be more likely to mean doing what is popular with and for government.

Deconcentration and regionalization

Locality allied to laity are two key concepts driving the administration of justice until very recently. The tradition was a corps of local magistrates who were wedded to their local communities and represented the communities they served, although in practice this was always a somewhat romantic view of arrangements as working class, minority ethnic groups and the disenfranchised were not adequately represented, although they were over-represented among magistrates' clientele. However, the attractiveness of a lay magistracy to a modernising government was much reduced by its apparent lack of professionalism and inability to deliver standardized efficient practices. It has been argued that they are over 30 times less efficient than a professional magistrate (Fitzpatrick *et al.* 2001: 111), but the old commitments do not disappear overnight and care is taken to keep the traditional magistracy on board. This is reflected in a quote by the then Lord Chancellor Irvine when in 1999 he said, 'Local diversity is your unique strength – the factor which can take into account the idiosyncrasies of local culture and behaviour. But society can be hard in its judgment on what it perceives as inconsistency' (Irvine 1999, cited in Fitzpatrick *et al.* 2001: 111).

The oft-quoted 'justice by geography' tended to reveal marked differences in sentencing outcomes in the youth and adult magistrates' court by region. Lord Warner in 2001 commented, 'This is resulting in a significant element of "justice by geography", which is inherently unfair'. This continued through the 1990s despite the attempts by the 1991 Act and subsequent guidance to seek to produce more consistent outcomes. This variation in sentencing was possibly justifiable, if you take an individualized approach to sentencing. In a government seeking to treat people as groups using actuarial justice concepts, there appears to be a growing demand for much greater standardization. Once the media became energized to react, any apparent sentencing disparity was seized upon as evidence of a system not working.

So the impact and processes of modernisation has been to challenge this commitment to localism to produce a more centralized agenda. This has been accompanied in the first instance by growth in the size of areas covered by the Magistrates' Court Committees and amalgamation of local areas until they now fit the preferred model of 42 areas coterminus to the police. It would have been interesting if this process had continued attendant upon the merger of the police force into larger units, which has been temporarily resisted by the police themselves. This process has transformed them into local management boards with a high focus on efficiency and effectiveness.

This process has continued and in 2003 a unified service was instituted. The 2003 Act provides for a unified courts administration to be created which combines the functions of the court service and the magistrates' courts committees. The new organization, Her Majesty's Courts Service, was established in April 2005. The aim of the agency is to, 'deliver improved services to the community, taxpayer, victims, witnesses and all other users of the courts. It will help to ensure the department can deliver high quality services across all the courts and develop best practice with the most effective use of resources' (www.dca.gov.uk).

Audit and inspection

A new inspectorate was established via the Police and Magistrates Court Act of 1994. This inspectorate further creates a potential tension between local accountability and national direction, particlarly given its power to visit the courts in session which blurs boundaries between the sentencing and administration functions. With an information system in place, as discussed above, which tracks centrally defined performance measures, the existence of inspection and audit further distances the actualizing of local control.

However, an opposite trend has been developing more recently with devolution of some responsibilities. Of growing importance here may be the Local Criminal Justice Boards in their role in monitoring performance. Another aspect of improving witness care is the plan to devolve funding for the Witness Service to Local Criminal Justice Boards, which will allow a more locally responsive service to develop within the context of national standards. The latest Audit Commission Report sees a clear role for Local Criminal Justice Boards in monitoring service provision and value for money, as part of a comprehensive framework for the delivery of services (Audit Commission 2003).

Penal populism and risk management

The interference of the executive government is nowhere better illustrated than by how far it has sought to use legislation to ensure it can deliver on its electoral promises. In a penal populist climate the government has wanted to ensure that the courts deliver the kinds of sentences which the public purports to demand, though, of course, it is less clear that the public actually wants everything that the politicians believe they want. Research undertaken by Roberts and Hough (2002), which looks at public perception of sentencing and the extent to which they are in line with the reality of sentencing decisions, shows yet again a less punitive population than is believed. Nevertheless, as the Carter Review (2003) noted sentence lengths have continued to increase and the tariffs for the most heinous offenders (i.e., life sentence offenders) has continually risen since the then Conservative Home Secretary, Leon Brittain, proposed what was then a modest increase in 1983. The use of the executive arm of the law to ensure that the punitive sentencing climate is enforced often leaves the judiciary powerless and unable to intervene. Where a successful defence of the law against abuse is mounted this is usually countered by a change in the law to overcome that restriction.

How far is it possible for the worse excesses of a punitive sentencing climate to be resisted by attention to risk assessment and management? The judiciary still sits on parole hearings where 'risk to the community' is a key determinant of release when the tariff has been achieved. However, the cautiousness which a risk averse or, as Hudson (2003) puts it, a risk control strategy engenders in the present climate leads to very conservative definitions of dangerousness or the optimum time for release and of assumptions about certain categories of offenders who should never be released. Each isolated, if tragic, case of someone being released who commits a further heinous offence goes on to justify caution in exercising the discretionary application of early release systems. In a somewhat paradoxical moment on actuarialism it should be recalled that taken as a whole the parole and lifer system are quite successful in terms of outcomes, but that has not reduced the climate of moral panic and fear which accompanies the release of certain groups of potential releasees.

Pluralization

The professionalization of the court system in the last two decades is a reversal of the trend we have seen in other parts of the criminal justice system. There has been a clear trend to seek a more professional organization on the grounds of becoming efficient and cost-effective in carrying out the duties surrounding the court process. There have been particular attacks on the lay magistracy which despite some increase in training, remains defined by its own structural position as lay members, members from the local communities. Until relatively recently stipendiary magistrates were a restricted phenomenon and did not appear to be growing at all. The change of name to district judge has come at a time when they are growing in number and become a more central feature of courts. Research conducted in 2000 (Morgan and Russell 2000, quoted in Raine 2005: 296) 'estimated that a professional judge sitting alone on a full time basis could undertake the work of around 30 lay justices' (Morgan and Russell 2000). This professionalization can also be seen in the appointment of business managers to key administrative roles in both the court service and the CPS.

Pluralization can be seen to a limited extent in the ways the processes of recruitment to the magistracy and to Youth Offender Panels have been opened up creating opportunities for those previously denied the option of being appointed a magistrate, unless nominated by a restricted group of insider bodies. Of course, increasing the training and requirements of professionalism on magistrates may have an unintended effect of making it more difficult for some to give up the time required to serve on the bench.

The increasing use of legal assistants to carry a wider caseload than they were allowed traditionally and the setting up of the designated caseworkers in the CPS, are examples of the development of an increasingly plural workforce in the legal professions. On 1 October 1998 legislation was introduced permitting CPS staff who are not lawyers to review and present in magistrates' courts a limited range of cases involving straightforward guilty pleas. These may include shoplifting, possession of cannabis and non-contentious motoring offences. Under the supervision of experienced Crown Prosecutors, who assist and advise them, these designated caseworkers divide their time between police stations, where they review cases, and local magistrates' courts. Caseworkers have to pass a testing training course, validated by an external body, and be formally designated by the DPP before they undertake this work (www.cps.org.uk).

Joined-up justice

Describing experiments in 2006–7 of the CJSSS (criminal justice: simple, speedy and summary) system which has aimed to improve the way cases are managed and dealt with, Lord Falconer states:

> through focusing on the things that make the justice system work well. It is collaborative; with magistrates and the judiciary taking a lead, working with the police, with defence, with the prosecution, with court staff, clear of the benefits, the mutual benefits of such an approach. Each component of the justice system is dependent on the other for delivering these improvements and for making sure that time is not wasted.
>
> (Falconer 22 February 2007, Speech, www.dca.gov.uk/speeches/2007/sp070222.htm)

The emphasis is clearly here on efficiency and the single-minded way this has been pursued has produced joined-up working, but whether the quality of the outcomes has changed is less clear to see. There is however some increasing evidence of multi-agency initiatives within the court setting which may produce better not just quicker outcomes – multi-agency drug courts, CPS co-located with the police, community justice centres, involvement of the judiciary in local Criminal Justice Boards, but sometimes this is undertaken reluctantly and cautiously by the sentencers. This returns us again to the balance between judicial independence and participation in joined-up systems. Raine offers a cautionary remark about this concern:

> the danger is that, in the rush to 'join up' the value of independence is eroded to the point where we may unwittingly end up with a monolithic

> criminal justice process: one that lacks the healthy tensions that safeguard the integrity of the process and which give vital reassurance and confidence to the public as to the quality of justice.
>
> (Raine 2002: 330–1)

In 2000 the Legal Services Commission came into being. This was a product of the Access to Justice Act of 1999 and its prime motivation was to encourage the joining up of services. Creaton comments, 'The aim was to achieve a joined-up delivery of legal and advice services in the areas of law such as housing, welfare benefits and debt' (Creaton 2003: 123). However, Creaton goes on to identify the very complex regulatory mechanisms in existence in the court system. There remains much to do if the various regulators are to be enabled to work together and there have been recent moves in this direction including the unified HM Courts Services. On a policymaking level, the introduction of a National Criminal Justice Board represents an attempt to bring policy together across all criminal justice agencies but including the courts. This is replicated in the 42 areas across the country.

Responsibilization

One way in which responsibilization has occurred is the diversion from the courts to other fora within communities for tasks previously dealt with through the judicial process. There has been an increase in less formal, quasi-legal decisions being taken without the court setting. This includes the development of the Youth Offender Panel to administrate the Referral Orders now a common feature of youth justice. Introduction of video links between remand prisons and courts to reduce the need for court attendance is another reduction in the active use of the courts. Pilot projects in restorative justice which are offered as alternatives to normal prosecution and the development of the Community Justice Centres at Liverpool and Salford, which, copying an American model, have pioneered community-centred responses to crime and nuisance behaviour. Also the processing of thousands of young people into anti-social behaviour orders which only reach the court on breach. With administrative diversion of court fines and reductions in the requirement to be present at hearings, the courts may not be at the epicentre of some of the crucial legal developments which are taking place which draws in a wider community voice and participation.

Permanence of paradox

At the heart of sentencing has always been individualization of outcomes. It is the cornerstone of the sentencing process. This has, by implication, buttressed a court system with a great deal of freedom to act according to the facts of any case, although always bound by the dictates of legislation and in the higher courts case law. Since 1991, as part of a broader commitment to modernise and manage the courts system, attempts have been made to influence sentencing outcomes much further. This process is still an ongoing project for government despite the very clear way in which the court system has been modernised. At the heart lies this basic contradiction between discretion and control of action.

Faster vs. better

The evidence is strong that efficiency gains in the court system have created a modern outward looking service with a strong customer focus and developing systems for ensuring efficient and effective exchange between courts, the legal professions and the wider criminal justice sector. It is less certain that the core business of the court – the sentencing of offenders – has responded effectively to criticisms of disparity and inconsistency in the way it functions. Efficiency in the courts does not necessarily impact upon whether the business outcomes are improved. This is partly because the struggle to control sentencing through executive interventions is still unresolved. The failure of the 1991 CJA Act to provide a single overarching purpose, resulted in a further attempt in the 2003 Act which Tonry describes as a 'laundry list' of purposes (Tonry 2004: 110). Tonry believes:

> Creation of a sentencing council and development and implementation of meaningful guidelines could make English sentencing more consistent, transparent and predictable; reduce the scale of racial, ethnic and gender disparities, provide a tool for management and control of state resources devoted to punishment of offenders; and make judges more accountable for their decisions about citizens' liberties.
>
> (Tonry 2004: 119)

The battle for control between the executive continues with little sign that the new Sentencing Guidelines Council is having any more impact upon sentencing than any previous attempt. The judiciary is both part of the solution and in government terms part of the problem, and this remains a key concern.

Victim-centred vs. offender-centred

In a challenging editorial in the *British Journal of Community Justice*, Williams and Canton (2005) point to the unnecessary conflict which has developed in crime policy between the needs of victims and the needs of offenders. The government's recent declarations of the importance of rebalancing the system in favour of victims suggests a more even-handed approach to how the needs of both offenders and victims will be met. The editorial argues persuasively that in fact in the current penal climate the promotion of services and support for victims has counterpoised the previous attention to offenders. This can serve to embed the exclusionary tone of the system in operation. This illustrates how the negative penal populist attitudes towards offenders in the current climate undermines the apparently neutral language of rebalancing:

> One is bound to suspect that this politicisation is part of a deliberate strategy to flush out opposition to victim-focused changes, so that opponents can be accused of woolly-minded, sentimental support for the civil liberties of criminals. The attempt to justify harsher sentencing of offenders and curtailment of civil liberties in the name of victims is not new.
>
> (Williams and Canton 2005: 2)

Conclusion

Writing as recently as 2001, Fitzpatrick *et al.*, reviewing the battleground between what they called new court management and old court ideologies, concluded, 'the old court ideologies, such as principles of localism and laity, have acted to temper the thrust of new public management and have bolstered the traditional hierarchical values' (Fitzpatrick *et al.* 2001: 116). The battleground is still being fought at a higher level between the judiciary and executive government. But 95 per cent of the criminal business of the courts take place in the magistrates' court and the strategies for change are still being relentlessly propelled forward.

> The business strategy identifies seven key enablers for restructuring the organization:
>
> - improved use of our buildings;
> - removal of high volume bulk work from our courts;
> - centralization of some back office administration;
> - improved take-up of telephone and e-services;
> - new ways of administering the £20bn of money we handle each year;
> - consolidation of fines and enforcement activity in the national enforcement service;
> - improved electronic management of documents and case files.
>
> (Business Plan 2006–07)

It may have taken longer to impose the will of modernisation upon the courts services but gradually that will has been exerted and the price to pay for the courts system, though the benefits are there too, is adherence to this managed culture. Experiments in court design and operation are proceeding quickly. Now there is a single locus for planning and change and with resources following the experiments, if not in a contestable manner but certainly within a market testing frame of reference, then the courts seems bound to be subsumed under this modernised approach. The achievements of the HMCS, as set out confidently in its Business Plan, shows the way in which the old fragmented, generic, loosely structured, lay managed and administered courts are no longer present.

This is a consumer-orientated, victim-centred, cost-effective and efficient system, with specialized functions being dealt with through the roll out of national experiments and a target-driven management information system to plot its achievement. This is a sector which has been modernised, more slowly but no less surely than any other criminal justice sector.

Further reading

Creaton, J. (2003) Modernising the courts and the legal profession, *Contemporary Politics* (June), 9(2).

Raine, J. (2002) Modernisation and criminal justice, in D. Ward, J. Scott and M. Lacey (eds) *Probation: Working for Justice*. Oxford: Oxford University Press.

Raine, J. W. (2005) Courts, sentencing and justice in a changing political and managerial context, *Public Money and Management*, 25: 5, 290–8.

chapter eight

Modernisation and the police

This chapter is primarily concerned with tracing the way in which public policing has been affected by the modernisation agenda post-1997. It will be seen that in at least some ways, modernisation is a continuation of the kind of NPM sector reform initiated by the Conservative administrations post-1979. The chapter attempts to place the institution of public policing into some kind of historical context, paying particular attention to developments over the last 30 years or so. The first section provides historical context, while the second section attempts to contextualize the global drivers of crime and their impact on policing. The third section looks in far more detail at the key dimensions of modernisation specifically for the police institution. It takes into account the political tactics used by successive Conservative administrations in the 1980s and 1990s, and the New Labour approach since 1997, and analyses the reform orientation of the public police throughout recent decades. The final section concludes by identifying dominant themes which are likely to be pertinent in the future.

Historical context

Sir Robert Peel's Metropolitan Police, established in London, has been credited as being the first modern police force since the year 1829. Peel's uniformed patrol officers were controlled centrally in their mission to both prevent and detect crime and they replaced an 'old' police who were predominantly comprised of watchmen and parish constables (Reiner 2000). The creation of the 'new' Metropolitan Police was in itself inextricably linked to the wider social process of urbanization. Chapter 1 made reference to the nineteenth century process of industrialization and the associated growth of the manufacturing sector, including factories and mills which spawned the growth of cities. Reiner (2000) explained how both 'orthodox' and 'revisionist' accounts of history offer explanations of how policing was inextricably linked to urbanization. From an 'orthodox' perspective, the modern police was developed as a natural, progressive and inevitable response to urbanization in the mid-nineteenth century following the Industrial Revolution. 'Orthodox' historians viewed the development of Peelian-style policing as being a benevolent form of social control, with the new Metropolitan Force being a more efficient way of providing policing provision for all. 'Revisionist' historians, on the other hand, tended to point to the shift from an agrarian to a capitalist mode of production as requiring a new form of social control to be exerted to serve the interests of the bourgeoisie, protecting them from the threat posed by the so-called 'dangerous classes'. For them, the early Metropolitan Police was a more malevolent than benevolent form of social control, designed to serve the interests of the few and to subdue the threat posed by the masses. This has direct relevance to modernity in the sense that the gap between the 'haves' and 'have nots' has arguably never been wider (Carvel 2003) and because of the disempowerment of particularly young, working-class males, the police are increasingly having to be aware of the need to contain the 'underclass' (Crowther 2000, 2004).

The policing of the inner city riots in the early and mid-1980s, perhaps most notably in Brixton, Toxteth and Handsworth, undoubtedly represented a crisis point in British policing. 'Operation Swamp' in Brixton 1981, which involved high visibility stops and searches of young, black, Afro-Caribbean men led to the Scarman Report which severely criticized police tactics (Scarman 1982). While the Scarman Report itself alluded to a Peelian vision of public police as keepers of the peace, this posed a paradox as far as NPM was concerned. At precisely the time when the police were needed to be seen as providing a service for all sections in society, the Thatcher government were beginning to pursue an agenda around 'economy', 'efficiency' and 'effectiveness' (Home Office 1993), which would eventually require the police to pursue targets on crime fighting and enforcement.

The policing of inner cities still represents one of the biggest challenges for policing today in the twenty-first century (Stenson and Edwards 2001). Nowhere was this more evident than in the racialized disorders which occurred in the north of England, notably in Bradford and Oldham, in 2001 (Ousley 2001; Ritchie 2001). In addition to this there was significant inter-racial conflict in the Handsworth area of Birmingham, in 2005, following the unsubstantiated rumour that a young black girl had been raped by a group of Pakistani youths. While there was no evidence to suggest rape and no girl ever came forward, two people were killed as a result of the riots (Vulliamy 2005). The policing response to the resulting disorder was of paramount importance in how the police were judged as responding to the challenges of diversity and multi-culturalism in the post-MacPherson era (Marlow and Loveday 2000).

In the late twentieth and early twenty-first century, policing has been expected to respond to the increasing demands posed by diversity, not just with regard to ethnicity and race but also with regard to class, gender, sexual orientation and disability. The undoubted catalyst for this necessity to be responsive to differentiation and diversity was the stabbing to death of the 18-year-old black student, Stephen Lawrence, in Eltham, South London on 22 April 1993. The flawed police investigation into this overtly racist murder, led to the MacPherson inquiry in 1999. The report found that, 'The investigation was marred by a combination of professional incompetence, institutional racism and a failure of leadership by senior officers' (MacPherson 1999: para. 46.1). 'Institutional racism' was further defined as:

> The collective failure of an organisation to provide an appropriate and professional service to people because of their colour, culture or ethnic origin. It can be seen or detected in processes, attitudes and behaviour which amount to discrimination through unwitting prejudice, ignorance, thoughtlessness, and racist stereotyping which disadvantage minority ethnic people.
>
> (MacPherson 1999: para. 46.1)

Of the 70 recommendations made by the inquiry, which were aimed to increase both trust and confidence in policing among minority ethnic communities, significantly police forces were set targets to assist with the recruitment, retention and progression of so-called 'hard to reach' groups.[1] The setting of these targets, however, highlights the continuing tension between the attainment of quantifiable 'outputs' and the achievement of deeper improvements in 'social outcomes'. The former is a product of the NPM agenda whereas the latter is more associated with the modernisation agenda, yet it remains somewhat elusive in terms of how it can be captured and evidenced.

As well as diversity, it has been acknowledged previously that modernisation has brought about a greater degree of individualization in society. It was pointed out how neo-liberal politics was a direct assault on the more communally-based politics around class, gender and race/ ethnicity. According to Clarke and Newman (1997: 109):

> The New Right attack on state welfare identified monopoly provision by public sector organisations as an inhibition on consumer choice and much of the restructuring project was legitimated by reference to enabling the welfare user to exercise such choice.

Throughout the 1980s, management 'gurus', such as Peters and Waterman (1982), urged private sector companies to become more 'close to the customer' and this mantra was assumed to have a transferability to the public sector. Throughout the 1990s, public sector organizations ran the risk of censure (Sumner 1990, 1994; Long 2004), not least because it was felt that the public should be treated more like 'customers' (Clarke and Newman 1997). The 'Citizens Charter' was introduced by the then Prime Minister, John Major. The introduction of associated Charter Marks for organizations deemed to be successfully performing was a watershed in terms of the introduction of 'quality of service' agendas across the public sector (Barnes and Prior 1995). This agenda had a specific impact on policing with the involvement of all three staff associations[2] in producing *The Operational Review* back in 1990 (Police Joint Consultative Committee 1990). The police were criticized in terms of being 'unaccountable' to a public, whose confidence in them was declining. Waters (2000: 264) described the effect of this as forcing 'ACPO to review the strategic direction of the police and the ways in which it could embrace a "quality" approach to enhance its public standing in service provision'. The commitment of ACPO in terms of an embracing of the notion of 'quality of service' in the early to mid-1990s, was in the development of a suite of performance indicators, intended to measure the extent of 'customer satisfaction' in terms of areas, such as satisfaction with response to 999 calls and service at station enquiry counters.[3] In responding to the lead set by ACPO, numerous forces around the country responded by initiating their own 'quality' reform programmes either in the late 1980s and early 1990s. Most prominently, the Metropolitan Police had its 'Plus' programme, with Kent looking to a 'Way Ahead' and Thames Valley instituting its 'Make Quality Contact' programme.

This concentration on quality of service and attempt to improve levels of 'customer satisfaction' was compatible with social processes of fragmentation in society leading to greater individualization. The ethos of individual difference and choice were beginning to replace the taken-for-granted assumptions of the collectivized class-based politics which had characterized the 1970s.

Closely linked with the social processes leading to individualization was the fact that more and more classes of people across society were becoming increasingly mobile and less inclined to identify with a sense of geographically defined community.

Greater geographical mobility has posed challenges for the police particularly because career criminals are nowadays less likely to operate within the confines of traditional force boundaries. Having its legislative underpinnings in the Police Act 1997, the National Crime Squad was set up in 1998, as a policing response to counter the threat of organized crime. Separate regional crime squads were effectively replaced by a structure which was more nationalized in terms of co-ordination, with officers from across England and Wales being seconded to the Squad. The bulk of the work carried out by NCS was around drug trafficking but the organization also focused on the policing of kidnap and extortion, money laundering and counterfeit currency, illegal arms trafficking and immigration crime (Mawby and Wright 2003). Back in 1992, the National Criminal Intelligence Service (NCIS) had been founded by the Home Office. From the late 1990s onwards NCIS was intended to complement the work of the National Crime Squad in taking a strategic overview of organized crime through intelligence co-ordination. In 2006, the Serious and Organized Crime Agency (SOCA) was formed as a result of the amalgamation of the NCS and NCIS (www.soca.gov.uk).

The increased geographical and social mobility of criminals has required a policing response which takes into account the benefits of economic and technological change. According to Manning (1992) and Chan (2003) the organization of police work has been substantially altered due to developments in communication technologies such as the introduction of computer-aided dispatch systems (CAD) and mobile data terminals (MDTs), which forces use to assist them in becoming more proactive in the way that they police. Technological advancements have been made in crime investigation terms in recent years with the establishment of the National DNA Database in 1995. The Police Information and Technology Organization (PITO) was established in 1998 as a non-departmental public body, in order to assist the police in trying to provide the kind of technology that they need to tackle crime in the twenty-first century. In terms of information and communications technology, the portfolio of PITO has included the launching in 2005 of the airwave digital mobile radio service. Recent developments in custody and case preparation applications allow electronic case files to be directly imported into the judicial systems in both Magistrates' and Crown Courts and it is intended that in terms of crime investigation, PITO's Ident1 computerized system will provide more efficiency in terms of replacing the National Automated Fingerprint Identification Service (NAFIS) (www.pito.org.uk). Technological change is likely to continue to be a huge driver of change in terms of the future of policing, with the move towards implementing national standards in policing (Home Office 2004). This is not least because the National Policing Improvement Agency (NPIA) became operational in April 2007 and is taking on the much of the work previously undertaken by PITO (www.npia.police.uk).

With the massive growth of the Internet in recent years and the associated rise of cybercriminality (Wall 2001; Jewkes 2003), the policing response has been the establishment, in 2001, of the National Hi-Tech Crime Unit (NHTCU), which has predominantly been associated with the issue of child pornography on the Internet. The work of NHTCU received national media coverage back in 2002 after the Federal Bureau of Intelligence (FBI) passed the credit card details of over 7000 British subscribers to an American-based child pornography website. As well as illicit pornography, the NHTCU has also been involved in the policing of both electronic theft and identity theft (Jewkes 2003).

Technological advancements have, in turn, assisted the police in terms of being able to tackle the problems which require a more international, if not global response. Having been established by the Maastricht Treaty in 1992, Europol is the organization which manages law enforcement issues which affect the European Union. From 1998 onwards, Europol began increasingly to take on a role in terms of developing a counter-terrorism strategy. The International Criminal Police Organization (Interpol) was originally established in 1956. At the beginning of the twenty-first century it currently has in excess of 180 member countries spread across five continents. Its reason for existence is to secure international police co-operation. Nowadays Interpol is utilized particularly when investigations into terrorism extend beyond European borders (Matassa and Newburn 2003). Following the al Qa'eda 9/11 attacks on New York and Washington, and the 7/7 attacks on London, the work of these transnational policing organizations is likely to play an ever increasing role in responding to the threat of global terrorism.

Drivers of global crime: modernisation and policing

In discussing the role of the correctional services, Chapter 5 acknowledges the extent of penal punitiveness in the context of the crisis in terms of the overcrowding of prisons. While the philosophy of penal punitiveness does not directly impact on public policing, as it is primarily a matter for the judiciary (see Chapter 7), it is worth noting that the Association of Chief Police Officers (ACPO) are very keen to endorse a punitive philosophy with regard to criminal justice matters. In a relatively recent press release, the President of ACPO, Ken Jones, made the following statement:

> The police service is working hard to tackle violent crime and despite a reduction of 13% last year on the more serious offences, violent crime overall is up 2% . . . Sentencing must always be a matter for the courts but I do believe that tough sentences for the most serious and prolific offenders is one of a range of factors that can help deter criminality.
>
> (www.acpo.police.uk)

Closely associated with the notion of 'penal punitiveness' is the belief that the rehabilitative ideal is in decline. While Chapter 5 suggests that the 'Nothing Works' mantra is too pessimistic, not least because there are those, such as probation officers, who follow a vocation built on the idea of offender redemption and rehabilitation, it seems that the staff associations who constitute the voices of the police as a collective are keen to emphasize retribution and incapacitation, which lends support to the idea that the rehabilitative ideal is in decline. In a recent *Sunday Times* newspaper article entitled, 'Police "let down" by prison chaos', the President of the Police Superintendent's Association, Rick Naylor, expressed the sentiment that hard working operational police officers were indeed being failed by the Home Secretary's failure to build enough prisons (www.timesonline.co.uk). The belief that the rehabilitative ideal is in permanent decline links in directly to the development of both penal populist and risk management strategies, which are explored in greater detail in the third subsection.

In terms of the commercialization of crime control, the installation and monitoring of security equipment, such as CCTV, has mushroomed over the last decade or so (Goold 2004). Additionally since the regulation of commercial security through the Private Security Industry Act 2001 and the establishment of the licensing and regulatory body, namely the British Security Industry Authority (BSIA), the sector has been able to claim that it is both more professional and more accountable. According to figures released from the BSIA in 2001, there were an estimated 8000 security companies in the UK, with the sector employing around 350,000 individuals (BSIA 2001). The mushrooming of the private security industry has, according to commentators, such as Shearing and Stenning (1981), occurred due to changes in wider society, most notably the privatization of what was previously public space. In many ways, like it or not, the public police have simply had to accommodate themselves to the inevitability of this process. The commercialization of crime control links in directly to moves towards mixed economy of service provision, plus the notions of 'contestability' and 'responsibilization' which are explored in the third subsection.

In terms of the assessment and management of risk, both crime analysis and offender profiling, have impacted on public policing in the UK massively over the last decade or so (Ainsworth 2001). The National Intelligence Model (NIM), which is referred to in greater detail in the following subsection, identifies crime problems following a risk-based model, suggesting when might be appropriate for police intervention (NCIS 2000). As acknowledged in Chapter 6 on community safety, this focus on risk cannot be separated from the wider belief that we live in a 'risk society', whereby problems can no longer be solved but they must simply be managed as best they can (Beck 1992). This idea has manifested itself within criminal justice thinking from the late 1980s onwards and in many ways has come to supersede the philosophy of rehabilitation which went into decline during the 1970s (Feeley and Simon 1994).

As part of the modernisation agenda, the Police Service has been required to engage more with the philosophy of victim-centred justice. In 1996, the second Victim's Charter was introduced, which heralded one-stop shops and victim statement schemes. With one-stop shops, the police had a responsibility to inform victims of crime about the progress made with their particular cases, and victim statement schemes gave victims the opportunity to articulate the various ways in which their experiences had impacted on them (Hoyle and Young 2003). Victim-centred justice has been legislated for in the context of the provision of Crime and Disorder Act (1998) for victims to be consulted when young offenders are given action plan and reparation orders. This legislation was consolidated by the Youth Justice and Criminal Evidence Act 1999, which required victims to be invited to attend youth panel meetings. This legislation, encouraging a more victim-centred approach, has to be seen in the context of the damning findings of the MacPherson Report (1999), which heavily criticized poor liaison between the police and victims and the families of victims. The shift towards victim-centred justice cannot be separated from the adoption of the kind of restorative justice approach advocated most notably by Thames Valley from the mid-1990s onwards (Pollard 2000). Despite the promotion of restorative justice at the policy level, the Halliday Report (2001) found evidence that acceptance of restorative justice was far from universal among the police culture in practice. The misfit between the philosophy of restorative justice and the ideology of 'penal punitiveness' is an example of the propensity for tensions to exist within the wider modernisation reform process.

In terms of crime prevention and reduction in policing, specialist crime prevention departments began to emerge following the Cornish Committee's report on the Prevention and Detection of Crime (Home Office 1965). Crime prevention departments began to appear within police force CID departments from the mid-1960s onwards (Byrne and Pease 2003). In the late 1970s and early 1980s following the Ditchley Circular (211/78), however, crime prevention increasingly came to be seen as the responsibility of the wider community rather than simply a function of public policing (Newburn 2003). The Standing Conference on Crime Prevention led the Morgan Committee in 1990 to recommend that local authorities take responsibility for both crime prevention and wider community safety. It was not until towards the end of this decade, with the introduction of the Crime and Disorder Act in 1998, that chief police officers and local authorities had a statutory responsibility, along with other agencies, to develop crime and disorder strategies (see Chapter 6). A specialist Crime Prevention College was established in Easingwold, North Yorkshire, in 1995 and, according to Byrne and Pease (2003: 292), the renewed emphasis on crime prevention and reduction, 'are slowly changing the craft of street policing from a focus almost exclusively on enforcement and detection to that of sustainable reductions in crime and disorder through prevention and problem solving'. The emphasis on crime prevention and reduction links in directly with specific policies around pluralization, joined-up justice and increasing attempts to 'responsibilize' (Garland 1996, 2001) citizens, all of which are explored in the third subsection.

In terms of the NPM, Home Office Circular 114 of 1983 (Home Office 1983) saw an attempt to further an agenda around the pursuit of 'economy', 'efficiency' and 'effectiveness' across the governance of public sector organisations (Long 2003, 2004). A focus on targets and league table-style results, rather than processes, was characteristic of the NPM as was the idea that organizations should be able to decipher their core competencies from non-essential responsibilities (Loveday 2000). Activities could be costed and market tested, with purchaser–provider splits being established where appropriate. Inter-agency co-operation and the treatment of clients as 'customers' was another characteristic of the shift away from welfare to a managerial mode of governance (Clarke and Newman 1997; McLaughlin *et al.* 2001). As far as policing was concerned, it would be fair to say that during the 1980s and early 1990s, they were able to resist many of the practices associated with NPM, while they were applied by successive Conservative administrations on other public sector agencies, most notably health and education (Harrison and Pollitt 1994; Rustin 1994). This was not least because of Prime Minister Thatcher's need to appease the police due to their work in quelling the urban unrest and their policing of organized labour in the form of the miner's strike in 1984–5 (Green 1990). The NPM agenda has continued in many respects under the modernisation programme and can be evidenced with reference to the continuation of performance management and audit and inspection (Power 1994), which are considered in the third subsection.

As well as needing to co-operate with the security services and international policing agencies, such as Europol and Interpol, in recent years public protection has taken the form of having to manage the demands posed by what Matassa and Newburn (2003) refer to as 'domestic political extremism'. The public police have had to play an increasing role, particularly with regard to animal rights protests. In utilizing recent legislation, such as the Protection from Harassment Act 1997 and Malicious Communications Act 1998, the police have had to respond to a variety of criminal offences associated with animal rights protest, such as letter bombs, raids on premises perceived to be exploiting animals for research purposes and violence against those thought to working in the field of animal experimentation. Most notable cases include the policing of the Huntingdon life sciences premises and the policing of Darley Oaks Farm, outside Burton-on-Trent in Staffordshire.

Having considered the specific impact on policing of the global drivers of crime, the next section considers in more detail how the key dimensions of modernisation have impacted on policing. In exploring the detail of the impact of modernisation, an assessment is made of both the political tactics used to attempt to secure change and the reform orientation of the police institution.

Mixed economy

Chapter 3 described how moves towards privatization in the criminal justice sector in the 1980s, were fought on ideological grounds. In terms of reform orientation, the public police were able to exert a relatively high degree of reform resistance during the 1980s and early 1990s precisely because their structural position in relation to government was more secure because of their usefulness to a government needing to control organized labour in the form of the miners and deal with the public disorder stemming from urban unrest (Crowther 2000). In terms of reform orientation, as the 1990s progressed the police position began to be characterized as one of 'reform vulnerability' rather than 'reform resistance'. After 1997, with the introduction of the modernisation agenda, the police began to find themselves in a position of reform vulnerability because the special relationship the police had enjoyed with the Conservatives, especially the Thatcher administrations, was to be threatened with the election of New Labour.

Back in the Thatcher era in the 1980s, as public sector employees, police officers tended to see themselves as having both a vocation and a lifelong commitment to the 'war on crime', which was at odds with the possible introduction of the profit motive. At the Police Federation Conference in 1992, the then Conservative Home Secretary, Kenneth Clarke, effectively launched the Inquiry into Police Responsibilities and Rewards (Home Office 1993). Under the chairmanship of Sir Patrick Sheehy, the then Chairman of British–American Tobacco Industries, the principles which guided the inquiry were manifested in the wider conventional wisdom of business management. The controversial Inquiry made recommendations around the flattening of the management pyramid, making fixed term appointments and employing staff on differential pay. The widespread police resistance to the possibility of privatization was evidenced by the strength of feeling among the rank and file officers who gathered at Wembley Stadium in 1993 to protest against the Sheehy Report (Leishman *et al.* 1995).

As Chapter 2 has pointed out, the Thatcher administrations were keen to censure 'monopoly' and during the Conservative-led John Major administration in the early 1990s, it was suggested that policing should be organized around a designated and more limited series of 'core tasks'. The Home Secretary announced a Home Office Review of Police Core and Ancillary Tasks, chaired by Ingrid Posen of the Home Office (Posen 1994). According to the Home Office (1995: 7), the terms of reference for the review were, 'To examine the services provided by the police, to make recommendations about the most cost-effective way of delivering core policing services and to assess the scope for relinquishing ancillary tasks.'

Posen (1994: 15) noted that the police had traditionally carried out a whole host of 'social work' type functions and questioned whether they should have a monopoly on carrying out such work in terms of their being called on, 'to fill any vacuum left by other services'. At the same time, the Police Foundation and Policy Studies Institute set up a separate Independent Committee of Inquiry into the Roles and Responsibilities of the Police, chaired by Sir John Cassels (1994). The then President of ACPO, Sir John Hoddinott (1994: 21), was a vehement critic of the Posen Inquiry and argued that:

> As the review team are rapidly discovering, policing does not divide easily. 'Ancillary' tasks have a vital role to play in forging links between officers and the communities they serve and it is increasingly apparent that neat divisions of labour do not provide solutions to setting priorities.

The Independent Committee of Inquiry into the Roles and Responsibilities of the Police, published its findings in 1994. According to Mawby (2000: 119–20):

> In attempting to head off recommendations for extensive privatisation, it offered instead two alternative models of two-tier policing, that would involve the establishment of locally based, less well trained forces to carry out routine and less demanding police tasks.

These locally based, well trained forces, would be under the direction of the public police, at least to some extent. Unlike Cassels, the report delivered by Posen (Home Office 1995: 11) was far more cautious in that, 'What emerged from the subsequent discussion of tasks is that there are relatively few areas where complete police disengagement could be achieved' and as a result (Home Office 1995: 5), the review team, 'concluded that there was little scope for the police service, broadly defined, to withdraw completely from large areas of current police work'. In reality, some 26 areas were identified where it was felt that police involvement could at least be reduced if not totally abandoned, such as escorting abnormal loads, defendant and witness summonses and stray dogs.

This pre-modernisation emphasis around exploring the possibility of contracting out services for private sector provision was possible to resist as the police were very much in a stronger bargaining position and were to a large extent reform resistant prior to 1997 (Leishman *et al.* 1995). Things began to change significantly with the introduction of the Local Government Act in 1999 and the associated 'best value' regime, which heralded the statutory demand that mixed economy provision be considered. It was precisely because of the threat of censure carried by Section 15 of this legislation that the reform orientation of the public police began to shift from 'resistance' to one which could be characterized as 'vulnerability'. The threat of censure carried by the legislation was enough to ensure compliance at least at the formal level.

Chapter 3 explored the inclination of New Labour to both encourage and enhance the arrangements which existed under previous Conservative administrations in the 1980s and 1990s. A policing-specific example of New Labour's preference for a mixed economy approach, was Surrey Police's introduction of so-called mixed economy teams. This is part of Surrey Police's wider Workforce Modernisation Programme. According to Loveday (2006) under this arrangement, highly skilled and well rewarded constables were made responsible for the management of these mixed economy teams, which consisted of both trained police staff and administrative assistants.

As indicated in Chapter 3, however, the goal in current policies is not for privatization *per se* but rather towards 'contestability'.

Contestability

According to Chapter 3, the rhetoric of 'contestability' is about creating the conditions for competition, rather than the insistence on a particular outcome in any area. A guiding principle of contestability is that service delivery should be open to competition without prejudice as to the outcome, thus opening up the possibilities for all the relevant sectors to apply – be it the public, private or voluntary sector.

In the context of policing specifically, New Labour's first administration saw the passing of the Local Government Act of 1999 which was referred to in the last subsection. The general duty of 'best value' authorities was to make arrangements to secure continuous improvements in the way in which its functions were exercised, having regard to a combination of economy, efficiency and effectiveness. (DETR 1998; Dobson 2000). This legislation signalled the end of the Compulsory Competitive Tendering regime which was formally abolished in 2000. Section 1(1)(d) of the Act made police authorities statutorily responsible for delivering best value. The best value review process was driven by Section 5(4) of the Act which required forces to ask the following questions, which are central to the notion of contestability:

1 *Challenge*

- whether they should be exercising the particular function;
- the level at which they should be exercising the particular function;
- its objectives in relation to the exercise of the function.

In characterising the ethos of the 'challenge' element of Best Value, Dobson (2000: 63) argued that:

> At the heart of the challenge stage is the need for an earthquake in respect of complacent orthodoxy. Adherence to old ways against the requirements of reason and circumstance gives no license for the present and no passport to the future. Practices which were once a dynamic reaction to a new environment can long have outlived their usefulness and have become empty rituals.

2 *Competition*
According to the local government White Paper, *Modern Local Government: In Touch with the People* (DETR 1998: para 7.29), competitiveness could be demonstrated in the following ways:

- The commissioning of an independent benchmarking report with a view to restructuring in-house services to match the performance of the best private and public sector providers.
- The provision of core services in-house and the buying in of top-up support from the private sector.
- The contracting out of a service to the private sector after competition between external bidders only.
- The forming of a joint venture or partnership following a competition for an external partner.
- The tendering of part of a service with an in-house team bidding against private sector and other local authority bidders before deciding whether to provide the bulk of a service internally or externally.
- The disposal or selling off competitively of a service and its assets to another provider.

The shift from 'privatization' towards 'contestability' was evidenced by the fact that the requirement for best value authorities to assess their competitiveness was not underpinned by an absolute statutory duty to subject services to competition. This is because unlike the compulsory competitive tendering regime, contracts, which were externalized, were not in themselves seen to be an automatic guarantee of best value. As far as political tactics were concerned the best value regime carried the threat of censure heavily under Section 15 of the Local Government Act (1999) with the threat that 'hit teams' of private contractors could be brought in to deal with 'failing' forces and even 'failing' Basic Command Units (Taylor 2001; Long 2004). The mere threat of censure in terms of the shift from exhorting and encouraging to demanding that best value reviews be carried out was enough to secure compliance rather than active commitment across police forces in England and Wales.

Performance management

The use of performance management as a tool to audit and assess performance in the public sector in general and in all the criminal justice agencies led, in practical terms, to the formulation of minimum standards, target settings and output controls.

The collection and publication of information based on performance indicators has been a statutory requirement for all local authorities since 1992, and was guided by the Audit Commission (Long 2004). Under New Labour's first term in office, a set of national best value performance indicators (BVPIs) was established by the Local Government Act 1999, along with the establishment of local authority performance indicators via the

Audit Commission Act of 1998. Along with Audit Commission indicators and local performance indicators were corporate health and service delivery performance indicators (Dobson 2000). Strategic objective indicators included the level and fear of crime, public safety and confidence. Indicators around cost and efficiency explored the resources committed to a service and their efficiency in terms of being turned into outputs. The assessment of how well a service had operated in order to achieve strategic objectives was achieved through indicators around service delivery outcomes. Examples of these included indicators around recorded crime including burglary, violent crime, theft of motor vehicles, youth crime, public disorder, files processed and road traffic collisions. 'Quality' indicators were intended to be a reflection of the experience of users of services, for example, around response times; 999 calls; victim and witness satisfaction; charges; summons and cautions; and custody suites with drug arrest referral schemes. The focus on ease and equality of access to services was achieved by 'fair access' indicators around the Police and Criminal Evidence Act PACE (1984) stops of white and minority ethnic persons and complaints for breach of PACE codes and racial incidents (Dobson 2000).

The government asked police authorities, along with other authorities, to set five year targets consistent with reaching the performance level of the top 25 per cent of authorities (Long 2003, 2004). At the time of laying the groundwork for the development of these league tables the DETR (1999: 13) argued that, 'This approach will put more pressure on those authorities that are performing poorly and will, over time, narrow the range of performance and improve the level of performance overall'. In celebrating the work and achievements of the so-called 'top quartile' or 'beacon' performers, it was anticipated that police forces would be able to learn from other 'centres of excellence'. In making applications for beacon status in particular areas, forces had to demonstrate results which could be disseminated to other forces and local Basic Command Units (BCUs), as the basis for promoting the adoption of *best practices*. The prospect of censure was intended to be a very real one for bottom quartile or 'failing' performers, with the intention that the inspection process be one where authorities were 'challenged' on their poor performance, with the possibility of referral to the Home Secretary for further consideration. Once again the threat of censure was enough to secure compliance among police forces, however, reform resistance continued in the form of performance data being manipulated. Data from Long (2004) indicated that 82 per cent of police middle managers in his sample thought that the best value regime would put pressure on police officers to massage and manipulate crime figures to better position their organization within the hierarchy of league tables. As a political tactic, this pointed to a more individualized form of resistance rather than a collectivized resistance built around a clear discourse of opposition to the reform process. Performance culture was here to stay, all one could do was to 'play the numbers game' (Hallam 1999; Davies *et al.* 2000).

To date, the best value regime in the context of policing has been superseded by the Police Performance Assessment Framework (PPAF). These assessments are carried out by the Home Office Police and Crime Standards Directorate, together with Her Majesty's Inspectorate of Constabulary (HMIC). In conducting this process, these two bodies take advice and support from both the Association of Police Authorities (APA), and the Association of Chief Police Officers (ACPO). In each force, 32 performance indicators plus 23 'baseline areas' are assessed and then aggregated to form an assessment of the following seven key performance areas: (1) reducing crime; (2) investigating crime; (3) promoting safety; (4) providing assistance; (5) citizen focus; (6) resource use; and (7) local policing (www.police.homeoffice.gov.uk). In terms of political tactics, the inclusion of more qualitative data to assess performance as well as indicators based around perceptions of local policing need has meant that New Labour has attempted to encourage the police to commit to rather than to simply comply with the demands of performance culture.

Deconcentration and regionalization

Chapter 2 explored how New Right rhetoric expressed the view that the state was too directly involved in the management, not just of criminal justice services, but also the public sector in general. Chapter 3 went on to discuss how the instruction to managers to manage their own practices was often done through an agreed set of centralized requirements (PSIs), targets and performance measures, as discussed above. The responsibility placed on middle management in terms of both policy and performance and standards has proved to be a feature of growing significance in all sectors under modernisation and certainly in criminal justice. According to governmentality theorists, such as Rose and Miller (1992: 187), 'centres of calculation', such as the Home Office, Audit Commission and HMIC, allow police managers what David Garland (1997: 192) would call a kind of 'responsibilized freedom'. The formulation of performance information requires 'action at a distance' (Rose and Miller 1992: 187) and is very much a double-edged sword for middle managers. While being given more power and autonomy than ever before in terms of how they spend money and make decisions on the one hand, they are on the other hand increasingly accountable to 'centres of calculation' who manage a political agenda underpinned by the threat of the censure of 'failure' (Long 2003, 2004).

Chapter 3 pointed out how 'deconcentration' implies a process whereby central government releases control and autonomy to a more localized level. It is an example of the 'permanence of paradox' that this process has occurred in the context of sustaining managerial oversight through the setting of central targets (Long 2003, 2004). The introduction of BCUs in the police and the recent emphasis on neighbourhood policing are examples of this deconcentration process. The permanence of paradox remains, however, in that 'bottom–up' neighbourhood policing does not sit easily with the introduction of more and more nationalized policing functions and central targets (Loveday 1999, 2000). Attempts at regionalization have become a distinctive feature of the modernisation agenda and this too provides supporting evidence for the permanence of paradox (Loveday and Reid 2003; Loveday 2005). To date, regionalization has been resisted by the police with Cleveland police threatening high court action should ministers have attempted to push through a merger between Durham and Northumbria constabularies. At present the Home Office finds itself having to repay some £4 million of an estimated £6.5 million which police forces claimed they spent preparing for the mergers which were eventually abandoned in July 2006 (www.policesupers.com).

Audit and inspection

The audit and inspection culture, so very much a facet of the NPM agenda in the 1980s and 1990s has continued to flourish with New Labour's modernisation agenda post-1997 (McLaughlin *et al.* 2001; McLaughlin *et al.* 2002).

Rather than a central, unified and cohesive state exerting social control, Rose and Miller (1992: 174) commented that, 'Political power is exercised today through a profusion of shifting alliances between diverse authorities in projects governing a multitude of facets of economic activity, social life and individual conduct'. While this was the case pre-1997, the number of 'diverse authorities' who monitor and attempt to regulate audit and inspection over policing has proliferated since 1997. Not only have HMIC and the Audit Commission continued to do the work that they were doing pre-1997, but more recently both the Police Standards Unit and the National Police Improvement Agency (established April 2007) have come to take on the kinds of roles associated with such 'centres of calculation' (Rose and Miller 1992). The governance of police forces has always taken place through a 'profusion of shifting alliances', and this tripartite arrangement was enshrined in legislation by the Police Act of 1964, whereby power was to be shared between the Home Secretary, individual chief constables and police authorities. Governance through 'a profusion of shifting alliances' has been greatly intensified in recent years. Rather than there being a unified state apparatus to monitor police performance, regulation nowadays takes place through the state devolving responsibilities to other agencies in order to do this. In the policing context, two classic examples of this are the Audit Commission and Her Majesty's Inspectorate of Constabulary. These bodies rely predominantly on what Latour (1987) refers to as 'inscription devices', or performance indicators, to monitor police performance. The social construction of performance data for police forces nowadays requires what Rose and Miller (1992: 185) refer to as 'centres of calculation', whose business it is to aggregate these inscription devices by means of comparison and evaluation of forces.

With reference to the social processes, described previously, Clarke and Newman (1997: 30) argued that, 'far from being a shift towards a "rolling back" of the state, these changes involve a "rolling out" of state power but in new, dispersed, forms'. They make the point that the dispersal of power has meant the simultaneous shrinking of the state and the enlargement of its reach into civil society (through its engagement of non-state agents). Dispersal of state power to bodies like the Audit Commission and HMIC is characteristic of, 'intensified forms of centralized power and control, through tighter fiscal control, new policy directions and an expanding apparatus of audit and evaluation' (1997: 29).

Under the auspices of the Audit Commission, the New Labour government established a new Best Value Inspectorate which began work in April 2000. In the specific context of policing, the Local Government Act amended the 1996 Police Act. This enabled HMIC to inspect and report to the Secretary of State on police authority compliance with the requirements of best value. Under the best value regime, the Home Secretary could direct a police authority to: (1) prepare or amend a performance plan; (2) follow specific procedures in relation to a performance plan; and (3) carry out a review of its exercise of specific functions. With regard to authorities labelled as 'failing', the Home Secretary had the power to transfer particular functions from local authorities to a private sector contractor (Dobson 2000).

While the best value regime required compliance on behalf of police forces simply because of its legislative underpinnings, the government had envisaged that the top quartile (top 25 per cent) performers would be given the status of so-called beacon councils or 'centres of excellence' (DETR 1998). In terms of political tactics, in an attempt to secure commitment to this agenda, the idea was that police forces and their authorities, who were 'responsibilized' (Garland 1997) under the Local Government Act, would strive to attain beacon status. Research conducted by Long (2004) revealed, however, that certain managerial practices were resisting this idea of striving to be the best. Many police managers interviewed were keen to discuss the disincentives of the quartile system. They referred to what could be called 'institutionalized disincentives', which effectively meant that forces and Basic Command Units would strive to be in the top half of the league tables but not in the top quartiles, as next time round they would not be able to demonstrate continuous improvements in service delivery. They also spoke about how in a competitive league table culture, there were no incentives to actually share best practice with neighbouring forces or BCUs who could effectively be seen as 'competitors'. In what was undoubtedly an example of the permanence of paradox, Smith (1995) pointed to this phenomenon across the public sector more generally as one of 'convergence'. This is the idea that organizations manage and manipulate the formal presentation of their performance data so as to fit in with the 'norm' or to hide themselves in the pack. This phenomenon of striving to be average or a little above average makes sense with the introduction of a regime whereby top league table performers would be inspected for 'best practice' that they could potentially spread, and 'failing' performers would be inspected on the grounds that they could be subject to censure.

The first National Policing Plan (Home Office 2003) was produced by the Home Secretary following the passage of the Police Reform Act 2002. The plan attempted to provide the strategic national overview against which chief officers and police authorities could prepare their own local three-year strategy plans as well as annual policing plans. This process has continued with the current arrangements for the Police Performance Assessment Framework. Audit and inspection takes the form of judgements made by comparing the performance achieved by a particular force to that achieved by a group of similar forces in terms of like for like comparisons. Forces are subsequently labelled 'excellent', 'good', 'fair' or 'poor'. Assessments are also made by comparing force performance in one year to that achieved by the same force in the previous year. In taking into account the priorities set by the Home Secretary in the National Community Safety Plan, forces are labelled either 'improved', 'stable' or 'deteriorated' (http://police.homeoffice.gov.uk).

Penal populism and risk management

Chapter 3 articulated how the modernisation agenda set in motion by New Labour was a reinvigoration of law and order politics under Tony Blair's oft quoted maxim of 'tough on crime, tough on the causes of crime'.[4] This penal populism can be evidenced by reference to the government's willingness to use policies, such as anti-social behaviour orders and 'youth curfew' schemes (Burney 2005; Squires and Stephen 2005) Along with penal populism is the associated growth of risk assessment and management policies and this has meant in the police-specific context, the development of intelligence-led policing. This is part of what Ericson and Haggerty (1997) referred to as 'policing the risk society'. The police have become increasingly involved in the production and dissemination of crime-related knowledge to bodies like traffic authorities and insurance companies (Chan 2003). According to Cope (2003: 341), 'Intelligence-led policing has developed within the broader context of the "risk society" that has influenced the proliferation of risk management strategies throughout criminal justice agencies'.

A major risk management tool used by the public police nowadays is the National Intelligence Model (NIM). The model identifies three levels of crime, namely Level 1 – local, Level 2 – cross border and Level 3 – national, transnational and serious and organized crime (Maguire and John 2006). The development of the NIM model, as a risk management tool, has to be seen in the much broader socioeconomic context of the globalization of crime control. To deal with the risks associated with both Level 1 and Level 2 criminality, crime analysts work in intelligence units within forces and Level 3 analysis is dealt with by SOCA. The shift towards risk management is symptomatic of what Cope (2003: 341) refers to as the move, 'away from demand-driven interventions towards proactive methods of crime control'.

In terms of political tactics, the police would seem to be far more committed to the ideals of both penal populism and risk management. This is because these ideals support the philosophies of crime reduction, crime detection and peacekeeping, which policing was founded upon.

Pluralization

Both Chapters 2 and 3 alluded to what could be referred to as the denigration of professionals by the Thatcher administrations. Chapter 3 looked at the 'combination of financial austerity and public disquiet' surrounding the roles being undertaken by professionals and about the corresponding reassignment of roles to what might be termed 'assistants'.

While Chapter 3 acknowledged that this trend was not unique to the New Labour agenda, its intensification since 1997 can be evidenced in the policing context with reference to terms like 'plural policing' and 'the extended policing family'. According to Crawford (2003: 141), 'A major driver in the pluralization of policing and the dispersal of responsibilities for crime prevention has been the impact of neo-liberal inspired reforms that have sought to rearticulate the relationship between state, market and civil society'. As well as the 43 Home Office police forces in England and Wales and a multitude of specialist policing bodies (such as Custom and Excise and the British Transport Police), Crawford (2003: 143) was keen to acknowledge the plethora of municipal, civilian and commercial policing enterprises. Municipal policing provision includes such things as environmental health officers, public auxiliaries (e.g., city guards, neighbourhood wardens and local patrols) and traffic wardens. Civilian policing includes the Special Constabulary, Neighbourhood Watch and other citizen patrols, as well as vigilantism. The diversity of commercial policing is reflected in personnel, such as security guards and door supervisors, private investigation services, plus security equipment, such as CCTV and alarm systems (Wakefield 2003).

Section 38 of the Police Reform Act 2002 introduced civilian patrolling officers, now referred to as Police and Community Support Officers. In late 2002/early 2003, some 1206 PCSOs were introduced across forces in England and Wales (Crawford 2003: 158). By focusing on low level anti-social behaviour and by providing a visible presence designed to reassure, it was intended that PCSOs be instrumental in releasing fully trained police officers from tasks which could otherwise be performed by civilians, leaving them to concentrate on tackling more serious crimes (Long *et al.* 2006).

In terms of political tactics, pluralization was greatly resisted by the public police as they became more reform vulnerable throughout the 1990s. According to Mawby and Wright (2003: 182):

> While the civilianisation of policing has consistently encountered opposition, principally from policing stakeholders, but also from other sources, on the grounds of 'policing on the cheap', effectiveness, competency and accountability, it is nevertheless, an integral part of the future of the police organisation.

This resistance has changed to compliance in many ways due to the creation of specialist civilianized jobs which are not considered to be directly threatening to the status or remuneration of uniformed police officers. The growth in numbers of crime and forensic analysts would be an example of this. This is likely to continue in the future with HMIC's (2004), with the roles, management and deployment of police staff further evolving under the 'Workforce Modernisation Agenda'. (Loveday 2006). Legislation, such as the Police Act (2002), further requires compliance with the pluralization agenda and the National Policing Plan for England and Wales (2003–06) attempts to move the police from compliance to commitment.

Joined-up justice

Chapter 3 spoke about how the emphasis on 'joined-up government' after New Labour's election in 1997 was very much intended to tackle what could be referred to as a 'silo' mentality which occurred as a result of the fragmentation of service provision across different criminal justice agencies. The impetus behind New Labour's promotion of partnership working was provided by the 1991 Morgan Report (Home Office 1991).

In terms of the impact of 'joined-up justice' specifically upon policing, at local level, police command teams (made up of superintending and inspecting ranks) have to work together with chief executives of local authorities under the statutory requirements of the Crime and Disorder Act 1998 (see Chapter 6). The philosophy of partnership working, underpinning the legislation, requires senior and middle management police officers to treat what were previously considered to be 'policing problems' as 'social problems' (Loveday 1999). While the Crime and Disorder legislation ensures a degree of compliance with the philosophy of joined-up working, this is no guarantee of genuine commitment. According to Long (2003: 641), 'It is a challenge to the traditional style of leadership in which officers were generally left to deal with the challenges presented by the daily management of their own functional "silos" '. In providing support for the notion of the permanence of paradox, Clarke and Newman (1997: 116) suggested that public sector managers are, 'constrained by a variety of often incompatible expectations'. As Long argues, this is precisely because of the existence of, 'an uneasy relationship between the government's message that crime is a social problem which requires "joined-up working" and the NPM-inspired performance culture in which success tends to be measured quite narrowly' (Long 2003: 641).

Responsibilization

Chapter 3 spoke about David Garland's (2001) notion of 'responsibilization' in terms of it being an attempt to increase the influence of state agencies on crime policy by actually giving more responsibility to non-state agencies in the private and voluntary sectors, as well as both empowering and responsibilizing citizens in local communities. The creation of new alliances and partnerships has meant the state no longer acting as a sovereign power in terms of both control and influence on crime policy. The recognition and commitment to controlling crime is expected to be pursued by a more diverse range of social actors and this is very much a continuation of the kind of citizen focus which began under John Major and further intensified with the New Labour administrations.

The government's White Paper, *Building Communities, Beating Crime* (2004) was instrumental in helping to launch the government's civil renewal agenda. The idea of civil renewal is underpinned by the notion of 'reponsibilization' in the sense that it is supposed to involve the government and the people working together to attempt to make life better. The notions of 'active citizenship', 'strengthened communities' and 'partnership in meeting public needs' received ideological backing in two speeches delivered in 2003 by the then Home Secretary, David Blunkett.[5] As a responsibilization strategy, civil renewal is first about generating a level of understanding among people so that they are aware of how they can exercise their powers as responsible citizens. Second, the civil renewal agenda encourages local citizens to organize themselves through groups, to pursue some common good for the benefit of wider society. Third, the agenda also responsibilizes state bodies in terms of demanding their support and execution of their public duties in assisting local citizens to become more actively involved in society.

In practical policing terms, the TOGETHER campaign (www.together.gov.uk) attempted to responsibilize local citizens to take a stand against anti-social behaviour and so-called 'low level' disorder. In West Yorkshire, for example, (see www.westyorkshirepolice.co.uk), the CIRCLE project was established as part of the wider civil renewal agenda. Six CIRCLE areas across the two districts of Wakefield and Calderdale were supported by the injection of a small amount of funding and the employment of civilian staff in the form of Community Advocate Project Officers, put in place to assist the community to tackle 'quality of life' issues identified by those in the communities themselves. Typically local residents, schools and local businesses have had representation on CIRCLE panels in attempting to come up with practical solutions to locally identified problems and these panels received assistance from the relatively newly appointed Police and Community Support Officers in the area. These practical solutions have included the construction of a youth shelter in Calderdale and the creation of a football club in Wakefield, both intended as diversionary measures to take young people away from criminal and anti-social behaviour (Long and Crowther-Davey 2007).

It is difficult to assess the level of commitment to responsibilization strategies, such as the civil renewal agenda, precisely because their successes do not easily satisfy the continuing desire of those who drive the modernisation for quantifiable demonstrations of performance. On the one hand, the idea that local citizens should take some responsibility for attempting to combat anti-social behaviour is attractive because it helps to tackle the idea that the police should have primacy as the agency with total responsibility for criminal problems. On the other hand, too much empowerment of communities may mean that expectations are raised too highly. Those who are most likely to be responsibilized within communities may be feared by local police commanders and those working within neighbourhood policing teams because they are politicized and may come with an agenda which challenges police orthodoxy.

Conclusion

This chapter has traced the way in which public policing has been affected by the modernisation agenda over the last few decades by placing the institution of public policing into a historical context. Having contextualized the global drivers of crime and their impact on policing, the key dimensions of modernisation were specifically explored. During the 1980s the strong bargaining power of the police in relation to other public sector agencies, such as health and education, meant that their reform orientation could be characterized as one of 'resistance'. With the urban unrest quelled and organized labour effectively destroyed, their orientation became far more vulnerable in the early 1990s. It has been found that censure was the dominant political tactic used to try and effect reform by the Major administration, while New Labour has attempted to secure compliance and to even try to achieve a degree of commitment to change. Although it would seem that the police are committed to the idea of penal populism and risk management in all other areas their endorsement is conditional and can best be characterized as compliance. While the collective leadership voice of the police, namely the ACPO, is sometimes keen to endorse governmental criminal justice polices this, the ability of rank and file officers to resist or even subvert through the practices that their great autonomy allows, does not equate to an organization which could be characterized as being reform transformative (Holdaway 1983).

The 'permanence of paradox' remains at the heart of understanding the impact of modernisation on policing. There is evidence of more interference and control from central government on the one hand, and on the other hand police managers seem freer than ever to make decisions which take account of local needs (Long 2004). Second, the modernisation agenda emphasizes the need for the police to work in collaboration with multi-agency-partners more than ever before to achieve cross-cutting targets which will ultimately improve social outcomes, yet conversely agency-driven targets have yet to shake off the worst excesses of competition between forces and BCUs characteristic of the league table culture engendered at the turn of the millennium.

Notes

1 Other recommendations covered stop and search; discipline and complaints; training; first aid; victim and witness treatment; family liaison; investigation and prosecution of racist crime, and the reporting and recording of racist incidents and crimes. (Newburn 2003).
2 Namely the Federation, the Superintendents Association and ACPO.
3 Other indicators included the percentage of victims satisfied with the initial response to a report of violent crimes, domestic burglary, police performance at the scene of road traffic accidents and perceived levels of foot and mobile patrols. These indicators were included in the annual report of the Audit Commission for the first time in 1996–7.
4 Phrase used by Tony Blair when addressing the Labour Party Conference in 1992 as Shadow Home Secretary.
5 Active citizens, strong communities – building civil renewal, the Scarman Trust Forum Lecture, 11 December 2003, and Edith Kahn Memorial Lecture, Civil renewal: a new agenda, 1 June 2003.

Further reading

Green, P. (1990) *The Enemy Without: Policing and Class Consciousness in the Miner's Strike*. Buckingham: Open University Press.
Home Office (2005) *National Community Safety Plan 2006–2009*. London: Home Office.
Loveday, B. (2005) Police reform: problems of governance and accountability. Management challenges surrounding proposals for police restructuring, *The Police Journal*, 78: 339–50.
Loveday, B. (2006) Workforce modernisation: implications for the Police Service in England and Wales. Evaluating HMIC, 2004. Thematic: Modernising the Police Service, *The Police Journal*, 79: 105–24.
McLaughlin, K., Osborne, S. and Ferlie, E. (2001) *New Public Management: Current Trends and Future Prospects*. London: Routledge.
Power, M. (1994) *The Audit Explosion*. London: Demos.

chapter nine

Modernisation and the voluntary and community sector

Introduction

This chapter is centrally concerned with those parts of the voluntary and community sector (VCS) who offer key services to the correctional sector mainly through funded and commissioned activity. The way in which the voluntary and community sector has been pushed centre stage by government as a key strategic feature of the modernisation agenda will be examined here, drawing in particular on the role of the voluntary and community sector in correctional services work. This will be based on a research project which was undertaken by the author (Senior *et al.* 2005) which investigated the enhancement of the role of the voluntary and community sector under NOMS. Issues of market testing, competition and contestability as well as joining-up justice appear at the forefront of debates concerning their role. It will be argued that modernisation represents a significant challenge to the traditions and mission of this sector even though, paradoxically, their role and place is supported and often lauded by a normally critical government.

Contextual outline

The overhaul of community sentencing and the introduction of new custodial orders, resulting from the Criminal Justice Act 2003, and the concurrent development of a new organization, the National Offender Management Service, following the Carter Report (Carter 2003) has created a fresh impetus for change in who delivers which services. This presents challenges to all stakeholders – public, private and voluntary – and any discussion of the enhancement of the role of the VCS has to take place within this larger policy arena and the modernising impulses of government.

The cross-cutting review on the role of the voluntary and community sector in service delivery conducted in 2002, noted:

> There are around half a million voluntary and community organisations (VCOs) in the UK. These range from small, local community groups to large, established, national and international organisations. Some have no income at all and rely on the efforts of volunteers; others are, in effect, medium-sized businesses run by paid professional staff.
> (HM Treasury 2002: 2.1)

The numbers in the sector are projected by Clinks based on surveys completed by the Voluntary and Community Sector Unit of NOMS as:

- Over 900 voluntary organizations are responsible for more than 2000 projects that provide services to offenders.
- Over 600 voluntary organizations work with offenders in the community.

- More than 7000 prison volunteers contribute to the rehabilitation of offenders.

(www.clinks.org)

Some definitional discussion is needed to clarify the parameters of the sector we are discussing. Although the sheer variety makes classification an inexact science added to the fact that the capture of data in relation to such agencies remains rudimentary (Senior *et al.* 2005). Five distinguishing features can be highlighted which help in shaping our understanding of this sector for the purposes of this discussion:

- the formal sector from community groups;
- VCS with offenders from generic VCS;
- varying size;
- varying focus;
- vision and business culture.

Distinguish formal sector from community groups

It is important here to focus on the formalized voluntary and community sector and not confuse this discussion with the many community groups which contribute to crime reduction in a rather more diffuse way and link more directly with community safety organizations and partnerships, which are the subject of Chapter 6. We are here concerned with organizations who, while many are community-based, have organizational structures which can take them a long way away from their locality. They tend to be formalized, have constitutions and often have charitable status. The informal community groups or local groupings which form around particular issues or concern do not share this formal character. This is of course not an absolute dividing line as community groups of all hues and sizes can contribute to the support of individual offenders. To describe it formally also is not to underestimate the sheer variety of organizational structures which can still be included under this heading. From the national large crime-focused agency, such as Nacro which has a campaigning arm, national and regional projects, with regional offices and many many individual projects across the country on a variety of programmes including housing, ETE, drugs, alcohol, mentoring and similar services right through to the single local agency based in a single area of work, such as an accommodation provider (e.g., Humbercare to the local groups who undertake prison visiting; Mothers Union). Diversity is the key adjective to describe the sector.

Distinguish VCS with offenders from generic VCS

In the work undertaken for NOMS in 2005, it was discovered that agencies which worked exclusively with offenders were a little distanced from the mainstream VCS groups. Indeed the core business of Councils of Voluntary Service around children, the elderly, people with learning disabilities and mental health problems, more than occupied their attention and there was a somewhat dismissive attitude, voiced by some of the directors of CVS to this specialized sector (Senior *et al.* 2005: 24). There were four main divisions:

- working solely with offenders (such as Nacro, SOVA or Apex Trust);
- working with disadvantaged groups where offenders were identified as a priority group (e.g., Princes Trust, Turning Point or Shelter);
- working with people in the community of which some of their clientele may be offenders but enter the service as community referrals (e.g., Mothers Union);
- working in the mainstream VCS (Samaritans, Citizen's Advice).

(Senior *et al.* 2005: 23)

Distinguish by size

This has already been alluded to and is reflected in the different organizational structures seen in this sector. The small agencies appear to be most vulnerable under modernising imperatives as we shall discuss. The protective role that larger organizations can play in a contestability environment will be interesting to explore. However, the increasingly large contracts offered over regions, which has been a growing feature of prison and probation contracts in recent years, does not always guarantee that the needs of the small agencies will be protected. Under employment legislation individuals can be protected through 'tupeed' arrangements but smaller agencies may simply not survive.

Distinguish by focus

Again this is hard to classify. We have listed below the substantive areas of work where agencies have expertise and some of it is in highly specialized and unique provision. Many agencies developed out of the pioneering work of one individual who pursued an area with vigour, creativity and imagination enabling it to grow into a well respected though often idiosyncratic provision. Some can then build from this base. For instance, Sova was largely a prison visiting organization when it started in 1975 and it has grown into a national organization offering Education, Training and Employment (ETE), mentoring and a range of other offender-related services. One interesting feature of the last ten years is the decision by agencies on whether they alter their focus along with changes in government funding patterns. There appears to be different responses to this issue. Some agencies are asserting their independence by refusing to change their core areas, (e.g., Apex Trust) and others are showing a remarkable capacity to change direction, as government reorients what it needs. It was noted in Senior's research (*et al.* 2005) how some agencies had to change their focus midway through existing contracts to meet a changing government directive.

The introduction of Basic Skills targets for prisoners forced one such change on a range of ETE provision delivered by VCS organizations.

Distinguish by vision and business culture

In some respects these two issues can be seen separately. Many VCS organizations are driven by a particular vision, sometimes faith-based, which determines what it regards as possible, appropriate and consistent with its stated mission. Some have been prepared to revisit that, maybe pragmatically, where funding streams make demands which would have been anathema to its original mission. This is particularly acute for those agencies asked to take on a greater surveillance operation as a result of the punitive and risk averse nature of criminal justice today. There has been no single response to this and indeed some organizations have maintained their vision of voluntary contact and refused to engage in services where they may be required to log reporting and contribute, in effect and in practice, to the compulsory supervision of an offender. Others have seen this as a necessary evil, noting that the private sector will engage here and they have to remain competitive. Such an acceptance of changing roles does have an impact on the type of organization the VCS has traditionally been. The development of a culture, which is business minded, within the VCS has been a clear response to these challenges. It has become hard to distinguish the style and managerial operation of some VCS organizations from their public or private counterparts. The development of bid teams, accreditation structures, business plans, employment of business accountants, complex HR and marketing functions, etc., have been a necessary shift if the mysteries of ESF funding, commissioning bodies, procurement procedures and performance management requirements are to be addressed. If the VCS wants to get funded work in this sector then it has to have the capacity to provide such functions to convince commissioners and ultimately the government it is fit for this purpose.

Since 1997 there have been changing patterns in the way public service delivery is to be managed. The government has clearly promoted an agenda which emphasizes the importance and centrality of the VCS in delivering public services.

> The mainstreaming of the voluntary sector in England was a key means for Blair to deliver on his 'Third Way' themes of liberalized public service delivery and civil renewal . . . This close relationship between the voluntary sector and core government policies has been a critical factor in the development and maintenance of a strong policy and political relationship.
>
> (Elson 2006)

The VCS, the Third Sector as it is dubbed, is now an essential partner and a channel for the implementation of a wide range of government policy objectives. With the distinctive focus of much VCS work being located with disadvantaged people, crime and social exclusion figure highly on the government agenda for the VCS. The VCS now sits alongside the statutory providers – the Prison Service, the Probation Service and the emerging National Offender Management Service, and the private sector. This defines its position if not its characteristics. Government encouragement to the VCS can be seen in the £125 million identified as part of the Futurebuilders fund and the ChangeUp funding streams, which offer a clear indication that infrastructural support is to be created to ensure this sector can compete. It is important to note, however, that take-up of Futurebuilders by crime-related organizations has been slow reflecting perhaps, the uncertainties of the commissioning future. The VCS may not be entirely convinced about the new role government envisages for it.

New IT infrastructures have been seen as central to the achievement of many of the key modernising goals discussed in this book. If the goals of joined-up services, of increasing efficiency, of making targets outcome focused rather than output focused are crucial, then co-ordination and integration of communication strategies and information flow is vital. This issue is further complicated by the need to create structures which enhance the capacity of all stakeholders involved to access information on a routine basis. This is a challenge facing the VCS in working within correctional services. Indeed accessing reliable information and gathering data is an issue in discerning how the criminal justice system currently functions. Joined-up justice supports the development of partnership in service delivery as well as producing organizational and technological reform to develop the infrastructure to support and enhance partnerships. This is the challenge which all the stakeholders face in moving forward on an agenda which seeks explicitly to combine and develop service delivery in a more co-ordinated and 'end to end' fashion.

The initial moves of the 1990s brought the VCS as partners to statutory provision both inside prison and in the community; it points to the roots of potential further engagement and also to some of the potential stumbling blocks. However, the terms of this partnership were less positive and more contested than statutory agencies often publicly expressed. However, this period established the growth of partnerships as a way of combining expertise from across different agencies. There was seen to be clear potential for a partnership approach to contestability as also outlined by the NOMS Chief Executive, Martin Narey:

> To ensure cost effectiveness the Government is keen to encourage competition in the provision of correctional services. Opening up the 'corrections market' will allow many more organizations to bring their skills and expertise to bear in helping offenders to turn away from crime. The Government expects to see partnerships developing between public and private sector providers and the voluntary and community agencies that harness their respective strengths.
>
> (NOMS 2004)

The reforms of the criminal justice system have to be seen as part of a wider agenda which the government has identified as the civil renewal agenda. David Blunkett in the Scarman Lecture (11 December 2003) said:

> The civil renewal agenda is about supporting interdependence and mutuality, not simply leaving individuals or communities to fend for themselves. We are talking here about building the capacity, the social assets, and the leadership which will enable communities to take advantage of both the targeted help which is available and broader economic and social improvements and investment.
>
> (Blunkett 2003)

The foregoing has illustrated just how pivotal government and commissioners see the role of the VCS under the modernising agenda – at least rhetorically. How far this will be translated into active funding support and produce meaningful shifts and growth in the proportions of funding going to this sector will unfold in the next five years. But perhaps before considering the detailed impact of modernisation on the VCS some clarity over the conceptual boundaries of what constitutes the VCS is needed.

There has always been a tradition of volunteering in the criminal justice sector, indeed many individuals continue to visit prisoners and support them through the difficult experience that is custody. In a variety of important ways volunteers support visitors centres, play facilities and counselling services giving important back-up to the work undertaken by paid employees. As outlined at the start of this chapter, the focus here is on the development of a VCS as a key funded provider of services to offenders. This is a role which has grown in recent times and explicitly so since the so-called Peppermint Paper in 1990 (Home Office 1990a). Through that initiative Probation Services were required to have at least 5 per cent growing to 7 per cent in later years, of its budgets for partnership spending and this focused attention on the use of the VCS as providers. Typically the most common areas of engagement are in the following areas: advice, gambling, drugs, housing, ETE/learning and skills, alcohol, restorative justice, health/mental health, mentoring/support, prisoner's family support and sex offending. It has been noticeable that growth in provision in some areas – ETE, drugs, mentoring – has followed the setting of key government targets and other services have been more vulnerable to loss of funding as they fall outside targets which would generate cash for the purchaser. Welfare Advice, a long time VCS-driven support service to the Probation Service, has suffered such sidelining in recent times.

The identified partnership money of the 1990s is far from the whole story in terms of funding support for the VCS. Changing sources of funding have produced a rich variety of funding outlets which overall has meant less exclusive reliance on funding from the statutory sector. This has proved difficult to track accurately without systems which can accurately capture this information. The sources of funding assistance for service provision have been tentatively categorized as follows:

- services contracted directly by prison or probation;
- services which involve pooled budgets, e.g., supporting people and DAT, DIP;
- services where other funding is involved, e.g., ESF, SRB;
- services given by the VCS to the correctional services which involve no direct cost to the statutory services or which are self-supported.

(Senior *et al.* 2005)

Although the VCS can appear relatively free from government shaping of its role and purpose, and the independence of vision is part of the attraction of this sector to purchasers, increasingly survival and growth has meant being much more closely tied to commissioning frameworks. Agencies can continue to float free when they have independent sources of funding but apart from those lucky enough to be funded by underlying charitable donations many of the leading providers – Nacro, Sova, Rainer, Turning Point, Addaction and many others – need to search continually for new bidding streams and sources of funding. Their very instability as organizations makes them likely to be attracted to the proposals of the modernising aspirations of government. The potential costs to the VCS of such dependence can be seen in terms of loss of independence; requirement to develop new or adapted skill sets; greater business orientation; developing structures akin to a small business; partnership with the private sector; and the generation of new areas of business to suit new political priorities. These issues will be addressed below as we trace the impact of modernisation on the VCS.

Reforming the VCS

The atmosphere of modernising government rhetoric so censorious for some, particularly public sector agencies, has been absent, even inverted, for the VCS. Government has spent the last decade or more providing funds inclusive of this Third Sector as an essential player in the new provider markets of a modernised criminal justice system. This has been buttressed by the presence of many influential friends at high levels in government and in the Lords often providing key voices in policymaking (e.g., the impact on a range of personal safety policies of the Suzy Lamplugh Trust). This is reflected too in funding regimes through funding through trusts and the development of infrastructural funds to increase capacity and enable the VCS to compete in a contestable market.

The reform orientation, therefore of the VCS is certainly transformative. They have taken on board government changes but not just in a reluctantly compliant manner but with commitment. The courting of the sector by all layers of government has made it feel central to the future plans of government for criminal justice. There have been adjustments necessary in form, organization and vision to accommodate this change but the traditional strength of the VCS in being adaptive and innovative to manage change has helped it through this transition. This optimistic vision for the future is hedged in with some paradoxical consequences these changes bring, to which we will need to return following a more detailed exploration of how the VCS has responded to the key dimensions of modernisation.

Key dimensions of modernisation

Mixed economy of provision

This first dimension of modernisation has direct benefits for the VCS. It is time for them to come centre stage and take a bigger share of the funding for statutory corrections work. However, how far the sector wishes to expand and develop its role rather than consolidate or secure its own traditional focus and role, may be more debateable. The VCS has lived through the last decade on poor funding regimes and non-sustainable contracts. Its requirement for work in this field is that it can become a more secure provider of services. The question of robust resources for work undertaken was of high priority for respondents in the research work Senior *et al.* (2005) undertook. The discussion revolved around concerns about unrealistic demands and inadequate recognition of key costs, such as full cost recovery for management support. Funders seemed unwilling to extend to development costs, funding staff development, supporting the infrastructure and funding for an exit strategy. Probation Service cutbacks had forced them to refuse cost of living increases and in the case of one contract cancel it completely. This lack of recognition of 'full cost recovery' was blighting relationships between the Probation Service and the VCS and forcing them to re-evaluate their priorities and seek other funds. A key concern in the study was the proliferation of short-term contracts. This situation discourages proper planning cycles, leaves VCS organizations vulnerable to loss of work and the need to recycle staff among competing organizations, and it can mean that a lot of time is spent merely in securing work rather than developing good practice.

So despite the positive environment for VCS participation there are a number of key issues which would need to be addressed for the sector to feel secure about continuing to invest in this area. Added to this the potential for a growth in the role of the private sector further problematizes any expanded engagement.

Contestability

A key concern for the VCS is how far contestability will be conducted in ways which encourage partnership and co-operation and do not induce a competitive, adversarial approach to commissioning. Government regards competition as energizing but risks ignoring the very concerns that the VCS has expressed even prior to the move to new commissioning arrangements. The Senior *et al.* (2005) study revealed a lack of understanding and distinct nervousness around the concept of contestability. Relevant was the theme of partnership. Concerns were expressed that the way in which contestability might be conducted would be a disincentive to partnership. Partnership working and the mechanisms within which it can thrive, take time to foster. However, partnership also raises a key issue around cost-effectiveness. Initial set up costs for partnership are often greater than they would be for single agency bidding. However, the costs of preparation and developing working protocols must be set against the potential savings in better outcomes in the provision which develops. If partnerships can produce visible savings in the co-ordination of end to end offender management then contestability structures should seek to be more complementary then conflictual.

But is the environment for procurement a productive one? Again the Senior *et al.* (2005) study reflected on this. Procurement processes can be difficult to handle. Governed by complex 'treasury rules' and pressures to deliver quickly, it is difficult to create an environment where procurement is seen as a positive and supportive process. Certainly the VCS are concerned about such processes and the government did respond to criticism of its procurement procedures more generally (ACU 2004; HM Treasury 2003). The issues highlighted in the study concern:

- expertise of the procurers and the procurees;
- demystifying Treasury Rules and the restrictions of EU procurement;
- working within pooled budgets – problem or solution?
- capacity to enhance partnerships;
- maintaining a level playing field;
- impact of regionalization on procurement processes;
- developing alternative approaches to procurement.

One suggestion which was discussed in detail during the study and subsequently became a government recommendation in the NOMS and VCS Strategy, though not yet acted upon, was whether the procurement process could be improved by creating a neutral mechanism for the bidding process. This notion of a 'neutral bidding agency' was seen as attractive on a number of counts. Procurement expertise is unevenly spread around purchasing organizations and this can lead, unintentionally, to problems in the process. It is perceived to be and often operates on an adversarial model, discouraging partnering and best value is often subsumed under cost cutting. It can advantage those with dedicated bid writers, strong and flexible infrastructures and those who have existing contracts and thus staffing capacity. By the same token it can disadvantage smaller organizations with no capacity to respond quickly in a fast moving environment. A range of procurement bases across a region produces duplication of contracts and a distinct lack of coordination and business planning.

A neutral bidding body would have the following characteristics:

- It would concentrate expertise both in the procurement process itself and in releasing purchasers to concentrate on contracting post-award of contract.
- It would be independent of the purchasers.
- It would have an inquisitorial approach to investigate bids – this would put the onus on the bidding agency itself to gather information and assess bids.
- It would allow smaller agencies to bid with some sense of a level playing field.
- Within procurement guidelines, encouragement to partnering could take place which would achieve an ancillary goal of supporting joined-up practices.
- It would support the appointment of *Partnership Development Workers* – working on both sides of the fence – brokering the language barriers – supporting the bidding process but independent of the organizations tendering.
- It would be cost neutral if agencies currently undertaking procurement merely rechannel the existing funds into setting up a single agency to undertake this task.

(Senior *et al.* 2005: 41–2)

Positioning is certainty occurring as a result of this emphasis on contestability and the role of the private sector and in contrast the attitude of the public sector may drive the commissioning process down a conflictual rather than a complementary route. Private sector companies need quick and big wins if they are to invest in the provision of community services and they can enter this field in partnership with the voluntary sector. The attitude of the public sector may be crucial. How far the Probation Service and the prisons have maintained good relationships with the VCS may dictate how far they find themselves in co-operation or in opposition to the private sector and the voluntary sector. New arrangements may well emerge borne out of secret affairs rather than open and transparent processes.

Performance management

The pressure to meet targets has perhaps most fundamentally altered the relationship between the VCS and the state. Traditionally, as we have described, the sector operated with the public sector, innovating and working in ways which, while close to grass roots community provision, were almost entirely driven by the needs of their consumers. In this climate innovative relationships between service users and the agencies can flourish. The ways in which the VCS have structured their work in the criminal justice sector implies a high degree of client-centred-ness and consensual engagement. A holistic approach to assessment was taken, which was more akin to a welfare-orientation to practice than a risk management approach. We noted in the study that the reluctance of many of the VCS agencies to engage in work where compliance was a feature seemed to encapsulate an important boundary. From a statutory sector perspective this feature emerged as a resistance to working in ways which suited their approach and targets and it was expressed as a reluctance to be accountable and submit to the rigours of audit. Some VCS organizations were willing to cross this boundary and operate under a public protection umbrella. While it could be argued that all work with offenders is focused on needs, this is often expressed in terms of risk management or a more limited concept of criminogenic need than that implied in assigning this term to the VCS.

The performance management culture, so much a central plank of modernisation, has begun to challenge those presuppositions about the relationship between the service user, the agency and the government. Indeed the term 'service user' almost seems inappropriate in the context of work with offenders. The VCS are required to account more to government than ever before. Some seem prepared to do this while others have a principled objection which makes change less palatable. The real dilemma is how far innovation can prosper in an environment where meeting centrally set targets governs what you provide, how you provide it and in what form. Maybe the risk of a performance management culture is a risk to the 'extra' which the VCS brings and what remains are sets of workers who are 'tupeed' between voluntary, private and public sector agencies as the contracts rotate.

Deconcentration and regionalization

Local delivery is often seen as self-evidently good and all general government statements support the needs of small organizations of which the VCS contains many. Their very localism is seen as a distinctive feature which attracts usage of their agencies for providing local programmes and support. However, even within the VCS we have seen tendencies for these agencies to grow and develop regional and national structures to cope with change. Those that remain a single agency in a single locality have had to fight for continued contracts where previously local contracting gives way to regionalization.

Regionalization of contracts has become a feature of the contracting regimes of prisons and under the regional offender managers the move to regionalization may develop even further. However, there is a potential synergy between these contrasting elements of modernisation which could benefit the VCS and particularly those large numbers of small organizations which thrive in local areas and whose organizational structure offers a distinctive and worthwhile service. Again the concept of partnership is relevant here.

In this section we draw on two pieces of research conducted in 2004 and 2007 which sought to evaluate a partnership project in North Wales known as the DAWN Partnership (Senior *et al.* 2004, 2007a) The background to this partnership acts as a potential example of future arrangements:

> Umbrella organisations, such as the DAWN partnership, have brought together a range of different agencies to provide a coordinated service. DAWN, brings together the leading substance misuse and offender rehabilitation agencies in order to provide rapid response, assessment and referral to an appropriate service provider dealing with a wide range of issues such as substance misuse, offending behaviour, relationships, housing, debt, family, health, training, self-esteem, education and employment issues. Such services aim to bridge the gap to enable people to move from inactivity to meaningful activity, and help people become better equipped to take advantage of opportunities within mainstream education and employment. However, partnership work aimed at assisting drug users is complex and not without many challenges, including relationship issues, resourcing, and conflicting philosophies, agendas and priorities (Buchanan and Carnwell 2005). The nature and context of partnerships will alter as funding and processes and procedures for new collaborative arrangements change. The development of the DAWN Partnership has taken place at a time of turmoil and change in the organisation of correctional services (Carter 2003). In some ways the DAWN Partnership is a model of a mixed economy of provision building on the strengths of different parts of the sector but in a context where commissioning and contestability regimes can stretch a commitment to partnership. It is important therefore for partnerships to be flexible, self-critical and open to independent evaluation.
>
> (Senior *et al.* 2007)

One pressure on this project beyond the perennial issues of resourcing was to expand to a pan-Wales arrangement, in other words expanding the reach of the organization from a North Wales focus to a focus on the whole of Wales. This is easier for some organizations within it who are structured on a pan-Wales basis than for others who are locally based. It is difficult for organizations who, though working within a national structure like the Probation Service, have local areas operating separately. Both evaluations have evidenced the value of this partnership in the delivery of resettlement services and the role of agencies of differing size and expertise working together to achieve its goals. If funders put a primacy on regional (in the case of Wales, national) contracts then the DAWN partnership will have difficult decisions to make, which could result in fragmentation of delivery in expansion and consolidation across the whole of Wales or in counter bids from organizations based in South Wales leaving it without business. The government's mixed messages hardly help such organizations to plan the future with any degree of certainty.

Audit and inspection

If the VCS is to become accepted as a key provider of services then it is vital that the internal organization can demonstrate that they meet benchmarks for their practice, thus being fit for purpose. But there are an increasing number of bureaucrats who require such accounting: ESF rules; the Criminal Justice Inspectorates; Adult Learning Inspectorates; LSCs and OLASS; and the National Treatment Agency, to name just a few. This can stretch the resources of big public sector agencies and certainly challenges the VCS, both small and large. Sometimes there will be costs to innovation and creativity in responding to bureaucratic needs as has been noticed in some ESF funding strands.

The VCS is anxious that its services are seen as professional, appropriate, quality assured and meeting national standards. But this has to be balanced, if it can be in such a managed culture, with the off-beat innovative practice which makes breakthroughs in the way offenders are dealt with and produces a new evidence-base to guide practice. The scales are currently heavily tipped towards audit, inspection and box ticking. The chances of innovation recede in this climate.

Penal populism and risk management

Voluntarism and punitive surveillance are uneasy bedfellows for the VCS. Often fashioned by grass roots, evangelical or visionary individuals who are seen to care for those who are disadvantaged, vulnerable or simply unable to cope with life, they offer a client-centred approach which fits with a welfare orientation to practice. This is the VCS central mission. This altruistic, often selfless concern with the needs of individuals makes the rules of engagement different. How then with this perspective and approach can the VCS engage with the penal populist climate of late modernity? The short answer is, with difficulty.

It takes courage and determination to continue to sponsor work with offenders when the climate is so negative. It is interesting to look at community safety initiatives to see that there is a relative lack of focus on offender needs and a much greater focus on public protection, crime and disorder, the needs of victims and local communities. Yet if the VCS is to engage effectively in this climate it has to be prepared to work within this punitive climate and to some extent recognize and work with the risk averse approaches of current practice concerns.

Again partnerships may help achieve this balancing act between care and control. In some respects, perhaps ironically, the VCS is closer to the 'advise, assist and befriend' mantra of traditional probation practice than the Probation Service itself. Thus, certainly with regard to much community provision, it has replaced those services which we would have associated with the Probation Service itself. It suggests two policy issues for the VCS that are at stake here. First, if you remove and reshape public sector provision for offenders, their welfare needs do not disappear through government fiat. Despite the focus on cognitive behaviour programmes as a panacea for reducing offending, progress is limited unless the welfare needs – accommodation, employment, education, health, advice, support for fractured relationships, drug and alcohol counselling – are supported. This is now much more likely to be done by the VCS than the Probation Service.

Second, it asks crucial questions about mission and perhaps the overarching influence of the global drivers of crime, this moves the VCS from its communitarian roots to a more direct engagement with the public protection and risk management agencies of the government. This is thus both a threat and an opportunity for the sector.

Pluralization

Achievement of changes in service delivery are predicated on an increasing range and diversity of skills in the workforce. Increasingly the silos of professional expertise, with separate training requiring a specific skill set, are seen to be inadequate to deliver the services required. This is producing shifts of responsibility on who does what and demands practitioners' skills which are, more specifically, accredited and benchmarked. This trend is noticeable in the training requirements of accredited programmes, in the provision of offender management for low and medium risk offenders, in delivering basic skills training, housing advice or drug counselling. Such important subsets of skills demand a more varied and flexible workforce to be prepared to deliver quality and robust services. This means distinct challenges to all the stakeholders in meeting these new professional development demands.

Funds within the VCS to support staff development is limited and there has, traditionally, been little formal training available. However, as part of the social contract implied in undertaking key roles for government, there has been a need to increase the skill sets of this sector through accreditation of agencies and the training of individuals. Occupational standards have developed for drug and alcohol provision, for mentoring, for housing support, for ETE, indeed for all major areas of welfare provision. The sheer variety of agencies now engaged in these tasks has led to the ever-increasing numbers of staff employed to work with offenders.

A traditional objection to greater involvement of the VCS by the statutory sector has been the perceived lack of professionalism allied to other fears. This was noted by Nellis, 'It feared job substitution – loss of jobs, loss of professionalism and a diminished service to offenders, delivered either by amateurs' in the voluntary sector or by profit seeking entrepreneurs in the private sector' (Nellis 2002: 357).

In Senior *et al.* (2005) this concern about VCS standards was echoed (Senior *et al.* 2005: 27–8). There is little doubt that such stereotypes are in retreat and this is testimony to the way in which all agencies have begun to appreciate and develop an inter-dependency which is built on good relations and positive engagement. However, it is important not to be complacent about the stability of these relations. There is a need to continue to challenge stereotypes which can undermine the professionalism of all agencies upon which they impact. The proliferation of new roles and new para-professionals is part of the pluralization of the workforce and supported by modernisation. It weakens professional control and autonomy and risks a dumbing down of provision. Although the professionalization of the VCS is to be welcomed it does make them a different organization to what they once were and without being simply nostalgic this could be seen just as more of a loss than a gain.

Joined-up justice

The NOMS changes, end to end offender management, contestability and a mixed economy of provision are predicated on joining up agencies in what government sees as a mutual endeavour to ensure good practice is developed. A recurrent theme of the previous sections has been the interpretation of partnership which conceptions of joining up evokes and this is particularly pertinent in considering the role of the VCS. The Senior *et al.* (2005) study focused centrally on the important issue of working in partnership. Despite being central to the concept and practice of joined-up justice, partnership was still viewed by some respondents with reluctance and anxiety. There were a number of features of this reluctance which related to size of contracts, problems of sharing work, statutory versus voluntary engagement and the length of time involved.

Partnership for the VCS is what might be termed an 'aerosol' word. It is sprayed onto contractual relationships to give it legitimacy and a positive image of mutual endeavour, shared control and level playing fields. The Senior *et al.* (2005) research shows that in the region under study there was no level playing field and that often what was described as partnership by the statutory providers was seen as a purchaser–provider relationship by the VCS (Senior *et al.* 2005: 36–9). There may be new opportunities if the structures being proposed and piloted through Parliament, at the time of writing, come to fruition. If traditional commissioners, such as probation and prison, become just providers then their need to be in partnership with the VCS and with the private sector will become more urgent. In those circumstances the bargaining power of the VCS may grow to ensure it achieves a partnership outcome which reflects rather more than just rhetorical commitment to joining up.

Responsibilization

Responsibilized communities are at the heart of the commitment to the VCS. It is seen as part of engaging communities in the resolution of its own problems and the Third Sector has been recruited to the cause of criminal justice through operationalizing such concepts. VCS often has a better climate of partnership with service user organizations, such as those responding to the needs of the BME sector or women offenders. The diversity of its provision could be focused in five main areas:

- Provision of needs-based services.

- Ability to offer advice, assistance, service delivery and support in specialist areas.
- Engaging faith-based provision to support the needs of a diverse offender population.
- Active promotion of services for BME and other minority groups.
- Peer-led support and mentoring services.

(Senior *et al.* 2007)

This carries with it some clear responsibilities for the VCS itself if it is to be looked upon as a major provider of these services. It must ensure it offers a professional and accountable service; a willingness to work with the statutory sector in fulfilling their duty to secure public protection; and an ability to adapt its culture of independence and voluntarism to the culture of statutory requirements while maintaining its accessibility to service users.

Permanence of paradox

Change for the VCS while occurring in an atmosphere of positive regard from government, nevertheless, produces key contradictions it has to encounter and be willing to overcome if it is really to become a major provider of statutory interventions under the developing correctional commissioning. Four are highlighted here.

Client-centred vs. government priorities

This issue splits the sector itself. There is no single response to this but clearly it exercises the way in which the future is welcomed or resisted. The fierce independence associated with the VCS is still very evident. It is of course stronger among those agencies who are buttressed by independent funds or charitable resources. This is a luxury which is denied many of the smaller more financially unstable agencies. Here survival can depend on a single new contract. Grant aiding in the past had been a secure and relatively risk-free way of investing in new services. This tradition has receded and is not a significant part of the funding streams today. The experience of European Social Fund processes typifies the modern approach to funding. Circumscribed areas are defined for support often with partnership requirements which can be onerous. Delivering such contracts takes an in-house bureaucracy which swallows resources and needs careful management. Successful outcomes are not guaranteed. As the work entailed in preparing a bid is immense but not costed into the provision, VCS resources can be stretched simply preparing bids sometimes with only limited chances of success. This may be a model which government commissioning will follow.

There are costs in time, resourcing, expertise, training and failure. But this may be manageable if the costs of becoming part of the state apparatus is justified. Paradoxically the government is attracted to the VCS because of its ability to innovate and provide high quality specialist, client-centred services, yet its modernising agenda may well sound the death knell to these features of the VCS.

VCS and private sector working together

If working on government contracts causes concern, then working alongside the private sector may challenge values even more. This is a difficult agenda and one where there is as much variety of response as there is co-ordinated solutions. The private sector has shown itself capable of prizing key voluntary sector staff into its ranks to give it the contacts within the sector to build partnerships. At the same time some VCSs have not resisted the overtures of private partners in developing key bids for contracts. Indeed a fundamental issue here lies in making the distinction between the two sectors so water tight. The increasing business culture of some of the leading VCS shows a way of operating that seeks to copy the best private business practices: its not-for-profit orientation becomes the key difference rather than the way it operates.

Creating a mixed economy of provision brings with it some of these fundamental contradictions for the sector. Although it has always been hard to talk of a single sector, as discussed at the opening of this chapter, this is even harder to sustain today. For instance, there are now examples of VCS working across new areas of business and in new geographical locations which does stretch the community 'bottom–up' orientation taken as an axiomatic feature of the VCS.

Welfare orientation vs. penal populism

A value-driven organization can find itself challenged by inclusion in the grand plan for crime and disorder. It would be interesting to see how far VCS organizations have modified their mission statements to appear in tune with the new emphasis on public protection, punitive punishment of offenders and a victim orientation. What is clear is that mission statements and detailed statements of purpose – a clear business plan – are features of the bigger organizations who need an external facing programme attractive to commissioners. The rhetoric of commitment to strengthening communities or supporting those excluded from participation or listening to service users is still liberally spread through such statements but in a context where they can demonstrate they can meet the needs of government. It is an uncomfortable compromise but one worth holding onto. The person-centred values and concern for those disadvantaged should not be put aside to meet the government imperative for punitive and exclusionary measures of penal policy. John Pratt notes, 'Manageralism provides no barrier to populism; instead, it simply provides a mechanism which allows criminal justice organizations to be carried along in its wake, as it redefines their tasks' (Pratt 2007: 134).

Partnership vs. competition

At the heart of the discussion, in the foregoing pages, is the importance of partnership in ensuring that VCS agencies, big and small, can survive and prosper into the twenty-first century. This has been shown to sit very uneasily with the push towards greater competition, particularly where procurement of services takes place on a wider regional or national basis. In the fight for survival the potential win–win of productive partnerships can be lost in the desire for institutional survival. This presents fundamental contradictions for this sector. There are three responses to this:

- To position for growth by ensuring it has the capacity to bid competitively against others.
- To position for partnership with other key providers from whichever sector is appropriate and plan for growth through the partnership (e.g., the DAWN Partnership, Senior *et al.* 2007).
- Transfer locus of activity to other areas of disadvantage less dependent upon acquiescing to the field of criminal justice to conditions, values and approaches which feel anathema to mission.

I suspect we are seeing all these positions and sometimes at the same time from the same agencies!

Conclusion

The VCS as a whole occupies a unique position in providing public services in comparison to the statutory sector. The responsibilities of the statutory sector combined with the guarantee of funding, at least relative to the VCS, gives it powerful control in decision making. Given the requirements upon them to meet targets, it is not surprising that in the past decade the correctional services have had a degree of control over procuring and contracting services. This was viewed by the VCS with frustration at best and hostility at worst. The procedures and protocols they were required to meet were frequently unfair and created endless problems in delivery. Most do not dispute the need for regulation and are as keen as the statutory sector to be seen as professional and competent in delivering their services. But put simply they did not believe that this is a level playing field and considered themselves very much the junior partner in the arrangements.

The focus on achieving targets has dominated public services discourse in recent years. The bargaining power of those agencies, like the VCS, working with the public sector can be, somewhat paradoxically, both weakened and strengthened within this strategy: weakened where their services are dependent on public sector funding but deemed by the latter or by their funders, as not an essential service to meet their targets, and strengthened where their control over a particular area of service delivery makes the public sector dependent upon them to meet key targets (e.g., some ETE provision and drugs counselling or voluntary hostel provision).

Modernisation has brought the VCS further into these debates and possibly through contestability created a more level playing field against the traditional purchasers of prison and probation. However, we have seen that modernisation offers no solution to threats to mission and direction and that while the VCS has much to gain in the current climate, it is not a warm and inviting climate but rather a hostile and punitive one in which the clash of values may mean going a step too far for many in the VCS.

Further reading

Elson, P. R. (2006) Tracking the implementation of voluntary sector/government policy agreements: is the voluntary and community sector in the frame? *The International Journal of Not-for-Profit Law* (August), 8(4).

Nellis, M. (2002) Probation, partnership and civil society, in D. Ward, J. Scott and M. Lacey (eds) *Probation: Working for Justice*. Oxford: Oxford University Press.

Senior, P., Meadows, L., Feasey, S. and Atkinson, J. (2005) *Enhancing the Role of the VCS Under NOMS: A Case Study of Yorkshire and Humberside*. London: Home Office.

Part Three

chapter ten

Conclusions and ways forward

In this book we have outlined a brief history of the ongoing reform of criminal justice policy and practice focusing specifically on modernisation (1) as a stage in socioeconomic development and modernisation (2) as a specific reform agenda. It was argued that modernisation is a variation and progression on the theme of NPM, which substituted the post-war settlement manifest in the form of the Keynesian welfare state. In other words, this account is just one chapter in a long and troubled history of social reform and global change.

Modernisation as described in the preceding pages is, at least at the time of writing, still an emerging and evolving political project belonging to three successive New Labour governments (1997–200?) and although the developments we have described will continue to evolve it is quite feasible that a new vocabulary will be developed if, for example, a Conservative government were to be elected in the next general election. Even if that occurs, the next government will have to work with ideas, structures and practices that have been, in part, determined by the New Labour legacy. In short, modernisation is a sequel to NPM and, in turn, modernisation is a prelude to a new discourse about reform. What this concluding chapter does is highlight the main features of the modernisation of the criminal justice sector as we see them, synthesizing some of the themes that have been addressed earlier on in this book.

There are three main elements to this conclusion beginning with a discussion of what we have termed the '*permanence of paradox*', paying close attention to the key dimensions of modernisation. The sheer diversity of responses to reform and change at the level of individual agencies and practices actually institutionalizes contradications and paradox. What Stan Cohen remarked on over two decades ago remains germane:

> Consequences so different from intentions; policies carried out for reasons opposite to their stated ideologies; the same ideologies supporting quite different policies; the same policy supported for quite different ideological reasons.
>
> (Cohen 1985: 158)

Some of the most pertinent developments occurring with regard to the police, courts, correctional agencies, youth justice, voluntary and community sector and crime reduction partnerships are teased out in order that some general observations can be made. It is shown that modernisation is a political project, implemented as a result of political choices and the application of political agency. Modernisation impacts in innumerable ways in relation to different agencies and also increasingly in terms of the interaction of agencies that are only seemingly independent and autonomous of each other. More than that, it is shown that each of the aforementioned agencies have very different orientations to the modernisation agenda, which in turn influence what the architects of future change can plan and the political tactics they need to do this. In the second section we reflect on the Anglo-centric bias of the materials covered in the text, largely the result of the lack of published materials focusing on the themes covered by us here. It is suggested that it would be timely for the model developed here to be tested in other jurisdictions in order to ascertain the main drivers behind criminal justice reform across Europe, South-East Asia, Australasia and the United States. It is not possible to do justice to this in a book of this size given the conceptual and methodological difficulties of doing comparative research. At a more basic level criminal justice is not studied with the same degree of interest in some other parts of the world, especially in counties, such as Hong Kong, China, Japan, India, and many countries throughout Africa. Nonetheless an attempt is made to anticipate some of the possible characteristics of modernisation in different parts of the world. The third and final part engages in some futurology, attempting to anticipate some of the challenges and opportunities facing the modernisers – or, in plainer English, reformers – of an ever diversifying and fragmenting criminal justice sector.

The key dimensions of modernisation: some emergent and evolving themes

An important feature of modernisation striking us while producing this book is the sheer complexity of modernisation in agency specific contexts, but especially when the focus is on partnerships. The intricacies of this reform programme can sometimes seem overwhelming, nevertheless there are some discernible patterns and it is to these that we now turn.

Mixed economy

This political rationality grew out of the emphasis on privatization belonging to the key principles of the NPM, although New Labour distanced itself from any explicit agenda where private sector involvement was regarded as better than public provision. The mixed economy of provision presents an opportunity for a range of agencies to provide services and, at least on paper, there is no attempt to say that one provider is superior to another. New Labour effectively created an open market in the criminal justice policymaking process, although this market operated in different ways in relation to each of the different agencies. Having said that our observations have suggested there are two discernible broad developments, which we term *segmentation* and *regulated choice*. These changes, like many others, are presented as politically neutral although it would appear that in some instances there is the mobilisation of bias rendering some agencies either more reform vulnerable or reform resistant. In other words, there is the selective application of the principles of a mixed economy of service provision.

Taking the latter first, *regulated choice* affects the corrections agencies, the voluntary and community sector and youth justice. In essence, these players are in the business of providing rather similar services involving a variety of support and treatment services, such as drug and alcohol counselling, housing support, education, employment and training, mentoring, offending behaviour programmes, mental health services, and so on. Rather than this service being delivered as a matter of course by the public sector the service can in principle be delivered by any of the agencies. Thus there is competition over who is to take responsibility for particular forms of service provision. Although this method was introduced as a substitute for privatization there are some services which are overwhelmingly provided by the private sector, such as electronic monitoring and prison escorting. In some instances, public sector agencies may not be fundamentally opposed to such choices. The original engagement of the private sector in such work was a direct result of the unwillingness of the public sector to take on certain tasks – electronic monitoring, prison escorting, secure training centres – although on other occasions it may be seen as an attempt to undermine and dilute their organizational integrity. We can note here, for example, the way in which the traditional support roles of probation through officers themselves or through their own corps of volunteers is now the province of a range of voluntary agencies delivering mentoring programmes.

Other criminal justice agencies, including the police, the courts and crime and disorder partnerships are affected by a rather different process, labelled as *segmentation*. This refers to those tasks that an agency may contract out but this occurs not as a result of explicit governmental pressure but more as a consequence of decisions taken by the agencies themselves. In the courts, for example, the activities undertaken to reduce delays may be undertaken by nonpublicly funded officials. A more concrete example is the Police Service where many policing roles and responsibilities – including crime prevention/reduction and peacekeeping – are farmed out to companies in the private sector. The expansion of a night time economy is an example par excellence of how the alcohol and drug induced violence spilling out onto the streets of town and city centres at weekends is regulated by bouncers. The policing of this crime problem is typically carried out quite satisfactorily by private security firms, although the police are still there if required. A more striking example is the gated communities, modelled on those found in American cities, such as Los Angeles, which are being erected in some parts of London and Manchester and other Western European cities. These are protected by privately employed security guards, complementing state provided police.

A paradoxical feature of the mixed economy is that it is applied selectively and there does not appear to be an explicit and coherent rationale underlying this selectivity. The justification for appealing to the logic of *segmentation* or *regulated choice* is not clear, although a unitary feature of both these trends is that the public sector is no longer seen as the sole provider of services.

However, the outcome is uneven and impacts in markedly different ways on the key stakeholders in criminal justice administration.

The next section examines the theme of competition in the field of criminal justice, namely contestability.

Contestability

This is an idea that has its origins in economics but it is one that has been introduced into criminal justice discourse with considerable alacrity, although rather like the mixed economy its impact has been rather uneven. In Chapter 5 it was noted that Martin Narey, in his former capacity as head of Correctional Services, described contestability as a mechanism that may be used to raise the standard and quality of services by opening up major areas of work for competition. Functions and roles typically carried out by state agencies could also be delivered by the private and voluntary and community sectors. It signalled the end of a state monopoly over crime and public policy. The government perceived it as a mechanism that would enable change, particularly raising standards of performance, although crucially any changes that could occur were not politically driven. New Labour government ministers were keen to assert that in contrast to their Conservative antecedents, they were not concerned with privatizing public sector provision *per se*. Furthermore, they were not interested in who delivered a particular service: the relationship between supply and demand was left to key decision takers making choices. In essence contestability builds on some NPM values, in particular market testing and marketization, although less attention is directed towards discrediting the public sector. The public sector is seen simply as another provider alongside private and voluntary bodies. Rather like the mixed economy, contestability has not impacted upon all agencies in the same way, the idea was being particularly promoted at the time of the Carter Report (2003), a document focusing most on the NOMS and the functions of the correctional agencies. Despite attempts by civil servants and politicians to present contestability as a benign development it did result in a sense of vulnerability and insecurity among senior officials in the Prison and Probation Services. In the case of probation, the presence of private and VCS players competing for a contract to provide community-based sentences, for instance, could throw the organization into a sense of crisis. Thus the negative impact of contestability was felt most by the National Probation Service, which throughout the history of recent criminal justice reform has been repeatedly exposed as vulnerable. In contrast, the private sector and VCS see this as a new set of opportunities for business that hitherto did not exist although, in the case of the latter as it has been outlined in Chapter 9, this could turn out to be a poisoned chalice, particularly for some of the smaller organizations.

The police and courts are both in a position of strength regarding contestability. Similarly the crime and disorder reduction partnerships have not been involved in competitive bidding and act more as commissioners themselves. It would appear that the police and local authorities occupy a relatively powerful position which, while not making them immune to such influences, certainly equips them with a higher degree of bargaining power.

The case of contestability shows quite clearly the commitment of modernisers to improving the standard and quality of criminal justice products, in itself a laudable aim and not one that would attract too much opposition from any reasonably minded person. This observation does not hold, though, if we acknowledge that its application has been rather selective. Paradoxically, this political decision to enforce contestability in the correctional services has culminated in a situation where probation managers have nothing whatsoever to gain, apart from an impending sense of crisis. Meanwhile, commercial outfits and VCS agencies are in a position to grasp sometimes quite lucrative opportunities. In the last analysis, then, contestability is a vehicle for enhancing the roles of the private and voluntary sectors at the expense of the public sector. Answers about any questions concerning the extent to which this was the desired outcome of the modernisers are not found here, although it would be naive to assume that this course is politically neutral.

The politicization of crime and public policy had already become manifest as part of the culture of performance management, initially engendered as part of the neo-liberal-led NPM, and progressed further as part of New Labour's modernisation strategy.

Performance management

Throughout this book, it has been shown that every agency involved in the field of criminal justice has been deeply affected by this political rationality. The importance of targeting, outputs and outcomes, measuring quality and standards, is necessarily in the thoughts and deeds of all managers and many practitioners. Almost 30 years ago the idea that such principles could be applied in the public sector were widely seen to be anathema, contradicting the core values held by the personnel it employed. As such the performance culture was imposed on agencies and any resistance was met with criticism and censure in the 1980s and 1990s. Nowadays the need to demonstrate effectiveness, efficiency and economy in service delivery is generally accepted and where there is not commitment, compliance certainly exists.

There are several paradoxes which become evident when evaluating the thinking behind performance management. These can be split into three broad categories, although the general problem of 'what gets measured, gets done' is always behind the scenes influencing the behaviour of professionals. First, are the targets devised to measure performance the right ones and are they actually meaningful? If we take as an example the target of reducing delay in the courts, the aim was to cut the amount of time it took to process a case through the prosecution process right up until sentencing. Even if the waiting time is shortened, what does this actually mean? Does it have any bearing on important matters, such as fairness and justice or sentencing outcomes? The performance of prison and probation activities all too frequently involves practitioners ticking boxes to demonstrate their effectiveness and in doing this they are not measuring other more qualitative aspects of particular activities.

Second, the performance culture has, in numerous instances, created a conflict between different targets precisely because there are so many multiple and competing 'centres of calculation' (Rose and Miller 1992).

Third, there may be conflict between the targets set for different agencies. Chapter 5 focused on partnership working and showed, for example, that rather than there being inter-agency working many partnerships are simply multi-agency and that they are not working in unison towards the same aims and objectives. More fundamentally, correctional agencies may be delivering programmes that are intended to reduce reoffending yet their performance will be assessed according to various criteria. However, their efforts may not be matched by other social agencies who may cancel out their hard work. To take another example, as part of a resettlement strategy there may be targets relating to rehabilitation but the targets may be agency specific. Obviously, the incentives to attain organizationally specific goals are going to be stronger. This has been particularly enforced in recent years by the added sanction of cash penalties for failure to meet key targets.

The ultimate paradox is that this is a game which agencies cannot afford to ignore. Dependent on budget allocations, and in some cases their continued existence, no matter how irrelevant a target appears to those working directly on the ground, agencies run a great risk in ignoring the paper chase and functioning idiosyncratically if creatively rather than in a more considered, evidence-based way. In the case of the VCS the very values which government purport to covet – innovation, community and client-centredness, creativity and ground breaking approaches – will be compromised in the rush to seek public money and achieve externally imposed targets.

Audit and inspection

This is also an element of the accountancy culture, mentioned above, which forms part of the actuarial approach to justice so prevalent today. As part of the NPM all public sector bodies were exposed to the rigours of audit. The key criminal justice agencies have been subject to audit for many years, illustrated by the existence of the Audit Commission and of the service inspectorates. The inspectorates of police, probation and prisons have all been beefed up over the last few decades and they are in a position to impose sanctions against under-performing agencies. The private and VCS sectors are not immune to audits (e.g., the Adult Learning Inspectorates) as well as the criminal justice inspectorates. Everywhere agencies are being inspected and called to account for failing to deliver on what they promised.

Audit and inspection may paradoxically inculcate a sense of defensiveness among agencies because the activity of auditing is very much about checking that an agency has done what it is supposed to have done. An individual may be committed to the raison d'être underpinning auditing and comply with its requirements, yet a fear of mistakes and errors may sometimes lead to duplicitous behaviour. In this kind of increasingly litigious atmosphere it would not be surprising if officials from time to time covered their tracks. This can be evidenced with reference to the publication of various inquiries (Macpherson 1999; Laming 2003; Bichard 2004; to name but a few) which uncovered various actions that were not audited because auditors and inspectors were looking for different things to measure. Rather these inquiries show that the actions of police officers, for instance, may not be necessarily based on the correct professional judgements.

There are contradictions at the heart of the auditing culture, however, mainly because the focus is on practices and processes that are auditable. It is a culture that is not well attuned to the more messy reality of what is fundamentally a people-based service. The sometimes disorganized and chaotic lives of offenders and their experiences of criminal justice are not always readily quantifiable, raising questions about the appropriateness of this as a method of modernisation.

There has also been a fundamental mismanagement of the ways in which auditing can be routinely assessed and managed. The introduction of management information systems at great expense, representing another function for the private sector, has continued apace (Bellamy and Taylor 1998). We have had LIBRA, CREST, SCOPE, CRAMS, NOMIS and NIMS, to name just a few. Some have been expensive failures and the multi-million case management system in probation, CRAMS, is a notable casualty of this process. There may be something more fundamental here about the nature of IT systems and their somewhat under-theorized relationship with knowledge management, especially the distinction between data, information and knowledge. As Meadows and Senior put it:

> Knowledge Management is about much more than an IT system, it requires that organisations create cultures that support knowledge sharing and knowledge creating behaviours, that they embed these in their processes and where appropriate use IT to facilitate this.
>
> (Meadows and Senior 2006: 6)

Under New Labour's governance, a wealth of data (i.e., information) has been amassed where the purposes of collecting these data are not clearly articulated or where the uses of the data are not established before the system has been introduced. This is contrasted with the approach shaped by knowledge management considerations under which the new NOMIS system for offender management seems to have been constructed, which would see IT systems as the servant of the audit process not the driver. Unless organizations clearly know what data they require, how they want the information presented, and crucially have individuals who can use that information correctly then problems will ensue.

Deconcentration and regionalization

An often overlooked aspect of modernisation that interestingly reveals some contradictions at its heart is the multiple locations for decision making, where decisions are seemingly made at the same time, and in considerable tension, on a local, regional and national level.

This spatial dimension of modernisation exposes many of its internal contradictions, which it shares with NPM. In very simple terms, over the last few years the relationship between central and local government has been changed. This is a trend that is very evident in some areas of criminal justice. Deconcentration has affected all agencies in the sense that more and more responsibility for service provision is being handed down to officials at a local level. On the surface it would appear that local players have more authority, but such a view distorts the reality of the situation inasmuch as central government still sets targets that inform the activities of local agencies. Taking the example of Basic Command Units (BCUs) in policing, their strategies are required to reflect Home Office strategic plans and targets and Youth Offending Services are directed by the edicts emanating from the YJB.

There are also discernible effects resulting from regionalization, especially the confusion it has created in some instances regarding central and local relations. For example, regional offender managers (ROMs), working on behalf of NOMS, are to be the commissioning agents for service delivery of correctional services across each region. The details of this process are only just emerging (NOMS 2007). Other agencies do not have a regional presence, though, and in the domain of youth justice there is no effective regional presence. Youth Offending Teams (YOTs), for example, are attached to crime and disorder reduction partnerships at a local level. The government is committed to regionalization and seeks to steer, regionally, through the government offices. The power of these tracking servants is largely limited but they can open the doors to funding opportunities while also reminding local providers of central government responsibilities. Regionalization has met resistance in some quarters, most notably from the Police Service which in 2006 successfully opposed the amalgamation of the 42 forces of England and Wales into a smaller number of regional forces. If the police had accepted this proposal, the impact on the rest of the sector would have been massive.

An appreciation of spatiality and its relevance for modernisation can also be found if we consider the global threat of terrorism whereby national, centralized agencies, such as the Serious and Organized Crime Agency (SOCA) (formerly the NCS and NCIS) are assuming responsibility for managing the terrorist threat, which also involves the sharing of information with police forces and the security services in geographically vulnerable areas.

Penal populism and risk management

A topic that has global resonance is that of penal populism and risk management. New Labour's aspiration to modernise the body politic is characterized by ambivalence in many ways, although this aspect is a good example. Since the mid-1990s the government and policymakers have tended to conflate penal populism and risk management, although they are not necessarily part of the same thing. Penal populism has been in existence at least since 1979 with the Conservative party's law and order campaign resulting in a successful election victory. Public clamour for harsher punishments has met a positive response from politicians and sentencers, and sections of the Police Service. This is in spite of some evidence that the public are not as punitive as government and the media might claim they are, and certainly the relationship is rather more complex than the populist redtops and hawkish ministers contend (Roberts and Hough 2002). It is only necessary to look briefly at the rise of the number of people imprisoned in England and Wales to see that penal populism is thriving.

The practice of risk management is far from new where practitioners assess who is and who is not likely to offend at a particular time and in a particular place. Such judgements are an integral element of any practitioner's occupational repertoire and are based on knowledge accrued over many years of practical experience. It was taken-for-granted that any individual only had finite knowledge of risk and that mistakes could be made. In the current climate, risk evaluation has been elevated to the status of a science: something that is technical and there to produce apolitical and neutral knowledge.

Paradoxically, an increasingly punitive public sees risk management as a method of eliminating risk. This is presented as the production of lists for identifying offenders posing different degrees of risk and the convening of various panels to manage their assorted degrees of dangerousness. This has created a perception of public protection which feeds unrealistic and unrealizable expectations in the public. It is not possible to dispose of risk altogether and risk management is far from foolproof. The situation is that risk is not a neutral category, rather it is shaped by factors such as penal populism. Offender groups are targeted because of the perceived risks they represent. For example, sex offenders have been in the population since time immemorial although it took the moral panic about paedophilia, the legislative response of the Sex Offenders Act (1997) and the creation of MAPPAs to articulate an official discourse about the criminogenic risks posed by this group of offenders. Under the conditions of penal populism other groups could be identified and labelled as posing a risk. Risk management has, in Barbara's Hudson's terms, in this jurisdiction at least, become 'risk control' (Hudson 2003: 60–7).

This particular issue is certainly an important theme for future research. In jurisdictions which have a less punitive ethos about crime and offending the key question would be, can approaches to risk management and the ways the tools may be used produce a positive way to support a more inclusive approach to crime and punishment? We can go back to juvenile justice in the 1980s to see a systems approach clearly contributing to a reduction in custody. Bell and Haines (1991) make a related point when they state:

> Systems management of itself is a value free management tool that says nothing about the aims of intervention. But it is the linking of systems management with the critique of welfarism and the over-use of custody which creates such a powerful mixture.
>
> (Bell and Haines 1991: 121)

Pluralization

New Labour modernisers have created opportunities for a range of new players and stakeholders, as well as the expansion of the VCS and private sectors in the so-called crime reduction industry. In addition, the core players in criminal justice are being transformed by the deprofessionalization of their status. There has effectively been 'downward hierarchical theft' where the roles and responsibilities of criminal justice professionals are being handed down to those whom professional groups perceive to be relatively under-qualified or unqualified and inexperienced people. In the Police Service, there has been the introduction of the police community support officers (PCSOs) to perform a patrol function. These officers, dubbed 'scarecrows' in one evaluation (Crawford *et al.* 2005), do not have the full powers enjoyed by fully sworn in police officers and are seen as providing 'policing on the cheap' by some critics as well as by some police officers. In the Probation Service the introduction of probation service officers (PSOs) has brought about a deskilling of probation mirrored by the employment of unqualified youth justice workers. Similar developments are afoot in the legal professions.

As always paradoxical features are evident. Alongside deprofessionalization there have been attempts to professionalize the lay magistracy, indicating a flexibility in approach on who delivers what in criminal justice. Pushed to achieve efficiency in the court system while simultaneously weakening the power of the magistracy, moves are being made stealthily to replace the lay magistracy with district judges and to increase the underpinning training of the lay magistrate at the same time. A similar process can be seen within the voluntary and community sector where there has been the accreditation of agencies to deliver programmes on behalf of the government – offending behaviour programmes, ETE provision, Basic Skills work and so on – have produced moves to professionalize this sector.

Deprofessionalization has impacted on training and staff development. The so-called 'Rolls Royce' training of probation officers has produced, according to all assessments, a high quality fit for purpose training regime.

This model could be adapted to the needs of the different sectors but as we have seen previously, youth justice has gone down its own somewhat idiosyncratic approach and the police and prisons have continued a 'silo' approach to training. Maybe the government simply has not understood clearly the advantages of the control a command over training structures could bring them. By circumscribing the training regimes, and in the case of some services delivering training specific only to delivery of particular programmes, central control can be enhanced over the culture and operation of local services. Training and education is under-theorized as a way of inculcating centralized values in a managed system such as the one discussed here. The role of training in other jurisdictions may, in the medium-term, help us to understand the impact of this feature on all professionalized delivery agents.

Joined-up justice

This dimension perhaps best defines contemporary modernisation, although it is not without perplexing complications. Unlike their Conservative predecessors New Labour actively supported the idea of partnership and joined-up working, bringing together the work of different government departments. Crime and disorder would only be dealt with as part of a package of reforms oriented towards education and training, improved health, adequate housing, and so on. Rather than treating crime in isolation and as something requiring an exclusively criminal justice stratagem, the welfare state as a whole was incorporated into an inter-agency network. Added to this would be the energy and commitment of the private, voluntary and community sectors, as well as citizens. It was demonstrated in some detail, in Chapter 6, that New Labour's commitment to tackling the multiple forms and causes of social exclusion constituted the bedrock of its approach to crime and public policy. The partnership framework established by the Crime and Disorder Act (1998) is often cited as the main driver of joined-up justice and its achievements are unquestioned. Attempts elsewhere have been made to reform criminal justice by joining up its activities through reducing delays from the point of arrest to sentencing. There have also been attempts to create seamless sentencing purportedly to increase effectiveness and efficiency – the central mantra of the Carter (2003) vision, end to end offender management.

Unfortunately there are some anomalies which have prevented joined-up thinking, and policy and practice. CDRPs have effectively been dominated by the police and local authorities and, more crucially, a crime reduction agenda has overshadowed the emphasis on community safety. Related to this point, the relationship between crime reduction work and wider social policy initiatives (e.g., attempts to create a more inclusive society) are contradictory. Punitive populism involves increasingly tough minded public attitudes to offenders to the extent that rather than creating more socially inclusive communities the outcome is communities where intolerance of young people, sex offenders and various minority ethnic groups creates new forms of exclusion. The criminalization of the incivilities making up anti-social behaviour displayed by groups of marginalized young people is a prime example. Rather than understanding the difficulties of growing up as a young person in modern Britain, the response is the demonization and vilification of young people. Finally, and quite tragically, this element of modernisation is likely to result in under-achievement and lost opportunities because other components of modernisation are diametrically opposed to genuine, joined-up partnership working. All agencies involved in criminal justice matters have their own agency specific agendas and priorities. Joined-up working is something that is promoted but it is not necessarily an outcome that is measured as part of a mixed economy of provision. Audit and inspection, an interest in performance management and pluralization do not harbour creative inter-agency thinking and practice. Rather, organizational objectives and priorities take precedence due to what Smith (1995) refers to as 'suboptimization', and partnership is just another job that may or may not get done.

The complexity of joined-up working is further illustrated when the criminal justice agencies themselves need the influence and impact of other social agencies to achieve its own goals. Attempts in early 2002–3 to develop thoroughgoing resettlement strategies demonstrates just how many agencies, in and around criminal justice but located in health, welfare or education, need to work together, pursuing joint goals, to achieve meaningful change. The diagram, drawing on work in developing a regional strategy in Yorkshire and Humberside (Senior 2002, 2003a, b; Senior *et al.* 2005) below neatly illustrates this complexity.

This dilemma can be explained in more detail by widening the debate to consider the last, but not least, dimension of modernisation: responsibilization.

Responsibilization

This has proven to be an influential idea in criminological thought and its significance for understanding modernisation cannot be understated. Most of the writing on this subject has analysed changing configurations of crime policy, especially the movement of sovereign states away from its control and direction. Responsibilization has brought about greater responsibility among statutory, voluntary and private agencies, as well as private citizens, for crime reduction. The central state has created a new mode of governance where it governs at a distance, interfering only when responsibilized citizens and agencies fail in their duties. The inherent contradictions of this approach have been well documented yet there is another paradox relating to an important group of individuals who are rarely talked about in discourses on responsibilization: the offenders.

A task force set up by Clinks on user involvement in helping other

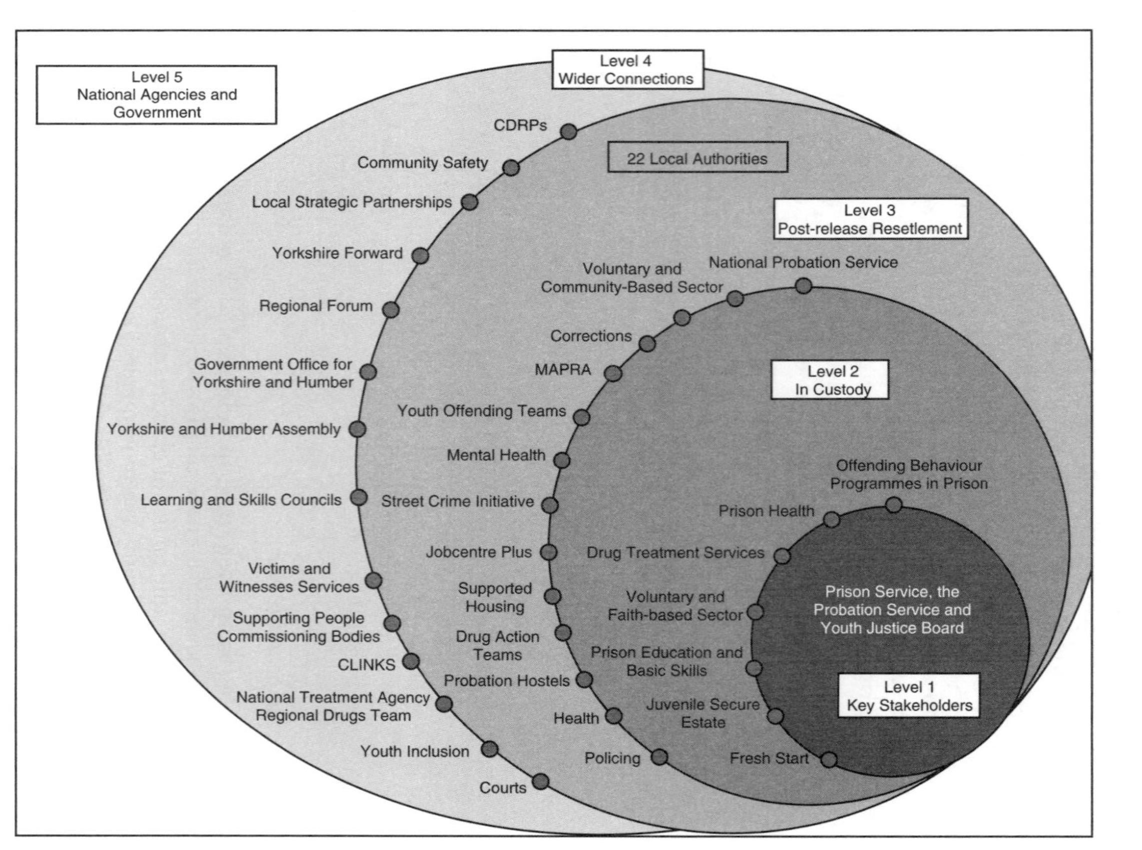

Figure 10.1 The complexity of a joined-up approach between criminal justice agencies

offenders was launched in 2007. The chair of this organization, Rob Allen, was quoted in *The Guardian* as saying that:

> Offenders currently have little influence in terms of their care and rehabilitation. But research suggests seeing offenders as active participants in their rehabilitation could lead to a reduction in reoffending.
>
> (Gaines 2007)

The notion of the responsibilized offender refers to ex-offenders who are able to play a part in helping other offenders to overcome the troubles they experience by drawing on their past knowledge and personal experiences. It could be argued that a truly responsibilized community would engage more with such offenders rather than endorsing penal populism and risk management. Instead of plugging crime reduction initiatives, such as target hardening, the use of CCTV and pandering to a victim-led criminal justice system, which all serve to exclude offenders, there are alternatives. Such protective strategies on their own all enhance the risk of social exclusion for the very population to which the goals of crime reduction are ultimately targeted (Young 1999). Effective crime reduction which is socially inclusive and genuinely restorative cannot ignore this dimension. Unfortunately responsibilitization for New Labour is twinned with rights, whereas those who offend, are anti-social or otherwise cause trouble to communities lose those rights and are at risk of exclusion through some of the mechanisms already discussed.

A key theme running throughout this book is that cognizance of the uneven, unwieldy and contradictory impact of the different dimensions of modernisation on each criminal justice agency is essential. Each dimension will resonate in different ways with some being more influential at particular times and in particular places. All that we can realistically aspire to do is to tease out some of the most readily discernible patterns. It has been argued that reform in general and modernisation in particular are influenced by the political tactics that are used to drive it forward and the reform orientation of particular agencies either as autonomous entities or in the context of a partnership.

We now briefly turn to consider two important mechanisms underlying modernisation and discussed in detail in Part One: political tactics and, in particular, the tactics of censure, compliance and commitment, and reform orientation with three component orientations – vulnerability, resistance and transformation.

Political tactics

Towards the end of the post-Second World War settlement, which met its demise with the ascendancy of the New Right and neo-liberalism from the late 1970s onwards, is a truism that the welfare state and public policy was cast into a crisis: an over-bureaucratic set of institutions was deemed to be ineffective, inefficient and perversely contributing to its own failure. The reforms to public and crime policy commencing in 1979 have been characterized as NPM.

Initially it was shown that public sector agencies were exposed to censure and coercion to encourage more effectiveness, efficiency and economy. This unpalatable approach was not widely accepted and the Thatcher reforms were met with largely ineffectual resistance. From the late 1980s and into the early 1990s, the Police and Probation Services were castigated for their perceived under-performance and failure to deliver their core services. This was an especially painful experience for the police who had given their support to the Conservatives, partly to secure them an election victory on the basis of a law and order vote and in their suppression of various 'enemies within' in the inner cities and mining communities. The disciplines applied in the Health and Social Services were transposed onto the criminal justice sector and greater parsimony became a defining feature. The inspectorates were given more power and authority to improve performance and to impose sanctions where failure was audited. The tactic of censure was time limited and gradually agencies began to comply to the new arrangements associated first with NPM and later with modernisation. The threat of censure (Sumner 1990) rather like an iron fist in a velvet glove (Clarke and Newman 1997) was still there, but compliance was the most effective mechanism.

Under New Labour and with the materialization of new players who were amenable to a modernising framework, there has gradually been more commitment. This in part can be attributed to the arrival of the VCS and private sector on the scene who were given a chance for new business that had previously been monopolized by the public sector. Their willingness to participate in the modernisation project compelled statutory agencies to get their act together to avoid being pushed out of the equation, an attitude and response seen nowhere better than in the Prison Service whose organization against further privatization has, however temporally, derailed that agenda in 2007.

The political tactics, referred to above, are quite clearly relational and they necessarily encounter the reform orientation of each agency.

Reform orientation

Over the last 30 years or so each agency has taken on various guises, appearing vulnerable at one time and resistant at another. The orientation of a particular agency is also related to other agencies and can result in fundamental reorientation. Over the years the Police Service has been subjected to numerous attempts to reform its structure and operation. The latter was resisted in the mid-1990s and in more recent times attempts to reduce the number of forces was actively and successfully resisted. The courts, who rather like the police, are shielded from certain reforms because of their legal independence, are in a position to resist fundamental change. The Probation Service has been shown to be particularly vulnerable with its mission being changed at regular intervals and with its current fragile status as the future of NOMS being decided. The Probation Service has rarely been able to muster resistance and its deprofessionalization is further weakening its power and status. The private, voluntary and community sectors are more willing to embrace the modernisation agenda and are reform transformative, not only in terms of their inner workings, but their commitment to reform has necessitated adaptation from public sector agencies. Interestingly the crime and disorder reduction partnerships are in principle more open to new ways of working – especially joined-up approaches – but, paradoxically, in practice the rhetoric of partnership is not always borne out. In actual fact, the police and local authorities end up shoring up their own position making their core activities yet more resistant to reform.

Now that the key dimensions of modernisation covered in this book have been rehearsed, it is necessary to briefly reflect on the salience of our analysis for understanding similar developments in other jurisdictions.

Modernising criminal justice: lessons to be learnt for an international analysis

This book admittedly is heavily Anglocentric in tone. It is customary in many texts nowadays to add a chapter looking at international developments. In a book of this size, it is not feasible to cover other jurisdictions in other parts of the world although some of the theoretical examples used are drawn from the American and Australian literature. It is possible for students to be introduced to comparative criminology later on in their course where they can compare criminal justice policy and practice across the world. However, this is a specialist subject and is not normally studied at an introductory level. Having said this, many of the ideas (e.g., risk, responsibilization) and theoretical debates are of universal significance and relevant in whatever part of the world the reader is based.

The work of Lacey (2003) is instrumental in encouraging one to acknowledge how the politics of criminal justice systems are so diverse when considering a range of countries. In terms of developing a comparative perspective at the global level of analysis, for instance, one would expect to see a marked difference between the kind of modernisation agendas being pursued across the western world in comparison with the type of governance being exerted in criminal justice contexts across the so-called 'developing countries'. In taking a global perspective, it is immediately apparent that some countries are more heavily industrialized than others. Those, like the UK and the US who have reached the stage of post-industrialization whereby post-Fordist modes of industrial production predominate, are likely to have different modes of governance being exerted over their criminal justice systems than countries that constitute cases of what might be termed peripheral capitalism. At the macro level, it is precisely because countries are at different stages of capitalist development or under-development that many developing countries simply will not have reached the stage where the modernisation agenda is being pursued as a political reform process. Some parts of Africa and the developing world, moreover, have not reached the stage whereby what we have referred to as the NPM has been developed. In the case of South Africa, for instance, according to van Zyl Smit and van der Spuy (2004) it was only after 1997 that new managerial policies, such as 'policing by objectives' and performance indicators, were introduced in a policing context, well after they had been introduced in the UK context and at a time when the UK was moving from a managerial to a more modernist mode of public sector and criminal justice governance.

When comparing Britain with the rest of Europe there are dangers in making the assumption that modernisation processes have been applied uniformly across different EU countries. This is largely because the political elites in some countries are keener than others to push the notion that political intervention is largely ineffective due to the increasingly globalized world which we inhabit. With reference to the work of Jospin (1998), Newman (2001: 49) argues that, 'Jospin suggests that the modernisation process in the UK is more "globalised" than that of other European nations, is less willing to take on the role of an active state, and is less willing to regulate capitalist economic processes'.

Even when comparing countries outside of Europe, which could be characterized as being at the stage of advanced capitalism or late modernity, there are inherent dangers in assuming simple policy transfer in terms of a modernisation agenda in the criminal justice context. According to Jones and Newburn (2004: 123), writers such as Christie (2000) and Garland (2000) are keen to emphasize their view that, 'fundamental shifts in economic and social structures and changes in cultural sensibilities have led political actors to adopt similar forms of penal response'. Jones and Newburn (2004) argue that to over-emphasize the continuities between countries is to run the risk of ignoring substantive differences in modernisation policies and practices. In the policing context, they challenge the assumption that Britain has followed the US example in recent years in relation to the adoption of policies, such as 'zero-tolerance' and 'Compstat'. The reality is, however, far more complex, with Jones and Newburn (2004) noting that in many cases what appears to have been transferred is illusory, remaining at the level of discourse. In reality actual policies and practices often remain markedly different in substantive terms.

One can say, however, that with a relative degree of certainty, the commercialization of crime control has had some kind of global impact. With specific reference to the phenomenal growth of CCTV, Karstedt (2004: 19) makes the point that, 'We find practices, strategies and technologies of crime prevention travelling around the globe'. With reference to the work of Braithwaite (2000), this same author makes the point that pluralization within criminal justice sectors has occurred to a degree in the global context. Karstedt (2004) adds that, 'Private policing has risen to or even overtaken the number of public police nearly everywhere' (2004: 19). On the other hand, strategies of responsibilization, which are becoming increasingly common in the UK criminal justice context are still the exception in other countries like Germany. According to Karstedt (2004) this is precisely because the notion of 'volunteerism' has sinister overtones in a political culture attempting to eradicate the collective, historical memory of a totalitarian regime.

The next section moves on from discussing the inherent epistemological problems of attempting to develop a neat, all encompassing, international model of modernisation. An attempt to explore the futures of modernisation is made.

The futures of modernisation

Futurology

The language used by criminologists alters over time and concepts, rather like fashion alter too. Concepts will be revived and there will be variations on old themes, but in the twenty-first century world absolute innovation seldom occurs in the social sciences. The concept of modernisation is no exception to this rule, though there is one certainty: criminal justice policy and practice will be changed and reformed for as long as there is crime and disorder and a systematic attempt being made to address it. Beyond this conviction there is little that we can be sure about although an attempt is made to consider some of the directions where change and reform will occur across the criminal justice sector. First, some comments are made about the future of the drivers of global crime because these will have a bearing on the capacity of governments to modernise. Second, some of the possible futures of the permanence of paradox relating to the key dimensions of modernisation, political tactics and reform orientations are then sketched. It is argued that modernisation is riddled with so many contradictions and imperfections that predictions of its unraveling are somewhat limited. There are so many consequences that cannot be anticipated. The internal workings of modernisation strategies coexist with a volatile external environment, exposing not just the limitations of modernisation but of the progressive values of modernity itself.

The future impacts of the global drivers of crime

The drivers of global crime, identified in the first part of this book, all seem set to remain of significance in understanding the dynamic processes belonging to modernisation, certainly in neo-liberal jurisdictions. The principles of the NPM developed throughout the 1980s and 1990s were adopted and reshaped by modernisers, although the underlying logic of the 3Es is still germane. There is scant evidence to suggest that there will be any diminution of its significance and authoritarian austerity is central to modes of governance across the world. All agencies nowadays are expected to achieve what they did in the past – and possibly more – by using existing funding regimes more prudently. It is likely that more will have to be done with less through working 'smarter' in an increasingly competitive environment. All criminal justice agencies are likely to be subjected to this disciplinary mechanism although it is feasible that this will become second nature as policymakers and practitioners comply with and commit themselves to these goals.

Public protection has been a consideration of fundamental importance as society becomes ever more fearful of various hazards and potential harms. Our homes, workplace and public spaces all feel less safe as people become more knowledgeable about the everyday significance of crime and anti-social behaviour. Sex offending, once confined to families, is now a virtual as well as an actual phenomenon and the rowdy behaviour of young people is increasingly criminalized as anti-social behaviour. High profile cases of seriously dangerous predatory violent criminals haunts not only the public but probation, parole and prison personnel who sometimes make flawed life and death decisions about the releasability of these offenders (e.g., Rice, Monckton). Human rights discourse is increasingly making the citizenry aware that governments should assume responsibility for looking after their safety and security. If this book had been written less than ten years ago, it is likely that few scholars could have anticipated the changes that are the long-term consequences of 9/11 in the US and 7/7 in the UK. While this is not explicitly a crime issue it has placed a burden on the criminal justice system, augmenting the work of the Police, Courts and Security Services. It is arguable too that the discourse of 'ordinary' crime has changed as a direct consequence of a focus on terrorism. In describing anti-social behaviour, for instance, some commentators make a subliminal connection to this global agenda in the way in which the debate is being conducted. References appear in the papers which exaggerate the nuisance behaviour of 11-year-olds as exerting terror on local communities.

At the time of writing in May 2007 the Home Office has been further modernised, being split into two separate bodies – justice and security – each with distinctive functions. Whatever happens as a result of this change it is clear that the terrorist threat not only occupies the intelligence and military services, it is also central to CDRPs at a local level although not all local communities are equally susceptible to such attacks. There is scant evidence to suggest that the terrorist threat will go away, as a war torn world generates a hardening of collective attitudes towards fundamentalist Christian and Islamic blocs in what, in other respects, is a secularized world. The politics of race and identity are inextricably bound up with this and inter-ethnic conflicts seem set to increase and worsen in terms of their scale and prevalence. There are ambiguities surrounding public protection, though, not least because resources are finite.

In response to fears about crime and the insecurity it generates, the *penal punitiveness* that has recently gathered momentum (especially in the UK and the US) does not seem to be waning. Governments throughout the world mobilize their electorates to demonstrate their mutual intolerance of offenders. The prison population in the United States is far too high and British society is going down a similar track with the prison estate reaching its capacity in 2007. Also, in that year John Reid, Home Secretary, made a firm commitment to building more prisons to accommodate more offenders in response to the punitive attitudes of sentencers and their tendency to ratchet up the penalties they mete out. Interestingly, Reid was told by the then Chancellor the Exchequer, Gordon Brown, that there were no resources to carry through this commitment. Overall, it would appear that *penal punitiveness* is becoming increasingly contradictory and irrational. The resignation of Rod Morgan in 2007, as head of the YJB, in response to the government's commitment to lock up more young people than in most other Western countries, indicates that modernisation is not always progressive and not necessarily based on the principles of scientific rationalism. At the moment there does not appear to be anything likely to curb the moderniser's commitment to punish anyone who steps out of line, whether they be terrorists or errant children. There is some justification for targeting terrorists but the wisdom of applying overtly Draconian measures against what, in many instances, are innocent citizens must be questioned.

The decline of the rehabilitative ideal belongs to the past and this pessimism was effectively challenged in the 1990s by the 'What Works' agenda and the burgeoning of 'evidence-based' research suggesting that future offending behaviour may be reduced. It is all about making sure interventions are targeted at the right people, at the right time and in the right place (Tilley 2005). Initiatives designed to reduce crime need to be tailored to meet individual requirements. The insights gleaned from this evidence-base are likely to be of limited use, though, because *risk assessment and management* are explicitly underpinned by the logic of actuarial justice. Rather than individualized justice, offenders are assorted into groups whose members share characteristics in common. Such an approach to *risk assessment and management* provides a useful profiling tool, sometimes to predict who is going to offend. Such reasoning is evidenced by attempts to bring into the criminal justice system individuals who are potentially dangerous before they have committed an offence. This pressure has been resisted thus far, but we anticipate further calls being made for predicting patterns of offending behaviour. Professionals will continue to call for rehabilitation but the punitiveness referred to in the previous paragraph could lead to calls for the segregation and exclusion of offenders rather than their rehabilitation.

The future looks like being a lucrative place for the private sector as the *commercialization of crime control* seems set to continue. The correctional services have already been exposed to privatization in various jurisdictions and policing functions are increasingly being performed by private security agencies. In the United States, for example, gated communities exist in many urban areas, existing as a testament to the limitations of federal and state funded law enforcement. Surveillance systems, such as CCTV and electronic tagging, were once the stuff of science fiction novels and new technological innovations are materializing all the time. Similar developments are occurring throughout Western European cities but not on the scale found across the Atlantic. Caution must be exercised because technological fixes, such as CCTV, are not able to address the underlying causes of crime and disorder. We do not anticipate any reversal of this trend and suggest that it may expand at an unprecedented rate. This is not without controversy, though, as it is likely to lead to a re-awakening of debates about accountability and further undermine any of the remaining significance attached to the principle of both criminal and social justice. More than that, the *commercialization of control* will see mechanisms of control reflecting the interests of those paying for it without any wider reference to democratic values.

In less than two decades *victim-centred justice* has come to dominate criminal justice policy and like the other global drivers, mentioned above, there is no reason to suspect that this will not continue into the future. Popular assumptions about the incorrigibility of many offenders and the need to punish them more forcibly are based on a sympathy with the victim. Western European criminal justice systems still have safeguards to protect suspects and offenders and they enjoy formal rights not enjoyed by victims, however the victim has a new status. It seems impossible that at any time a government will give up on victims. The modernisation of criminal justice partly depends on the effective valorization and inclusion of victims as a justification of its other more punitive and exclusionary policies. There is, of course, restorative justice, although its future is likely to be limited because of growing public intolerance with nuisance offenders (e.g., the current criminalization of anti-social behaviour) and because it is of little utility in the case of serious and violent offenders.

The future of *crime prevention and crime reduction* is very interesting and it is quite feasible that crime science could exert more of an influence on the modernisation of criminal justice (Laycock and Webb 2005; Farrell and Pease 2006). The use of technology has already been referred to, to which we can add the advances being made by geneticists and suggestions that there is a criminal gene, although the situation may not go as far as that portrayed in the movie *Minority Report* where criminals can be identified before they even commit an offence. The natural and environmental sciences also offer new methods of reducing criminal opportunities and there is every indication that target hardening will continue to be a priority.

The key dimensions of modernisation: future paradoxes

Many of the paradoxes inherent in globalizing modernisation strategies have already been identified and they are currently being played out in polities throughout the world. Accordingly the future is an uncertain one, although we suggest there are some discernible patterns.

The view that criminal justice best operates if there is a *mixed economy* is not as controversial as it once was and there are both pockets of resistance as well as compliance and commitment. Any resistance to the imposition of this political rationality will not result in its overturn but what is at stake is the extent to which it restructures the traditional and core functions of an agency. The Police Service does not seem to be threatened by private and voluntary sector involvement in policing-related activities and the commodification of security will not totally supplant the public sector in any society. In some societies, especially in the US, the tendency towards two-tiered policing will be further accentuated, but modernisers in the UK do not have this as their over-arching goal. The core functions of the magistracy and judiciary are also relatively immune and while some roles can be undertaken by the private sector, this is likely to be limited to IT. As noted in Chapter 5, the correctional agencies, especially probation, could be sidelined by the introduction of a mixed economy. The question remains, how committed are modernisers to privatizing, or to be more accurate de-publicizing, state sector roles and responsibilities? An answer to this question may be found by predicting the implications of *contestability*. This is not about privatization *per se* but the introduction of a competitive system of this ilk could erode the public sector's confidence in its own competencies. A demoralized Probation Service could quite easily be pushed aside by voluntary and community sector organizations and private sector players who enter the fray with a reform transformative orientation.

The NPM principle of *performance management* will undoubtedly continue to feature in modernisation programmes although there are likely to be tensions arising because of growing scepticism about their utility. Modernisers have tweaked the performance measures to include more qualitative indicators rather than relying on the more tangible quantitative measures. However, there is growing criticism that there is a lack of clarity about what exactly it is they are supposed to be measuring. The emphasis on *audit and inspection* leads to similar difficulties. There is commitment to the general principle of being audited and inspected but a growing concern over the evidence-base employed by the Audit Commission gives us a health warning about its efficacy.

In this final section we make some attempts to predict what is likely to happen as part of the future of modernisation in key areas.

Penal populism and risk management

As a key global driver of crime, penal populism and risk management would appear to be more or less unstoppable forces in Anglo-American societies, although, as noted earlier, other nation states are less punitive. For various years some commentators have critiqued the tendency of British governments to follow what was done in the United States, hence the policies of mass imprisonment in both countries. However, this has not been followed throughout all Western European countries, so there is the need to be cautious about thinking punitiveness is inevitable because other governments have exercised their political agency and decided to use alternative methods of tackling offending behaviour. This is perhaps an over-optimistic reading.

Perhaps the most worrying trend is that the more punitive a society becomes the more importance is attached to risk assessment and management paradigms. A punitive society is an intolerant society, demonstrated well by the UK where anti-social children and potential terrorists are seen as equal threats, at least at a discursive level. The problem that may occur is that the effectiveness of a punishment regime is often judged on the basis of risk assessment tools that are not necessarily scientific and so are prone to human error and misjudgment. The uses of risk to determine releasability are limited. The overarching danger is that there are limits to what punitive populism can achieve, beyond detaining individuals who pose risks that cannot be adequately predicted. There may come a day when assessing risk is seen as too risky and people are detained indefinitely, or at least for longer periods, on the spurious grounds that they might just present a risk if released.

Pluralization

It is difficult to tell how much further this logic can be applied. In terms of the UK, para-professionalization is well established in other public sector agencies and it came to criminal justice relatively late. It raises complex issues about the attitudes of ministers and policymakers to professionals, although professional interests can be potentially reform resistant. The British Medical Association is an example, and in criminal justice the police have resisted some pressures towards this, although the introduction of PCSOs shows that even the traditionally more robust agencies can buckle under pressure. A worrying development is that professional expertise is being disregarded. This is illustrated well by the case of Louise Casey, a government appointed Tsar for anti-social behaviour, who upset an audience of youth justice practitioners by undermining their professional wisdom and practical experience (*Observer*, 18 February 2005). Casey is an example of a person with no criminal justice experience, or even commitment to its knowledge base, coming in to challenge established ways of working and thinking. Casey also represents a growing lobby of anti-social behaviour specialists who are contributing towards the criminalization of incivilities and essentially social rather than problems.

Joined-up justice

Agencies have worked in partnership since time immemorial and this tendency is global although the commitment of particular governments will vary over time. However, there are variations in terms of the nature of partnership inasmuch as, is it genuinely joined-up or is it more a matter of sitting around a table and ticking boxes? Joined-up thinking and practice presents an exciting opportunity for cross-departmental co-operation and collaboration but partnerships are always going to be fragile because each organization has its own priorities. In the UK, for example, there are numerous frameworks for joined-up working – CDRPs, NOMS, YOTs, MAPPAs – other incentives encourage the maintenance of silos and monopolization, though. In the correctional agencies this creates openings, not only for the voluntary and private sectors, but also for para-professionals, all of whom may eventually usurp public sector service providers. In contrast the police and courts, with their law enforcement agendas, are likely to remain relatively robust, even for the former whose monopoly is being compromized through pluralization. Finally, it is possible that the advances made as a consequence of identifying complex social problems requiring joined-up responses could be reversed if policymakers recognize that such a policy response is fraught with contradictions and is also expensive. This latter point is a negative appraisal but bear in mind that neo-liberal governments in the past have been reluctant to sanction the kind of thinking associated with social democracy.

Deconcentration and regionalization

The chapters in the main body of this book have described in detail this spatial dimension in the UK. It seems to us that the processes of globalization will continue to exert a powerful influence on modernisation, especially its political economic dimensions: the maintenance of economic competitiveness will be central to all government activity. At the same time there will be pulls in the opposite direction as regions within countries and continents attempt to assert their autonomy. At a local level, responsibilized communities and citizens will either reap the benefits or dis-benefits of globalization.

Responsibilization

The days where individual nation states assumed sole responsibility for service delivery are now gone. State welfare is likely to remain, albeit in a residualized form, although all agencies participating in the crime industry are likely to be responsible for their actions, even though what they are required to do will be determined by power elites at the heart of government, or more accurately, the networks of governance. There is clear scope here for politicians to blame service providers for failures, although the greater danger is that competition and division between agencies may be accentuated. The individual citizen has been made more and more responsible for their day-to-day security than ever before. The gated communities in the US may be a sign of things to come as the fearful affluent in society decide to design out and excluded criminals.

In the final analysis, this book has demonstrated how 'modernisation' is an important stage in the history of criminal justice reform. Indeed, the ideologies, policies and practices associated with it will continue even if in a transmuted form in the years to come. While this book closes at this point, it is certain that the police, courts, correctional agencies and all stakeholders with an interest in crime will continue to confront government-led initiatives to which they will require a response in a changing world. As is the case with any programme of reform, the intentions behind it may be misunderstood or even actively subverted. This book has shown that a variety of forms of resistance have occurred and that, equally, agencies can transform their world through practice. However, the overriding trend is for government policymakers to influence the form of political agency that may be exercised by criminal justice professionals and practitioners.

References

6, Perri and Peck, E. (2004) New Labour's modernisation in the public sector: a neo-Durkheimian approach and the case of mental health services, *Public Administration*, 82(1): 83–108.

Active Communities Unit (2004) Think Smart . . . think Voluntary Sector Home Office.

Ainsworth, P. (2001) *Offender Profiling and Crime Analysis.* Cullompton: Willan.

Armstrong, M. (2006) *Performance Management: Key Strategies and Practical Guidelines*, 3rd edn. London: Kogan Page.

Armstrong, P. and Harrison, J. (1984) *Capitalism Since World War Two: The Making and the Break-Up of the Great Boom.* London: Fontana.

Audit Commission (1989) *The Probation Service: Promoting Value for Money.* Abingdon: Audit Commission.

Audit Commission (1996) *Misspent Youth: Young People and Crime.* London: Audit Commission for Local Authorities and NHS in England and Wales.

Audit Commission (1998) *Misspent Youth '98 The Challenge for Youth Justice.* Abingdon: Audit Commission.

Audit Commission (1999) *Misspent Youth '99 The Challenge for Youth Justice.* Abingdon: Audit Commission.

Audit Commission (2003) *Local Criminal Justice Boards: Supporting Change Management.* Abingdon: Audit Commission.

Audit Commission (2004) *Youth Justice 2004: A Review of the Reformed Youth Justice System.* Abingdon: Audit Commission.

Bailey, R. and Williams, B. (2000) *Inter-agency Partnerships in Youth Justice: Implementing the Crime and Disorder Act 1998.* Sheffield: University of Sheffield Joint Unit for Social Services Research.

Barnes, M. and Prince, D. (1995) 'Spoilt for Choice? How consumerism can disempower public service users'. Public Money and Management, July–September, p. 53–59.

Bauman, Z. (1989) *Modernity and the Holocaust.* Oxford: Polity Press.

Bauman, Z. (1991) *Modernity and Ambivalence.* Oxford: Polity Press.

Bauman, Z. (1998) *Work, Consumerism and the New Poor*. Buckingham: Open University Press.

Bauman, Z. (2000) *Liquid Modernity*. Cambridge: Polity Press.

Beck, U. (1992) *Risk Society*. London: Sage.

Becker, H. (1963) *Outsiders: Studies in the Sociology of Deviance*. New York: The Free Press.

Bell, C. and Haines, K. (1991) Managing the transition: implications of the youth court in England and Wales, in T. Booth (ed.) *Juvenile Justice in the New Europe*. Sheffield: University of Sheffield, Joint Unit for Social Services Research.

Bellamy, C. and Taylor, J. (1998) *Governing in the Information Age*. Buckingham: Open University Press.

Berger, P. and Luckmann, T. (1996) *The Social Construction of Reality*. London: Allen Lane.

Beveridge, W. (1942) *Social Insurance and Allied Services* (The Beveridge Report), Cmnd 6404. London: HMSO.

Bichard, R. (2004) *The Bichard Inquiry Report*, House of Commons HC 653. London: HMSO.

Blunkett, D. (2003) Scarman Lecture 11.12.03 Active Citizens, Strong Communities building Urban Renewal. Home Office.

Bottoms, A. E. (1977) Reflections on the renaissance of dangerousness, *Howard Journal of Penology and Crime Prevention*, 16.

Braithwaite, J. (2000) The new regulatory state and the transformation of criminology, in D. Garland and R. Sparks (eds) *Criminology and Social Theory*. Oxford: Oxford University Press.

Brittan, S. and Lilley, P. (1977) Delusions of Income Policy. MTSmith.

Brown, S. (2005) *Understanding Youth and Crime: Listening to Youth*. Maidenhead: Open University Press.

BSIA (2001) Interesting facts and figures in the UK security industry. Available at: www.bsia.co.uk/industry.html

Burnett, R. and Appleton, C. (2004) *Joined-Up Youth Justice: Tackling Crime in Partnership*. Lyme Regis: Russell House Publishing.

Burney, E. (2005) *Making People Behave: Anti-Social Behaviour, Politics and Policy*. Cullompton: Willan.

Burrows, R. and Loader, B. (1994) *Towards a Post-Fordist Welfare State*. London: Routledge.

Butler, T. and Watt, P. (2007) *Understanding Social Inequality*. London: Sage.

Byrne, S. and Pease, K. (2003) Crime reduction and community safety, in T. Newburn (ed.) *Handbook of Policing*. Cullompton: Willan.

Cabinet Office (1999) *Modernising Government*, Cmnd. 4310. London: HMSO.

Carter, P. (2003) *Managing Offenders, Reducing Crime: A New Approach*. London: Cabinet Office.

Carvel, J. (2003) 'Postcode survey finds widening gap between rich and poor'. *The Guardian*, Thursday 12th June.

Cassels, Sir J. (1994) *Independent Committee of Inquiry into the Role and Responsibilities of the Police*. London: Police Foundation.

Cavadino, M. and Dignan, J. (2006) Penal Systems: A Comparative Approach. London: Sage.

Chan, J. (2003) Police and new technologies, in T. Newburn (ed.) *Handbook of Policing*. Cullompton: Willan.

Christensen, T. and Lægreid, P. Trust in government, *Public Performance and Management Review*, 497 (June): 12.

Christie, N. (2000) *Crime Control as Industry*, 3rd edn. London: Routledge.

Clarke, J. and Newman, J. (1997) *The Managerial State: Power, Politics and Ideology in the Remaking of Social Welfare*. London: Sage.

Clarke, J. and Newman, J. (2004) Governing in the modern world, in D.L. Steinberg and R. Johnson (eds) *Blairism and the War of Persuasion*. London: Lawrence and Wishart.

Clarke, J., Gerwittz, S. and McLaughlin, E. (2000) *New Managerialism: New Welfare*. London: Sage.

Clarke, R. (1980) Situational crime prevention: theory and practice, *British Journal of Criminology*, 20(2): 136–47.

Cohen, S. (1985) *Visions of Social Control*. Cambridge: Polity Press.

Cohen, S. (2002) *Folk Devils and Moral Panics: Creation of Mods and Rockers*, 3rd edn. Oxford: Blackwell.

Cook, D. (2006) *Criminal and Social Justice*. London: Sage.

Cope, N. (2003) Crime analysis: principles and practice, in T. Newburn (ed.) *Handbook of Policing*. Cullompton: Willan.

Cope, S. (2001) Analysing criminal justice policymaking: towards a policy networks approach, in M. Ryan, S.P. Savage and D.S. Wall (eds) *Policy Networks in Criminal Justice*. Basingstoke: Palgrave Macmillan.

Crawford, A. (1997) *Local Governance of Crime*. Oxford: Clarendon Press.

Crawford, A. (1998) *Crime Prevention and Community Safety*. London: Longman.

Crawford, A. (2003) The pattern of policing in the UK: policing beyond the police, in T. Newburn (ed.) *Handbook of Policing*. Cullompton: Willan.

Crawford, A., Lister, S., Blackburn, S. and Burnett, J. (2005) *Plural Policing: The Mixed Economy of Visible Patrols in England and Wales*. Bristol: Policy Press.

Creaton, J. (2003) Modernising the courts and the legal profession, *Contemporary Politics*, (June) 9(2).

Crick, M. (1986) *The March of Militant*. London: Faber.

Crick, M. (1997) *Michael Heseltine: A Biography*. London: Hamish Hamilton.

Crowther, C. (2000a) Thinking about the underclass: towards a political economy of policing, *Theoretical Criminology*, 4(2): 149–67.

Crowther, C. (2000b) *Policing Urban Poverty*. Basingstoke: Macmillan.

Crowther, C. (2004) Over-policing and under-policing social exclusion, in R. Hopkins-Burke (ed.) *Hard Cop, Soft Cop: Dilemmas and Debates in Contemporary Policing*. Cullompton: Willan.

Crowther-Dowey, C. (2007) The police and drugs in M. Simpson, T. Shildrick and R. MacDonald (eds) *Drugs in Britain: Supply, Corruption and Control*. Basingstoke: Palgrave.

Dahrendorf, R. (1998) Changing Social Values under Mrs. Thatcher, in R. Skidelsky (ed.) *Thatcherism*. London: Chatto and Windus, 191–201.

Davies, H., Nutley, S. and Smith, P. (eds) (2000) *What works? Evidence-Based Policy and Practice in Public Services*. Bristol: Policy Press.

Davies, N. (2003) 'How Britain is losing the drugs war.' *The Guardian*, May 22, 2003.

Dean, H. (2006) *Social Policy*. Cambridge: Polity Press.

Dean, M. (1999) *Governmentality*. London: Sage.

Denman, G. (1982) *Intensive Intermediate Treatment with Juvenile Offenders: A Handbook of Assessment and Groupwork Practice*. Lancaster: Centre for Youth, Crime and Community, Lancaster University.

Department for Constitutional Affairs (2006) *Review of the Implementation of the Human Rights Act*. London: Department for Constitutional Affairs.

DETR (1998) *Modern Local Government: In Touch with the People*. Wetherby: DETR Free Literature.

DETR (1999) *Performance Indicators for 2000/2001: A Joint Consultation Document Produced by DETR and the Audit Commission on Best Value and Local Authority Performance Indicators for 2000/2001*. Wetherby: DETR Free Literature.

Devine, F., Savage, M., Crompton, R. and Scott, J. (eds) (2004) *Rethinking Class, Identities, Cultures and Lifestyles*. Basingstoke: Palgrave.

Dixon, J. A., Levine, M. and McAuley, R. (2006) Locating impropriety: street drinking and the ideological dilemma of public space, *Political Psychology* 27: 187–206.

Dobson, N. (2000) *Best Value: Law and Management*. Bristol: Jordan.

Driver, S. and Martell, L. (2006) *New Labour*, 2nd edn. Cambridge: Polity Press.

du Gay, P. (2000) *In Praise of Bureaucracy*. London: Sage.

Durkheim, E. (1964) *The Division of Labour in Society*, trans. W. D. Halls. New York: Free Press.

Eadie, T. and Canton, R. (2002) Practising in a Context of Ambivalence: The Challenge for Youth Justice Workers, *Youth Justice*, 2(14).

Edwards, A. and Benyon, J. (2000) Community governance, crime control and local diversity, *Crime Prevention and Community Safety: An International Journal*, 2(3): 35–54.

Elias, N. (1978) *The Civilising Process, Vol. 1. The History of Manners*. Oxford: Blackwell.

Elias, N. (1982) *The Civilising Process, Vol. 2. State Formation and Civilisation*. Oxford: Blackwell.

Elson, P. R. (2006) Tracking the implementation of voluntary sector/government policy agreements: is the voluntary and community sector in the frame? *The International Journal of Not-for-Profit Law* (August), 8(4).

Emsley, C. (2003) The birth and development of the police, *Handbook of Policing*. Cullompton: Willan.

Ericson, R. and Haggerty, K. (1997) *Policing the Risk Society*. Oxford. Clarendon Press.

Farrell, G. and Pease, K. (2006) Criminology and security, in M. Gill (ed.) *The Security Handbook*. Basingstoke: Palgrave.

Farrall, S. (2002) *Rethinking What Works with Offenders*. Cullompton: Willan.

Farrall, S. and Gadd, D. (2004) The frequency of fear of crime, *British Journal of Criminology*, 44(1): 127–32.

Faulkner, D. (2002) Prisoners as citizens, *British Journal of Community Justice*, 1(2).

Feeley, M. and Simon, J. (1994) Actuarial justice: the emerging new criminal law, in D. Nelken (ed.) *The Futures of Criminology*. London: Sage.

Fitzgerald, M., Stockdale, M. and Hale, C. (2003) *Young People and Street Crime*. London: Youth Justice Board.

Fitzpatrick, B., Seago, P., Walker, C. and Wall, D. (2001) The courts: new court management and old court ideologies, in M. Ryan, S. P. Savage and D. S. Wall (eds) *Policy Networks in Criminal Justice*. London: Palgrave.

Foucault, M. (1977) *Discipline and Punish*. London: Allen Lane.

Foucault, M. (1991) Governmentality, in G. Burchell, C. Gordon and P. Miller (eds) *The Foucault effect: Studies in Governmentality*. Brighton: Harvester, 87–104.

Fox, C. and Jenkins, D. (2005) The development of the National Offender Management Service (NOMS) and the implications for community safety, *Community Safety Journal*, 4(1): 4–11.

France, A. (2007) *Understanding Youth in Late Modernity*. Maidenhead: Open University Press.

Friedman, M. (1977) *Inflation and Unemployment*. London: IEA.

Fussey, P. (2004) New Labour and new surveillance: theoretical and political ramifications of CCTV implementation in the UK, *Surveillance and Society*, 2(2/3): 251–69.

Fyfe, N. (2001) *Geography of Crime and Policing*. Oxford: Blackwell.

Gaines, S. (2007) Ex-inmates who have found success after prison now want to help others avoid the trap of reoffending, *Guardian*, 19 February. Available at: SocietyGuardian.co.uk

Gamble, A. (1983) Thatcherism and conservative politics, in S. Hall and M. Jacques (eds.) *The Politics of Thatcherism*. London: Lawrence and Wishart, 109–31.

Gamble, A. (1994) *The Free Economy and The Strong State: The Politics of Thatcherism*, 2nd edn. London: Macmillan.

Garland, D. (1996) The limits of sovereign states: strategies of crime control in contemporary society, *British Journal of Criminology*, 36(4): 445–71.

Garland, D. (1997) 'Governmentality' and the problem of crime, *Theoretical Criminology*, 1(2): 173–214.

Garland, D. (2000) The culture of high crime societies: some preconditions of recent 'Law and Order' policies, *British Journal of Criminology*, 40: 347–75.

Garland, D. (2001) *The Culture of Control*. Oxford: Oxford University Press.

Garside, R. (2006) *Right for the Wrong Reasons: Making Sense of Criminal Justice Failure*. London: Crime and Society Foundation.

Gerth, H. and Wright-Mills, C. ([1946] 1958) *From Max Weber: Essays in Sociology*. New York: Galaxy Books.

Giddens, A. (1994) *Beyond Left and Right*. Cambridge: Polity Press.

Giddens, A. (1999) *The Third Way*. Cambridge: Polity Press.

Giddens, A. (2007) *Over to You, Mr Brown: How Labour Can Win Again*. Cambridge: Polity Press.

Gilling, D. (1997) *Crime Prevention: Theory, Policy and Politics*. London: UCL Press.

Gilling, D. (2005) Partnership and crime prevention, in N. Tilley (ed.) *Handbook of Crime Prevention and Community Safety*. Cullompton: Willan.

Glendinning, C. (2002) *Partnership, New Labour and the Governance of Welfare*. Bristol: Policy Press.

Goodey, J. (2005) *Victims and Victimology: Research, Policy and Practice*. Harlow: Longman.

Goold, B. J. (2004) *CCTV and Policing: Public Area Surveillance and Police Practices in Britain*. Oxford: Oxford University Press.

Gramsci, A. (1971) *Selection from the Prison Notebooks*. London: Lawrence and Wishart.

Green, P. (1990) *The Enemy Without: Policing and Class Consciousness in the Miner's Strike*. Buckingham: Open University Press.

Hadfield, P. (2007) *Bar Wars: Contesting the Night in Contemporary British Cities*. Oxford: Oxford University Press.

Hallam, S. (1999) Policing the numbers. The Sociology of a Performance Bureaucracy. Unpublished thesis. ?????? Police Staff College Library.

Halliday Report (2001) *Making Punishments Work: Report of a Review of the Sentencing Framework for England and Wales*. London: Home Office.

Halsey, A. H. (1988) A sociologist's view of Thatcherism, in R. Skidelsky (ed.) *Thatcherism*. London. Chatto and Windus, 173–89.

Ham, C. and Hill, M. (1993) *The Policy Process in the Modern Capitalist State 2nd Edn*. New York: Harvester Wheatsheaf.

Harfield, C. (2006) SOCA: a paradigm shift in British policing, *British Journal of Criminology*, 46: 743–61.

Harrison, S. and Pollitt, C. (1994) *Controlling Health Professionals*, Buckingham: Open University Press.

Harvey, D. (1989) The *Condition of Postmodernity*. Oxford: Blackwell.

Hatton, D. (1988) *Inside Left: The Story so Far*. London. Bloomsbury.

Hay, C. (1996) *Re-Stating Social and Political Change*. Buckingham: Open University Press.

Hay, C. (1999) *The Political Economy of New Labour: Labouring Under False Pretences?* Manchester: Manchester University Press.

Hayek, F. (1944) *The Road to Serfdom*. London: Routledge.

Hebenton, B. and Thomas, T. (1996) Sexual offenders in the community: reflections on problems of law, community and risk management in the USA, England and Wales, *International Journal of the Sociology of Law*, 24: 427–43.

Heseltine, M. (2000) *Life in the Jungle: My Autobiography*. London: Hodder and Stoughton.

Hewitt, M. (1992) *Welfare, Ideology and Need: Recent Perspectives on the Welfare State*. London: Harvester-Wheatsheaf.

Heywood, A. (2000) *Key Concepts in Politics*. Basingstoke: Palgrave Macmillan.

Hicks, J. (2002) Waking from a fading dream? An analysis of two key influences on the early work of crime and disorder reduction partnerships, *British Journal of Community Justice*, 1(3).

Hills, J. and Stewart, K. (eds) (2005) *A More Equal Society: New Labour, Poverty, Inequality and Exclusion*. Bristol: Policy Press.

HM Treasury (2002) *The Rob of the Voluntary and Community Sector in Service Delivery: A Gross Cutting Review*. HM Stationery Office.

HM Treasury (2003) *Guidance to Funders*. HMSO.

HMIC (2004) *Modernising The Police service: Thematic Inspection of Workforce Modernistaion* – The Role, management and deployment of Police Staff in the Police service of England and Wales. London: HMSO.

HM Inspectorate of Probation (2006a) *An Independent Review of a Serious Further Offence Case: Anthony Rice*. London: Home Office.

HM Inspectorate of Probation (2006b) *An Independent Review of a Serious Further Offence Case: Damien Hanson and Elliott White*. London: Home Office.

Hoddinott, J. (1994) Core questions, *Police Review* (August), 102(5279): 20–2.

Holdaway, S. (1983) *Inside the British Police*. Oxford: Basil Blackwell.
Home Office (1965) *Report of the Committee on the Prevention and Detection of Crime*. London: HMSO.
Home Office (1983) *Manpower, Effectiveness and Efficiency in the Police Service*. London: HMSO.
Home Office (1990a) *Partnership in Dealing with Offenders in the Community*. London: HMSO.
Home Office (1990b) *White Paper: Crime, Justice and Protecting the Public*. London: HMSO.
Home Office (1991) *Safer Communities: the Local Delivery of Crime Prevention through the Partnership Approach* Home Office Standing Conference on Crime Prevention
Home Office (1993) *Inquiry into Police Responsibilities and Rewards*. London: Home Office.
Home Office (1995) *Review of Core and Ancillary Tasks*. London: HMSO.
Home Office (1997) *No More Excuses: A New Approach To Tackling Youth Crime In England and Wales*. London: Home Office.
Home Office (1998) *The Crime and Disorder Act: Community Safety and the Reduction and Prevention of Crime – A Conceptual Framework for Training and the Development of a Professional Discipline*. London: Home Office.
Home Office (1999) *The Government's Crime Reduction Strategy*. London: Home Office.
Home Office (2000a) *A Guide to the Criminal Justice System in England and Wales*. London: Home Office.
Home Office (2000b) *The Victim's Charter*. London: Home Office.
Home Office (2003) *The National Policing Plan, 2003–2006*. London: HMSO.
Home Office (2004) *Building Communities, Beating Crime: A Better Police Service for the 21st Century*. London: HMSO.
Home Office (2005) *National Community Safety Plan 2006–2009*. London: Home Office.
Hope, T. (2002) The road taken: replication, evaluation and crime reduction, in G. Hughes, E. McLaughlin and J. Muncie (eds) *Crime Prevention and Community Safety: New Directions*. London: Sage.
Hope, T. (2005) The new local governance of community safety in England and Wales, *Canadian Journal of Criminology and Criminal Justice* (April), 369–87.
Hopkins-Burke, R. (ed.) (2004) *Hard Cop, Soft Cop: Dilemmas and Debates in Contemporary Policing*. Cullompton: Willan.
Hough, M. (2004) Modernisation, scientific rationalism and the Crime Reduction Programme, *Criminal Justice*, 4(3): 239–53.
Hough, M., Allen, R. and Padel, U. (2006) *Reshaping Probation and Prisons: The New Offender Management Framework*. Bristol: Policy Press.
Hoyle, C. and Young, R. (2003) Restorative justice, victims and the police, in T. Newburn (ed.) *Handbook of Policing*. Cullompton: Willan.
Hudson, B. (1993) *Penal Policy and Social Justice*. Basingstoke: MacMillan.
Hudson, B. (2003) *Justice in the Risk Society: Challenging and Re-affirming justice in late modernity*. London: Sage.
Hughes, G. (1996) Strategies of multi-agency crime prevention and community safety in contemporary Britiain, *Studies on Crime Prevention*, 5(2): 221–45.
Hughes, G. (2007) *The Politics of Crime and Community*. Basingstoke: Palgrave.

Hughes, G. and Edwards, A. (2005) Crime prevention in context, in N. Tilley (ed.) *Handbook of Crime Prevention and Community Safety*. Cullompton: Willan.

Hughes, G., McLaughlin, E. and Muncie, J. (eds) (2002) *Crime Prevention and Community Safety: New Directions*. London: Sage.

Hutton, W. and Giddens, A. (2000) *On the Edge. Essays on a Runaway World*. London: Jonathan Cape.

Jessop, B. (1990) *State Theory: Putting Capitalist States in their Place*. Cambridge: Polity Press.

Jessop, B. (1994) The transition to post-Fordism and the Schumpeterian workfare state, in R. Burrows and B. Loader (eds) *Towards a Post-Fordist Welfare State?* London: Routledge.

Jessop, B. (2000) From the KWNS to the SWPR, in G. Lewis, S. Gerwitz and J. Clarke (eds) *Rethinking Social Policy*. London: Sage, 171–84.

Jessop, B. (2003) *From Thatcherism to New Labour: Neo-Liberalism, Workfarism, and Labour Market Regulation*. Lancaster: Department of Sociology, University of Lancaster. Available at: www.comp.lancs.ac.uk/sociology/soc131rj.pdf

Jewkes, Y. (ed.) (2003) *Dot.cons: Crime, Deviance and Identity on the Internet*. Cullompton: Willan.

Jewkes, Y. and Johnston, H. (eds) (2006) *Prison Readings: A Critical Introduction to Prisons and Imprisonment*. Cullompton: Willan.

Johnson, P. (1980) *The Recovery of Freedom*. Oxford. Blackwell.

Johnston, L. (2000) *Policing Britain*. Harlow: Longman.

Jones, D. (2001) 'Misjudged youth': a critique of the Audit Commission's reports on youth justice, *British Journal of Criminology*, 41: 362–80.

Jones, T. and Newburn, T. (2004) The convergence of US and UK crime control policy: exploring substance and process, in T. Newburn and R. Sparks (eds) *Criminal Justice and Political Cultures: National and International Dimensions of Crime Control*. Cullompton: Willan.

Joseph, M. F. W. (1944) The British White Paper on employment policy, *The American Economic Review* (September), 34(3): 561–7.

Jospin, L. (1998) *Modern Socialism*. London. The Fabian Society.

Kanter, R. (1990) *When Giants Learn To Dance*. London: Unwin Hyman.

Karstedt, S. (2004) Durkheim, Tarde and beyond: the global travel of crime policies, in T. Newburn and R. Sparks (eds) *Criminal Justice and Political Cultures: National and International Dimensions of Crime Control*. Cullompton: Willan.

Kelly, L. and Regan, L. (2000) *Stopping Traffic: Exploring the Extent of, and responses to, trafficking in women for sexual exploitation in the UK*, Police Research Series, Paper 125. London: Home Office.

Kemshall, H. (2003) *Understanding Risk in Criminal Justice*. Maidenhead: Open University Press.

Kemshall, H., Mackenzie, G., Wood, J., Bailey, R. and Yates, J. (2005) *Strengthening Multi-Agency Public Protection Arrangements (MAPPAs)*. London: Home Office.

Kerr, P. (2002) *Post-war British Politics: From Conflict to Consensus*. London: Routledge.

Kershaw, C., Chivitie-Matthews, N., Thomas, C. and Aust, R. (2001) *The 2001 British Crime Survey*, Home Office Statistical Bulletin, 18/01. London: Home Office.

King, A. (1998) Margaret Thatcher as a political leader, in R. Skidelsky (eds) *Thatcherism*. London: Chatto and Windus, 51–64.

Knight, C., Dominey, J. and Kemshall, H. (2007) Gathering offender perceptions of probation programmes: potential, pitfalls and limits, *British Journal of Community Justice*, 5: 1.

Kooiman, J. (2003) *Governing as governance*. London: Sage.

Lacey, N. (2003) Principles, politics and criminal justice, in L. Zedner and A. Ashworth (eds) *The Criminological Foundations of Penal Policy: Essays in Honour of Roger Hood*. Oxford: Clarendon Press.

Laming, H. (2003) *The Victoria Climbie Inquiry*, Report of an Inquiry by Lord Laming, Cmnd. 5730. London: HMSO.

Latour, B. (1987) *Science in Action*. Milton Keynes: Open University Press.

Laycock, G. and Webb, B. (2005) Designing out crime from products and systems, *Crime Prevention Studies*, 18.

Lea, J. (2002) *Crime and Modernity*. London: Sage.

Leishman, F., Cape, S. and Starie, P. (1995) Reforming the police in Britain: new public management, policy networks and a tough 'old bill'. *The International Journal of Public Sector Management*, 8 (4) 26–37.

Leonardsen, D. (2004) *Japan as Low Crime Nation*. New York: Palgrave Macmillan.

Levitas, R. (1998) *The Inclusive Society? Social Exclusion and New Labour*. Basingstoke: Macmillan.

Levitas, R. (2005) *The Inclusive Society? Social Exclusion and New Labour*, 2nd edn. Basingstoke: Macmillan.

Lewis, D. (1997) *Hidden Agendas: Politics, Law and Disorder*. Essex: Farringdon Books.

Liebling, A. (2006) Lessons from prison privatization for probation, in M. Hough, R. Allen and U. Padel *Reshaping Probation and Prisons: The New Offender Management Framework*. Bristol: Policy Press.

Liebling, A. and Maruna, S. (eds) (2005) *The Effects of Imprisonment*. Cullompton: Willan.

Lister, R. (2004) *Poverty*. Cambridge: Polity Press.

Lodemel, I. and Trickey, H. (eds) (2000) *'An Offer you can't Refuse': Workfare in International Perspective*. Bristol: Policy Press.

Long, M. (2003) Leadership and performance management, in T. Newburn (ed.) *Handbook of Policing*. Cullompton: Willan.

Long, M. (2004) Naming, shaming and the politics of blaming: Police middle management perceptions of the impact of best value. Unpublished PhD thesis, University of East London.

Long, M., Robinson, A. and Senior, P. (2006) *A Visible Difference: an Evaluation of the Second Phase of the Police Community Support Officers in West Yorkshire*. Hallam Centre for Community Justice. Sheffield Hallam University.

Long, M., Senior, P. and Crowther-Dowey, C. (2007) *An Evaluation of the Circle Project undertaken as part of West Yorkshire Constabularys Civil Renewal Agenda. 2004–2005. Hallam Centre for Community Justice: Sheffield Hallam University.*

Lords (2000) *Hansard* 2 Oct 2000 co. 1202.

Loveday, B. (1999) Government and accountability of the police, in R. I. Mawby (ed.) *Policing across the World: Issues for the Twenty-First Century*. London: UCL Press.

Loveday, B. (2000) The Crime and Disorder Act 1998 and Policing, *The Police Journal*, 73(3).

Loveday, B. (2005) Police reform: problems of governance and accountability. Management challenges surrounding proposals for police restructuring, *The Police Journal*, 78: 339–50.

Loveday, B. (2006) Workforce modernisation: implications for the police service in England and Wales. Evaluating HMIC, 2004. Thematic: Modernising the Police Service, *The Police Journal*, 79: 105–24.

Loveday, B. and Reid, A. (2003) *The Challenge of Police Reform in England and Wales*. London: Policy Exchange.

Luckmann, T. (1983) *The Life World and Social Realities*. London: Heinemann.

Lukes, S. (1974) *Power: A Radical View*. London: Macmillan.

MacPherson, Sir William (1999) *The Stephen Lawrence Inquiry – Report*, Cmnd. 4262-0. London: HMSO.

Maguire, M. (2004) The crime reduction programme in England and Wales: reflections on the vision and reality, *Criminal Justice*, 4(3): 213–37.

Maguire, M. and John, T. (2006) Intelligence-led policing, managerialism and community engagement: competing priorities and the role of the national intelligence model in the UK, *Policing and Society*, 16(1): 67–85.

Maguire, M. and Kemshall, H. (2004) Multi-agency public protection arrangements: key issues, in H. Kemshall and G. McIvor (eds) *Managing Sex Offenders Risk*. London: Jessica Kingsley Publishing.

Mair, G. (2004) *What Matters in Probation*. Cullompton: Willan.

Manning, P. K. (1992) Information technologies and the police, in M. Tonry and N. Morris (eds) *Modern Policing: Crime and Justice, A Review of Research, Vol. 15*. Chicago, IL: University of Chicago Press, 349–98.

Marlow, A. and Loveday, B. (eds) (2000) *After MacPherson: Policing after the Stephen Lawrence Inquiry*. Lyme Regis: Russell House Publishing.

Marquand, D. (1988) The paradoxes of Thatcherism, in R. Skidelsky (ed.) *Thatcherism*. London: Chatto and Windus, 51–64.

Martin, D. (2003) The politics of policing: managerialism, modernisation and performance, in R. Matthews and J. Young (eds) *The New Politics of Crime and Punishment*. Cullompton: Willan.

Martinson, R. (1974) What works? Questions and answers about prison reform, *Public Interest*, 55 (Spring): 22–54.

Maruna, S. (2001) *Making Good: How Ex-Convicts Change and Rebuild Their Lives*. New York: American Psychological Association.

Matassa, M. and Newburn, T. (2003) Policing and terrorism, in T. Newburn (ed.) *Handbook of Policing*. Cullompton: Willan.

Matthews, R. and Francis, P. (1996) *Prisons 2000*. London: St Martin's Press.

Matthews, R. and Pitts, J. (eds) (2002) *Crime, Disorder and Community Safety*. London: Routledge.

Mawby, R. (1999) *Policing Across the World*. London: UCL Press.

Mawby, R. (2000) Core policing: the seductive myth, in F. Leishman, B. Loveday and S. Savage (eds) *Core Issues in Policing*, 2nd edn. Essex: Pearson, 107–23.

Mawby, R. and Wright, A. (2003) The police organization, in T. Newburn (ed.) *Handbook of Policing*. Cullompton: Willan.

McCourt, W. (2002) New public management in developing countries, in K. McLaughlin, S. Osborne and E. Ferlie (eds) *New Public Management: Current Trends and Future Prospects*. London: Routledge, 227–42.

McLaughlin, E. (1994) *Community, Policing and Accountability*. Aldershot: Avebury.
McLaughlin, E., Muncie, J. and Hughes, G. (2001) The permanent revolution: New Labour, public management and the modernisation of criminal justice, *Criminal Justice*, 1(3): 301–18.
McLaughlin, K., Osborne, S. and Ferlie, E. (2001) *New Public Management: Current Trends and Future Prospects*. London: Routledge.
Meadows, L. and Senior, P. (2006) *Knowledge Management Briefing*. Available at: www.clinks.org
Minkes, J., Hammersley, R. and Raynor, P. (2005) Partnership in working with young offenders with substance misuse problems, *Howard Journal of Criminal Justice*, 44(3).
Minogue, K. (1988) The emergence of the New Right, in R. Skidelsky (ed.) *Thatcherism*. London: Chatto and Windus, 125–42.
Moe, R. (1994) The re-inventing government exercise: misinterpreting the problem, misjudging the consequences, *Public Administration Review*, 54(2): 111–2.
Monk, D. (2007) Presentation, *Serious Incidents: The Role of the YJB*. Available at: www.yjb.gov.uk (accessed 21.2.07).
Mooney, G. (ed.) (2004) *Work: Personal Lives and Social Policy*. Bristol: Policy Press.
Morgan (Home Office) (1991) *Safer Communities: The Local Delivery of Crime Prevention Through the Partnership Approach (Morgan Report)*. London: Home Office.
Morris, A. and Giller, H. (1987) *Understanding Juvenile Justice*. London: Croom Helm.
Murray, C. (2000) The British underclass, *The Sunday Times*, 13 February.
Narey, M. (2003) Available at: www.cbi.org.uk/ndbs/press.nsf/0/de45447ba2aa5ffa80256d40002c8f38?OpenDocument
Nash, M. and Ryan, M. (2003) Modernising and joining up government: the case of the prison and probation services, *Contemporary Politics* (June), 9(2).
NCIS (2000) *The National Intelligence Model*. London: NCIS.
Nellis, M. (1999) Towards the 'fields of corrections': modernising the Probation Service in the late 1990s, *Social Policy and Administration*, 33(3).
Nellis, M. (2002) Probation, partnership and civil society, in R. Ward, J. Scott, and M. Lacey, (eds) *Probation: Working for Justice*. Oxford: Oxford University Press.
Nellis, M. (2004) 'I know where you live!': electronic monitoring and penal policy in England and Wales 1999–2003, *British Journal of Community Justice*, 2(3).
Nelson, A. and Griffiths, C. (2001) Perception of risk among minority groups: causes and consequences, *Crime Prevention and Community Safety: An International Journal*, 3(1): 55–65.
Newburn, T. (2002) Modernisation, New labour and criminal justice policy, *Criminal Justice Matters*, 46.
Newburn, T. (2003) Policing since 1945, in T. Newburn (ed.) *Handbook of Policing*. Cullompton: Willan.
Newburn, T. and Sparks, R. (2004) *Criminal Justice and Political Cultures: National and International Dimensions of Crime Control*. Cullompton: Willan.

Newman, J. (2000) Beyond the new public management? Modernising public services, in J. Clarke, S. Gerwitz and E. McLaughlin (eds) *New Managerialism, New Welfare*. London: Sage.
Newman, J. (2001). *Modernising Governance: New Labour, Policy and Society*. London: Sage.
NOMS (2004) NOMS Update Issue No. 4, Home Office.
NOMS (2007) *National Commissioning Plan 2007 / 2008: Commissioning Framework*. London: NOMS.
Nozick, R. (1974) *Anarchy, State and Utopia*. Oxford: Basil Blackwell.
OECD (2005) *Modernising Government: The Way Forward*. London: OECD.
O'Keeffe, C. (2004) Object and subject: the challenges of peer research in community justice, *British Journal of Community Justice*, 3(1).
Osborne, D. and Gaebler, T. (1992) *Reinventing Government*. Panagon, MA: Addison-Wesley.
Ousley, N. (2001) *Community Pride not Prejudice. Making Diversity Work in Bradford*. Bradford Vision 2001.
Padfield, N. and Maruna, S. (2006) The revolving door at the prison gate, *Criminology and Criminal Justice*, 329.
Park, R. E., Burgess, E. W. and McKenzie, R. D. (eds) (1925) *The City*. Chicago, IL: University of Chicago Press.
Pattison, S. (1997) *The Faith of the Managers*. London: Cassell.
Pearson, G. (1983) *Hooligan: A History of Respectable Fears*. Oxford: Blackwell.
Pease, K. (1997) Crime prevention, in M. Maguire, R. Morgan and R. Reiner (eds) *The Oxford Handbook of Criminology*, 2nd edn. Oxford: Oxford University Press.
Pease, K. (2002) Crime prevention, in M. Maguire, R. Morgan and R. Reiner (eds) *The Oxford Handbook of Criminology*, 3rd edn. Oxford: Oxford University Press.
Peters, T. (1987) *Thriving on Chaos*. Basingstoke: Macmillan.
Peters, T. and Waterman, R. (1982) *In Search of Excellence: Lessons from America's Best Run Companies*. New York: Harper and Row.
Phillips, C., Jacobson, J. Lewis, R., Carter, M. and Considine, M. (2002) *Crime and Disorder Reduction Partnerships: Round One Progress. Police Research Series Paper 151*. London: Home Office.
Pitts, J. (1988) *The Politics of Juvenile Crime*. London: Sage Publications.
Pitts, J. (2001a) *The New Politics of Youth Crime: Discipline or Solidarity*. Basingstoke: Palgrave.
Pitts, J. (2001b) Korrectional karaoke: New Labour and the zombification of youth, *Youth Justice*, 1(2): 3–16.
Pitts, J. (2003) Changing youth justice, *Youth Justice*, 3(5).
Police Joint Consultative Committee (1990) The Operational Police Review.
Pollard, C. (2000) Victims and the criminal justice system: a new vision, *Criminal Law Review*, 5.
Pollitt, C. (1993) *Managerialism and the Public Services: Cuts of Cultural Change in the 1990s?* 2nd edn. Oxford: Blackwell.
Pollitt, C. (1995) Justification by works or by faith? Evaluating the new public management, *Evaluation: the International Journal of Theory, Research and Practice* (December), 1(2): 133–54.
Posen, I. (1994) What is policing? *Police Review* (February), 102(5254): 14–15.
Power, M. (1994) *The Audit Explosion*. London: Demos.

Pratt, J. (2007) *Penal Populism*. London: Routledge.

Raikes, S. (2002) A model for community safety and community justice, *British Journal of Community Justice*, 1(1).

Raine, J. W. (2001) Modernising courts or courting modernisation? *Criminal Justice*, 1(1): 105–28.

Raine, J. (2002) Modernisation and criminal justice, in D. Ward, J. Scott and M. Lacey (eds) *Probation: Working for Justice*. Oxford: Oxford University Press.

Raine, J. W. (2005) Courts, sentencing and justice in a changing political and managerial context, *Public Money and Management*, 25: 5, 290–8.

Ramsbotham, Sir David (2003) *Prisongate: The Shocking State of British Prisons and the Need for Visionary Change*. New York: Free Press.

Reed, M. (1992) *The Sociology of Organizations*. Hemel Hempstead: Harvester Wheatsheaf.

Reiner, R. (2000) *The Politics of the Police*, 3rd edn. Oxford: Oxford University Press.

Reiner, R. (2007a) *Law and Order: An Honest Citizen's Guide to Crime and Control*. Cambridge: Cambridge University Press.

Reiner, R. (2007b) Success or statistics? New Labour and crime control, *CJM*, 67(Spring).

Respect Task Force (2006) *Respect Action Plan*. London: Home Office.

Rhodes, R.A.W. (1997) *Understanding Governance*. Buckingham: Open University Press.

Rhodes, R.A.W. (2000a). New Labour's civil service: summing up, Joining up, *Political Quarterly*, 71(2): 151–66.

Rhodes, R.A.W. (2000b) Governance and public administration, in J. Pierre (ed.) *Debating Governance: Authority, Steering and Democracy*. Oxford: Oxford University Press.

Ritchie, D. (2001) Panel report, 11th December 2001: One Oldham, One Future Government Office for the North West.

Roberts, J. V. and Hough, M. (2002) *Changing Attitudes to Punishment: Public opinion, Crime and Justice*. Cullompton: Willan.

Robertson, R. (1992) *Globalisation: Social Theory and Global Culture*. London: Sage.

Rose, N. (1999) *Powers of Freedom: Reframing Political Thought*. Cambridge: Cambridge University Press.

Rose, N. and Miller, P. (1992) Political power beyond the state: problematics of government, *The British Journal of Sociology*, 43(2): 172–205.

Routledge, P. (1994) 'Scargill. The Unauthorised Biography'. Toronto. HarperCollins.

Russell, C. E. B. (1910) *Young Gaol-Birds*. London: Macmillan.

Rustin, M. (1994) 'Flexibility in higher education'. In R. Burrows and B. Leader, (eds), Towards a Post-Fordist Welfare State. London: Routledge.

Ryan, M., Savage, S.P. and Wall, D.S. (eds) (2000) *Policy Networks in Criminal Justice*. Basingstoke: Palgrave Macmillan.

Savage, M., Warde, A. and Ward, K. (2003) *Urban Sociology, Capitalism and Modernity*. Basingstoke: Palgrave Macmillan.

Savage, S. P. (2003) Tackling tradition: reform and modernisation of the British police, *Contemporary Politics* (June), 9(2).

Scarman, Lord (1981) *The Brixton Disorders 10–12 April, Report of an Inquiry by the Rt. Honourable Lord Scarman*, Cmnd. 8427. London: HMSO.

Scarman, Lord (1982) *The Scarman Report*. Harmondsworth: Penguin Books.

Schedler, K. and Proeller, I. (2002) The new public management: a perspective from mainland Europe, in K. MacLaughlin, S. Osborne and E. Ferlie (eds) *New Public Management: Current Trends and Future Prospects*. London: Routledge, 163–80.

Schuster, L. and Solomos, J. (2004) New directions or the 'same old story'? New Labours policies on race relations, immigration and asylum, in D.L. Steinberg and R. Johnson (eds) *Blairism and the War of Persuasion*. London: Lawrence and Wishart.

Senior, P. (2002) *Regional Resettlement Framework: Consultative Document for GOYH* (July). London: SHU Press.

Senior, P. (2003a) *Pathways to Resettlement: A Strategy Document for Yorkshire and the Humber* (June). London: SHU Press.

Senior, P. (2003b) Tackling social exclusion through positive pathways to re-settlement *Yorkshire and Humber Regional Review* (Winter).

Senior, P., Crowther, C. and Haith, A. (2002) *A Time Limited Evaluation of Bradford Anti-Crime Partnership Officers*. Sheffield: Hallam University, Research Centre for Community Justice.

Senior, P., Buchanan, J., Madoc-Jones, I. and Baker, S. (2004) *The Dawn Project Evaluation 2004*, NEWI.

Senior, P., Meadows, L., Feasey, S. and Atkinson, J. (2005) *Enhancing the Role of the VCS under NOMS: A Case Study of Yorkshire and Humberside*. London: Home Office.

Senior, P., Buchanan, J., Evans, M. and Baker, S. (2007a) *The Dawn Project Evaluation*. London: HCCJ.

Senior, P., O'Keeffe, C. and Monti Holland, V. (2007b) Barriers to employment, training and education in prisons and beyond: a peer-led solution, in R. Sheehan, G. McIvor and C. Trotter (eds) *What Works with Women Offenders*, Cullompton: Willan.

Shearing, C. and Stenning, P. (1981) Modern private security: its growth and implications, *Crime and Justice* 3: 193–245.

Silvestri, M. and Crowther-Dowey, C. (2007) *Gender and Crime*. London: Sage.

Skidelsky, R. (ed.) (1988) *Thatcherism*. London: Chatto and Windus.

Smith, A. (1776) *An Inquiry into the Nature and Causes of the Wealth of Nations*. New York: The Modern Library Random House.

Smith, P. (1995) Outcome-related performance indicators and organizational control in the public sector, in J. Holloway, J. Lewis and G. Mallory (eds) *Performance Measurement and Evaluation*. London: Sage, 192–216.

Smith, R. (2003) *Youth Justice: Ideas, Policy and Practice*. Cullompton: Willan.

SOCA (2006) *SOCA Annual Plan 2006–2007*. London: SOCA.

Solanki, A., Bateman, T., Boswell, G. and Hill, E. (2006) *Anti-Social Behaviour Orders*. London: Youth Justice Board.

Solomon, E. and Edgar, K. (2004) *Having their Say: The Work of Prisoner Councils*. London: Prison Reform Trust.

Solomos, J. and Schuster, L. (2004) Race, immigration and asyulum: New Labour's agenda and its consequences, *Ethnicities* 4(2): 267–87.

Spalek, B. (2006) *Crime Victims*. London: Palgrave.

Squires, P. (ed.) (2006) *Community Safety: Critical Perspectives on Policy and Practice*. Bristol: Policy Press.

Squires, P. and Stephen, D. (2005) *Rougher Justice: Anti-Social Behaviour and Young People*. Cullompton: Willan.
Steinberg, D.L. and Johnson, R. (2004) Distinctiveness and difference within New Labour, in D. L. Steinberg and R. Johnson (eds) *Blairism and the War of Persuasion*. London: Lawrence and Wishart.
Stenson, K. (1998) Displacing social policy through crime control, in S. Hänninen (ed.) *Displacement of Social Policies*. SoPhi: University of Jykväskylä, 117–44.
Stenson, K. (2005) Sovereignty, biopolitics and the local government of crime in Britain, *Theoretical Criminology*, 9(3): 265–87.
Stenson, K. and Edwards, A. (2001) Crime control and liberal government: the Third Way and the return to the local, in K. Stenson and R.A. Sullivan (eds) *Crime, Risk and Justice: The Politics of Crime Control in Liberal Democracies*. Cullompton: Willan, 117–44.
Stenson, K. and Edwards, A. (2003) Crime control and local governance: the struggle for sovereignty in advanced liberal polities, *Contemporary Politics*, 9(2): 203–17.
Stern, V. (2006) *Creating Criminals: Prisons And People In A Market Society*. London: Zed Books.
Sumner, C. (1990) *Censure, Politics and Criminal Justice*. Milton Keynes: Open University Press.
Sumner, C. (1994) *The Sociology of Deviance: An Obituary*. Milton Keynes: Open University Press.
Taylor, D. (2001) New hit squads to target failing police, *Evening Standard*, 11 June, 6.
Thatcher, M. (1977) *Let Our Children Grow Tall: Selected speeches, 1975–1977*. London: Centre for Policy studies.
Thorpe, D., Smith, D. Green, C. J. and Paley, J. H. (1980) *Out of Care: Community Support of Juvenile Offenders*. London: Allen and Unwin.
Tilley, N. (ed.) (2005) *Handbook of Crime Prevention and Community Safety*. Cullompton: Willan.
Tonry, M. (2004) *Punishment and Politics: Evidence and Emulation in the Making of English Crime Control Policy*. Cullompton: Willan.
Touraine, R. (2001) *Beyond Neo-liberalism*. Cambridge: Polity Press.
Townsend, P. (1990) Underclass and overclass: the widening gulf between the social classes in Britain in the 1980s, in G. Payne and M. Cross (eds) *Sociology in Action*. Basingstoke: Macmillan.
Travis, A. (2006) Prisons inspector role to be abolished by Reid, *Guardian*, 29 June.
Travis, A. and Wintour, P. (2007) Reid proposes splitting Home Office into ministries of national security and justice, *Guardian*, 22 January.
van Dijk, T. (1998) *Ideology: A Multi-Disciplinary Approach*. London: Sage.
van Zyl Smit, D. and van der Spuy, E. (2004) Importing criminological ideas in a new democracy: recent South African experiences, in T. Newburn and R. Sparks (eds) *Criminal Justice and Political Cultures*. Cullompton: Willan.
Vulliamy, E. (2005) Rumours of a riot, *Guardian*, 29 November.
Wakefield, A. (2003) '*Selling security: The Private Policing of Public Space*'. Cullompton: Willan.
Walker, A. (1984) *Social Planning*. Oxford: Blackwell.
Walker, A. (1991) The strategy of inequality: poverty and income distribution in

Britain, 1979–1981, in I. Taylor (ed.) *The Social Effects of Free Market Policies*. Hemel Hempstead: Harvester Wheatsheaf.
Walkerdine, V. and Johnson, R. (2004) Transformations under pressure: New Labour, class, gender and young women, in D. L. Steinberg and R. Johnson (eds) *Blairism and the War of Persuasion*. London: Lawrence and Wishart.
Walklate, S. (1999) Some questions for and about community safety partnerships and crime, *Crime Prevention and Community Safety: An International Journal*, 1(3): 7–16.
Wall, D. S. (2001) *Crime and the Internet*. London: Routledge.
Waters, I. (2000) Quality and performance monitoring, in F. Leishman, B. Loveday and S. Savage (eds) *Core Issues in Policing*, 2nd edn. Essex: Pearson, 264–87.
Weber, M. (1961) *General Economic History* (trans. Frank H. Knight). New York: Collier.
Weber, M. (1964) *The Theory of Economic and Social Organisation* (originally trans. in 1947). Glencoe, MN: Free Press.
Weber, M. (1978) *Economy and Society*, 2 vols. California, CA: University of California Press.
Webster, C. (2007) *Understanding Race and Crime* Maidenhead: Open University Press.
Weeks, J. (2004) Labour's loves lost? the legacies of moral conservatism, in D. L. Steinberg and R. Johnson (eds) *Blairism and the War of Persuasion*. London: Lawrence and Wishart.
Wiles, P. (1999) The contribution of research to policy. Speech given at the Centre for Criminal Justice Studies (ISTD) AGM, November.
Williams, B. (2003) Where do victims of crime fit in? *British Journal of Community Justice*, 2(2).
Williams, B. and Canton, R. (2005) Editorial: victims of crime, offenders and communities, *British Journal of Community Justice*, 3(2).
Williams, F. (1994) Social relations, welfare and the post-Fordism debate, in R. Burrows and B. Loader (eds) *Towards a Post-Fordist Welfare State?* London. Routledge.
Wilson, W.J. (1996) *When Work Disappears: the World of the New Urban Poor*. New York: Knopf.
Winlow, S. (2001) *Badpellas: Crime, Violence and New Masculinities*. Oxford: Berg.
Young, J. (1999) *The Exclusive Society: Social Exclusion, Crime and Difference in Late Modernity*. London: Sage.
Young, J. (2007) *The Vertigo of Late Modernity*. London: Sage.
Young, J. and Matthews, R. (2003) New Labour, crime control and social exclusion, in R. Matthews and J. Young (eds) *The New Politics of Crime and Punishment*. Cullompton: Willan.
Zimring, F. (2007) *The Great American Crime Decline*. New York: Oxford University Press.

Websites

www.acpo.police.uk/pressrelease.asp (Ref. 61/06).
www.npia.police.uk
www.pito.org.uk
www.police.homeoffice.gov.uk
www.policesupers.com
www.soca.gov.uk
www.timesonline.co.uk/tol/newspapers/sunday.times/britain/article129583.ece
www.together.gov.uk
www.westyorkshirepolice.co.uk

Index